Communication
Research

Communication Research

Robert N. Bostrom
University of Kentucky

WAVELAND
PRESS, INC.

Prospect Heights, Illinois

For information about this book, write or call:
    Waveland Press, Inc.
    P.O. Box 400
    Prospect Heights, Illinois 60070
    (847) 634-0081

To Ann

Contents

Preface

This book studies research methods as one endeavor—the discovery of meaningful relationships among the ways in which human beings communicate with one another. To this end, we have attempted to integrate qualitative and quantitative methods, together with examples of the many forms of reasoning that go into research. Students should achieve understanding, but also know procedures for conducting research on their own. No previous training in mathematics, statistics, or communication theory is assumed.

Research methods courses range from experiences in appreciating research to hard-nosed courses in statistics. This book takes the point of view that research is a continuous process, ranging widely in depth, extension, and utility. Understanding and predicting are both important aspects of research, and the close relationship between the two is often overshadowed by proponents of one methodological school or another. The "received view" is that there is a logical progression of discovery, usually starting with openminded observations, then proceeding to more careful investigation and the formal construction of theories. The orthodox approach would be to begin with qualitative research in order to understand the problem in depth, and then proceed to more formal investigations, such as surveys and textual analysis. This form of inquiry should continue until the researcher understands the problem well enough to formulate hypotheses around which more formal theories can be constructed. But the process is not a single-minded progression in the direction of greater understanding. Sometimes we begin with formal hypotheses without subjecting ourselves to deeper, more intensive analysis, and consequently totally miss the most important parts of the problem. At other times, our testing of formal hypotheses derived from inductive principles shows that the induction was incorrect, and we should start over.

However, most of us attack problems by beginning with inductive, open-ended inquiry, followed by tentative hypotheses and testing of same. John Dewey's approach to "thought" still remains a fairly well-accepted method: begin with exploration and deep analysis of the situation, and proceed to more formal hypotheses and application. Dewey's disciples, however, center on problems as the ultimate rationale for research, and quite often research is more interested in the answer to a theoretical question rather than the solution to a specific social problem. Any study of research methods, however, must clearly treat both the inductive and deductive forms; each is incomplete without an understanding of the other.

In communication, as well as social science in general, inductive methods are receiving greater and greater attention, being studied as qualitative methods, or ethnomethodological research. The goal is to address a particular situation as openly as possible, recognizing that the researcher is a participant as well as an observer, and seek relationships or characteristics that might have been overlooked by a less intense method. However, induction as a prelude to more formal hypothesis testing is only part of qualitative research. Anderson writes that the ideal form of qualitative research is "inductive, eidetic, subjective, contextual, mundane, textual, preservationistic, interactive, and interpretive" (Anderson, 1987, p. 253).

Both qualitative and quantitative methods depend in some degree upon statistical reasoning. This reasoning in turn involves some calculations using simple procedures. However, working problems is not an end in itself, in that calculations should illustrate, not exhaust, the range of statistical tests. Other extremely important processes in research are selection of theoretical frameworks, judging the importance (practical and theoretical) of problems, designing assessment procedures, and interpreting findings.

Teachers of communication research are accustomed to routinely assigning exercises in which students calculate z scores, t tests, F ratios, chi-squares, and other simple statistics. Now we are confronted with a student population that not only suffers from mathematical anxieties, but who are poorly prepared in calculating abilities. The ubiquity of the computer and the statistical package adds weight to the argument "I won't ever have to do this" that students use as an excuse to evade mathematical activity. The connection between simple calculation is bridged in this book by the introduction of simple computing methods, Excel for the personal computer, and SAS for the mainframe. We have substituted SAS for SPSS, because it is simpler and widely available. Clearly no book of this kind can go into detail concerning the use of the computer—what we aim for is just a sampling.

Most instructors of research methods testify that students *can* do research, including very sophisticated statistical analyses. Routine calculations of chi-square, analysis of variance, and regression (correlation) are not easy at first, but students soon get in the swing of the process and learn that they are able to do it. This is not to minimize the role of the computer (both large mainframes and desktop packages) in modern research, but some students who graduate with a B.A. or M.A. may be working in an office with nothing but a calculator. These students will often be confronted with instances where a statistical test is valuable and worthwhile, and if they can work problems with a hand calculator, they will be far better off than a student who can't. Then, of course, many feel that those who *can* calculate are more critical consumers of research than those who can't.

In short, what is proposed is a continuous "seamless web" approach to research, which stems from a pragmatic view of communication as a process. Even if we don't accept pragmatism as a personal philosophy, almost everyone realizes that pragmatic research is valuable, especially for those who would like to use communication to solve important problems. Two questions generally guide work in theory and research:

Why do people do what they do?
What does communication have to do with it?

The first concerns general principles of human behavior, and the second concerns the role that communicative activity has to do with altering or shaping this behavior. Physicians are fond informing patients about the dangers of smoking and then assuming that people guide their behavior with rational principles. They think that to speak with a smoker is enough to make sure that these principles are present in an individual's mind. Neither of these assumptions are true. People begin to smoke for irrational reasons (image building, group conformity) and continue because of physiological addiction. Rational use of information has little connection with either process.

In short, whether we consider ourselves to be doing practical (applied) research, or whether our interest is in extending and establishing theoretical statements, sooner or later we will be involved in "reality" testing, to see if the phenomenon at hand is due to a theoretical relationship, or whether chance alone can suffice as an explanatory device. Chance is a numerical ratio and can only be analyzed as such. Most of the communication research reported in our research journals, such as *Communication Monographs, Human Communication Research*, or *Communication Research*, have practical significance as well as theoretical significance. We would hope that working in a communication research course will not only bring about the ability to do communication research, but a larger appreciation of the role of this research in our culture.

PART ONE

Introductory Principles

Research is a familiar term to most of us and some of us may even have read a research article. So the fact that there is research in communication should be no surprise to any of us. Many interesting aspects of communication research appear in our studies; some involve effects of the media, others tell us about our relationships, and still others predict how political messages will be received. The quality of this research is a fundamental aspect of how and when the research ought to be applied.

Learning about research includes many fundamental processes. We may have distinguished between theory and data, and may be familiar with various statistical procedures, but for many of us, this is the first exposure to the concept of *communication research* in a real way. First we will explore why people conduct communication research, and then examine the nature of data used in this research.

As with so many things, definitions will be crucial, and we will spend some time on them. At the same time, we will focus on a basic rationale concerning why communication research is done and what can be done with it. In this first section, we will begin the exploration of the many different approaches to communication research, and examine the reasons various researchers take the approaches they do. Much communication research depends on science as a foundation, so we will briefly look at some of the characteristics of science. But communication research also includes exploratory analyses, as well as confirmatory ones, so we must expand our approach to include more qualitative methods, as well as quantitative.

Research is a continuing process, beginning with choice of topic and ending with implications and extension. Some parts of this process are fairly well spelled out, and others are personal ones.

Chapter One

Introduction to Communication Research

COMMUNICATION AND SOCIAL PROBLEMS

Recently on the *Today* show, a prominent physician expressed his concern about the use of tobacco among the general public. This doctor felt that people who smoked should quit. He went on to say that he didn't understand patients' behavior. He said that everyone in his office informed all of their patients, especially the smokers, about the dangers of using tobacco. The fact that people continued to smoke, even after receiving these anti-smoking messages, puzzled this physician. The presence of this irrationality among the people who use tobacco made him feel that stronger measures should be taken, and he recommended that the federal government regulate nicotine as a drug.

The doctor may have been right. Smokers may well be crazy. But at the same time we must also consider the possibility that the doctor's *theory of communication* may be flawed. His theory, apparently, is that *information alone* can bring about changes in smokers' behavior. This theory predicts that if health professionals provide good information to smokers, less smoking will result. When the theory is tested, however, typically no change occurs in behavior when information is provided to smokers. Most of them keep on smoking. Since rational people don't do this, according to the doctor, smokers are irrational. Therefore it would be acceptable for the government to regulate their behavior. This conclusion may seem like a good one to doctors, but to smokers it seems dictatorial and paternalistic.

Tobacco isn't the only thing we consume that might be bad for us. We also eat the wrong things. To combat this, the Food and Drug Administration (FDA) requires package labelling. In the supermarket, food containers have labels that tell us how much fat and how many carbohydrates are in a can of spaghetti or a bag of potato chips. It seems

3

logical to assume that if the vendors of food products inform consumers of the nutritional value of foods (printing nutritional analyses on the outside of food packaging), good things will result. Unfortunately, research has shown that this available knowledge about the nutritional value of foods has had no appreciable effect on consumers' choices of foods at the supermarket. Nutritional knowledge, as such, doesn't seem to bring about any alteration in nutritional habits.

The doctor on the *Today* show and the FDA are not the only ones to draw conclusions based on overly simplistic ideas about communication. Well-meaning people are constantly attempting to improve the rest of us. They generate messages to influence our driving behavior ("seat belts save lives"), our language ("he's not a poor learner, he's cognitively challenged"), and our personal hygiene ("brush your teeth"). Many message generators are puzzled when the recipients of the messages react in ways that weren't intended—or sometimes don't react at all.

Communication is clearly a superior way to solve social problems. However, it will not be successful if it is applied mindlessly or simplistically. The sad fact is that many of those who would solve society's problems know a good deal about the particular problems but not as much about communication. So if our doctor on the *Today* show had looked into the subject extensively, he would have discovered that smokers need not only information, they need "involving" activities as well. The best place for him to have found this information would have been in the large body of knowledge about the relationships among sources, receivers, and messages, which we usually call communication theory. **Theories** are collections of statements that we use in explaining, predicting, and controlling the world about us. We often think of theory as an explanatory activity, but it is also involved in our attempts to predict and control the world about us. A simpler way of putting it is that theories are what we know about a given subject.

Theory and research are closely interrelated—without research there can be no theory, and without theory there can be no research. Good research builds good theory—and good theory will help us in solving problems. So a good way of starting our study of communication research would be to assert that the purpose of *communication research* is to help solve problems by creating, extending, exploring, and testing *communication theory*.

COMMUNICATION THEORY

If we are trying to solve a social problem and we see that our communicative strategies aren't working, the first thing we should do is ask if the communicative strategies we chose are the best ones available. Since the choice of strategy comes from a communication theory of some kind, we should take the advice of Kreps, Frey, and O'Hair (1991), and draw on the broadest theoretical base possible. Our first step will always be to review the theory involved. If the theory includes knowledge that is already available to help us solve the problem, there is little value in conducting yet another research project.

Here's a typical example: Suppose that you have been asked by the employee benefits office at your corporation to find out why employees don't seem to be interested in signing up for a new health maintenance organization (HMO) in your company. You are informed that the employee benefits personnel have sent out two circulars describing the wonderful benefits of the new plan and only briefly describing alternatives. If you have a good background in communication theory, you would already know that two-sided, refutational messages are much more effective (Allen et al., 1990). In other words, you probably already know enough about the problem to solve it without further engaging in an elaborate research effort. You need to prepare a message that presents both sides and strongly refutes the desirability of the old plan. If this message doesn't work, you might consider research as the next step.

Up to this point, we have been using the term communication theory as if it were a unitary, well-defined entity. Nothing could be further from the truth. There are many approaches to communication theory: historical, philosophical, scientific, esthetic, political, cognitive, metaphorical, narrative, dramatistic, and so forth. We have already identified the key purposes of theories: *to explain, to predict,* and *to control.* These three uses stress very different approaches to knowledge. In a very broad sense, explaining examines phenomena in depth, while predicting and controlling stress a narrower range, focusing on the future. Research is used to generate theory and to test it. The following sections review a few basic aspects of communication theory.

Generating Theory

Theories begin with our observations of the world about us. Basically, we begin theoretical study by examining this world carefully, looking to see what happens or what characteristics a given object might have. **Empiricism** is an extreme point of view that asserts that only observable phenomena determine what is true and what isn't true, and leaves little room for differences of opinion. In fact, an early group of empiricists, the logical positivists, asserted that any definition not based on observation was meaningless. Few people hold that view today, because most of us derive a good deal of meaning from non-empirical activities, such as reading poetry, watching a sunset, and decorating a Christmas tree. Even when we try to be as objective as possible, our values interact with our observations in important ways.

Nonetheless, empiricism has served well as a starting point, especially in the physical sciences and medicine. B. Aubrey Fisher (1978) expressed the traditional view of empiricism in this way:

> A nonscience is also divorced from reality—to some extent, at least. To the extent to which explanations do not reflect real-world phenomena or events, these explanations are nonscientific. A science must inevitably return to those things or events that actually occur and cannot indefinitely remain analytically separate from proceedings in the world without soon being rejected as fruitless. (p. 23)

This view of explanation implies that we can trust only our senses. This means that in studying other persons, since we can't see what others are *thinking*, we must content ourselves with what they are *doing*. Confining ourselves to visible events means that we are studying behavior.

However, the definition of behavior can be a broad one including contractions in the pupil of an eye, pushing levers, writing statements, buying soap, and voting for president. This view has come to be called *behaviorism* because of its basic dependence on "external" behavior. Communicative behavior would include spoken words, written messages, nonverbal signals, and our reactions to all of these. In other words, empirical theories are those that rely on observation only and not some other source of knowledge.

Probably one of the most central characteristics of the present-day empiricists is objectivity. Empiricists seek to objectify their data, in spite of the difficulty in doing so. Perhaps a better word to describe this research might be "objectivist," but current usage clings to "empiricist" as a basic term.

The empirical interest in objectivity and rationality sounds like an excellent approach to research, but it may be a total impossibility when applied to human problems. Most research is influenced by social values, even if we follow what we think are objective methods. While this may seem like a contradiction in terms, it is a common occurrence for the practice of scientific research to be affected by an individual's values. Examples of the intrusion of value questions in scientific research are common. Think about what value questions come to mind when genetic research or human cloning is discussed.

Some theorists have proposed that total empiricism is impossible and "action" theories (value-oriented science) should be substituted.[1] "Action" theories contend that our interpretation of others' behavior is more important and meaningful than the behavior itself. Also, the individual's intentions (plans) leading to social behavior are considered to be much more interesting than the specific behavior.

One basic contention of "action" theory is that empiricists themselves bring values to the research process. Most empiricists acknowledge that that is probably true, but the proper role of research methods is to minimize the human variation in observation and inference as much as possible. For research findings to be usable in solving problems, a fairly stringent standard must be applied before we can declare a theoretical statement to be true or false. In the next section we will examine what we mean by "true" in communication research and how the process contributes to solving human problems.

Testing Communication Theory

Communication theory is a related collection of statements describing specific relationships among communication activities. Statements are "true" in different ways. Let's take a common principle in communication theory and look at some of the ways in which it could be "true." In our daily lives, we might have noticed that sometimes people seem to give off contradictory signals about their inner states. A teacher may say to a student, "Come in—I've got lots of time," but then look at the clock several times throughout the conversation. The words say that time is not a problem, but the behavior contradicts the words. After many instances of such observations, communication researchers may see that people tend to take nonverbal cues as better indicators of the "real" state of affairs than verbal cues. When Judee Burgoon (1994) reviewed research in nonverbal communication, she concluded: "Adults generally rely more on nonverbal than verbal cues in determining social meaning" (p. 235). This means that we tend to think nonverbal cues are "truer" than verbal ones.

When evaluating a communication theory, our first step ought to be an assessment of the "kind" of truth that we think it represents. It may be that the theory is true for one group but not for another. It may be that the theory is true for only a small group of people, while we assumed it was true for a larger group. It may also be "true" because of cultural differences or physiological differences.

Peter Anderson (1989) has proposed five separate categories of regularities in human behavior: (1) natural forces (such as physiology or physics), (2) cultural rules (customs or taboos), (3) personal traits, (4) relational patterns (such as an organizational position, or a marriage), and (5) intentional, goal-oriented behavior. In other words, people behave in particular ways because of nature, their culture, their personalities, their relationships, and their goals or plans. To a greater or lesser extent, communication involves all of these regularities in behavior.

"Academic" vs. "Applied" Theories

Another way of classifying theories is to group them into academic as opposed to applied theories (Kreps, Frey, & O'Hair, 1991). An **academic theory** is one that exists primarily for the sake of knowledge alone, and an **applied theory** is one that we can use in solving a significant social or organizational problem. The theory that the doctor on the *Today* show used would clearly be an applied one and a theory that told us that there was life on Mars would be an academic one. Belief in life on Mars has little to do with whether we go to work or not, and what we choose to wear to work. Knowledge for its own sake alone is a typical goal of much university research; knowledge to help bring about social change is somewhat different. However, the distinctions are not truly clear. If we can discover a communication effect that helps doctors persuade others that they should stop smoking, the effect might well tell us something fundamental about communication in and of itself. When Michael Faraday discovered the principle of magnetic induction (which would be considered an academic theory), his primary interest was examining competing theories about electricity. But his discovery made possible the invention of transformers and electric motors—highly practical devices!

Let us recapitulate for a moment. It is perfectly possible to do research for theory's sake alone, and never worry about possible application. At the same time, it is also possible to do research that is theory-free, to solve some personal or organizational problem. Research that aims at the generation of theory will of necessity be theory-free, at least in its initial stages. But most everyone agrees that the best research involves both theory and practice. If we are committed to using communication as a means to solve problems in our society, then we need to explore the relationships involved with theory and application.

WHAT HAPPENED TO THE DINOSAURS?   For millions of years, dino-saurs roamed the earth. Then, abruptly they disappeared. Paleontologists hypothesized that they grew too large, or that other kinds of predators may have killed them off. Dr. Louis Alvarez, working in another field entirely, noticed that an interesting geological formation, a layer of a different color and different chemical composition, appears in geological formations that would correspond roughly with the time that the dinosaurs disappeared. This layer contained an unusual amount of chemicals that are associated with comets. Dr. Alvarez hypothesized that an exceptionally large comet had struck the earth and created an ecological disaster, one that included occlusion of the sun for at least three years, and extremely high levels of dust and contaminants in the atmosphere. This disaster could have easily extinguished the dinosaur population on the earth, or at least, reduced it to the level that many species then existent could not survive.

THE NATURE OF RESEARCH

Why would anyone want to do research? The primary reason is *uncertainty*. Human beings are very uncomfortable with uncertainty; we continually seek answers to questions. It matters very little whether the questions are ordinary or cosmic. Clearly, uncertainty motivates much interpersonal communication (Berger & Calabrese, 1975; Berger, et al., 1976). While it is true that some of us are more or less comfort-able with uncertainty, it is safe to say that information seeking is the product of the cognitive state of uncertainty.

Each of us engages in "research" every day. If while in London we wish to visit the British Museum, we might well begin by examining Lon-don maps to see where the closest underground stop is that would take us there. After determining that it is the Russell Square station, we still might be uncertain and ask a friend, "If you were going to the British Museum, would you use the Russell Square Station?" When we have enough data firmly in mind, we board the underground and find our way to the museum.

Most of us use the word *research* fairly broadly, applying it to library searches, to interviews while passing out pizza samples in the grocery store, and to careful scientific study. In a sense, we are all researchers, in that we seek information in a variety of situations. We look into the facts about a given car before we buy it; we ask others about prospective vacation locations; and we try on clothes at the mall.

Obviously we do not consider an investigation into the location of the British Museum or the payment schedule on a new car to be "real" research in the sense of a formal investigation of a developed theory. Such exploration would not justify the expenditure of public money to solve a social problem, or be sufficient to change the way in which we administer our public schools. Sometimes we need our information to be more convincing, or to be more worthy of effort on the part of others. In other words, sometimes we want to do research that would lead others to regard our findings in a different way than they would react to our findings about the London subway or recommendations about a good movie to rent. To do this, we need to do formal, serious research—research that follows certain rules and carries a degree of credibility that "personal" research does not. Historical research can answer certain categories of questions, and scientific research concentrates on different kinds. A good way of envisioning this process is to look at it as making the "truth" of our theory as general as possible. Science is one approach that we use to achieve general truths. In order to make our investigations as broad as possible, it is necessary to learn more about the nature of science.

THE NATURE OF SCIENCE

News magazines proclaim that a public opinion poll was "scientifically selected"; we hear that someone has made a "science" out of figure skating; we know that entomology and geology are sciences. One aspect of science has to do with proving principles and another has to do with convincing other persons that you have done so. It is this second aspect of science that has convinced many contemporary writers to speak of the "rhetoric of science" in a way that asserts that science is not much different from critical study or artistic expression. This is a lot like saying that astrology is a science. Science is "rhetorical" in that it aims at belief, but it is not rhetorical in the same way that a message urging us to vote for the Labor Party might be, and it should not be judged in the same way that typical rhetorical theory should be.

Taylor (1991) gives us a good description of the rhetoric implied in science. He notes that the "boundary work" of scientific discourse is affected by the publicness of the audience for which it is intended. To abandon rhetorical forms would be to abandon their rhetorical force. In other words, science is rhetorical in a particular way, and this way includes the four characteristics of *universalism, communalism,*[2] *objectivity,*[3] and *skepticism*. While it is true that these characteristics are rhetorical in nature, they are actually more than that, in that they imply methodological and cognitive orientations to the world. To see how this is so, let us look at them in some detail.

Universalism

Science aims at statements which are universal; that is, they are the same wherever or whenever they occur. The gravitational constant is such an expression—when things fall in outer space they are accelerated at the rate of thirty-two feet per second every second that they fall. Gravity pulls on them to produce motion, whether it is the orbit of Mars around the sun or the flight of a skydiver. Hydrogen and chlorine combine to make salt, and the proportions are exactly the same every time. In the social sciences, we are content with statements which are *probably* true, not necessarily true all the time (Fetzer, 1974). Nonetheless, we want some sense of the universal in these probabilistic statements. Yet the assumption that the hard sciences deal with laws (highly specific statements), and the social sciences deal with less exact ones is fairly widespread. Cushman and Pearce (1977, p. 346) present this view: "The number of staunch advocates of this approach [objectivist thinking] has been steadily declining. Social scientists have simply been unable to discover *laws* which have generality and necessity comparable to those in the natural sciences." Nonetheless, we would not call a study scientific if we couldn't rely on its results to hold true in different times and places, and under different conditions.

Let's look at an example. In communication research, we distinguish argumentative persons from verbally aggressive persons (Infante & Rancer, 1982; Infante & Wigley, 1986). The argumentative person tends to question ideas, and the verbally aggressive person tends to attack others' personal worth. A number of relational and organizational outcomes can be associated with the behavior of each of these personality types, some of which are desirable and others which are not. These statements take on a universal nature, in that we expect the verbally aggressive person to behave the same way tomorrow as he or she did today, and we expect verbally aggressive persons in Spokane, Washington to behave the same way that verbally aggressive people in New Haven, Connecticut behave. If we don't have this characteristic of universality, the whole idea of differentiating people according to their verbal aggressiveness is a waste of time. Another way of expressing universals is to say that they are **replicable**, or repeatable under different times and different circumstances. Instead of investing all the time, ability, and energy in carrying out all the research to prove this statement is replicable, we depend on the efforts of Dominic Infante of Kent State, who has investigated the phenomenon in great detail. Through Infante's papers and published work, we are able to understand the argumentative personality, and when we try his procedures with other persons, we get the same result he does.

Replicability seems like such a commonsense idea—a concept or a principle has utility only if someone else can perform the same process and produce a similar result. The statement "verbal hostility produces poor problem solving" implies future problem solving as well as past problem solving, and is therefore nonverifiable in the Humean view of logic. David Hume demonstrated that since we cannot know the future, cannot say that a principle will always hold true in the future. This seems silly when we apply it to commonsense events, such as the decision about whether your car will start. If you don't *really* know whether your car will start, you might as well take the bus and leave it in the parking lot. Most of us are willing to give the car a chance. Hume pointed out that the proof of induction (the sun has always risen in the East, therefore, it will rise in the East tomorrow) depends on assuming that the principle of induction itself is valid, which in turn depends on the principle of induction. This is clearly illogical, so most of the time, we assume that logical questions sometimes take a back seat to practical ones.

Hubner (1985) notes that this logical limitation applies to even very well-known concepts, such as the gravitational constant (pp. 4–5), and that the existence of physical laws must depend on something other than strict inferential logic. But we know that the gravitational constant is a powerful descriptor of falling bodies and that the descriptions of communication satellites as well as firmly struck baseballs can only be accomplished by use of this constant. These logical difficulties are dealt with in a number of ways, and various thinkers in the philosophy of science have proposed rules that they hope will enable people to justify the use of scientific concepts (Reichenbach, 1936).

Communalism

We expect that we all will use the term "verbally aggressive" in the same way. Each of us might have our own definition of the word, but if we are to achieve repeatable results, we have to agree on a common, or *communal* definition of the term. We achieve this through *operationalism*, a view that holds that scientific statements need to be grounded in specific actions in order to be meaningful. Language has meaning if and only if the terms embodied in it can be referred to some direct procedure. P. W. Bridgman (1938), who is generally associated with originating the strongest arguments in favor of operationalism, used the term *instrumental* operations. For example, to specify that one gram is the weight of a cubic centimeter of pure water, it is necessary to elaborate all the specific circumstances that are necessary to achieve a consistent result—terms like centimeter, pure (as applied to water), temperature, sea level, latitude, and so forth. Once all these conditions are satisfied, then a degree of agreement can be reached concerning the term in question. Exactly how good this agreement must be is usually not specified in the philosophy of science.

If we wish to talk sensibly about argumentative persons, we will probably use the definition proposed by Infante. His definition is useful because it has been tested in a number of circumstances and the results are well known. In other words, when we use his term, *we know more.* If we were to make up our own, we might know something, but not nearly as much as if we used a standard definition. The operational definition of argumentativeness, then, would be a certain level of responses on a test.

Objectivity

It seems strange to assert that the practice of scientific research should be done by persons that are disinterested in the outcome. What we mean by "disinterestedness" is that people should be objective about their work and not let their predispositions about the outcome distort what they do—or specifically what they observe in their study. Objectivity in a scientific sense has certain inherent difficulties. Since scientists are human, is it not possible that they are biased and therefore subjective?

Gunnar Myrdahl (1967) approached the problem by dividing knowledge into beliefs, which are based on knowledge, and valuations, which are not. Beliefs are intellectual and cognitive; valuations are emotional and volitional. Cunningham's (1973) definition of objectivism is one of the best in current usage. A system is objective if, and only if:

a. it is possible for its descriptions and explanations of a subject matter to reveal the actual nature of the subject matter, where actual nature means the qualities and relations of a subject matter as they exist independently of an inquirer's thoughts and desires regarding them, and

b. it is not possible for two inquirers holding rival theories about some subject matter and having complete knowledge of each other's theories (including the grounds for holding them) to both be justified in adhering to their theories. (p. 46)

In other words, we can avoid subjectivity and distortion if we are careful and build safeguards into our system.

Skepticism

In philosophy, the skeptics are those who don't believe in *a priori* knowledge, which is another way of saying that they will believe it only if they see it. This is a complicated idea, but worth thinking about. Can you "really" know anything that you haven't observed (or that someone else has observed)? If you believe the basis of knowledge is observation, then you are an *empiricist*. If you think there are metaphysical things out there that also deserve your belief, you are a *dualist*. If you think that all knowledge is mental only, you are probably in trouble, especially if you drive your car a lot.

How we think we know things and what it means for us to know is an important issue, and we will return to it in the next section. If a female classmate tells you that space aliens kidnapped her when she was a little girl, and she still gets messages from them, especially late at night—you might want to have a concrete demonstration of her statements. This would especially be the case if she wants you to give her money so that she can buy materials to build a space ship. Most of us are pretty gullible, but we would probably stop short at giving money to someone to build a space ship. The formal position of science is that whatever is at issue is probably not true unless it can be carefully tested.

Skepticism is an absolutely essential aspect of the scientific community. Earlier we spoke of *replicability* as the ability to repeat the results of a study or experiment. Researchers attempt to replicate previous work to test it. In 1994, the Federal Office of Research Integrity charged an MIT researcher with faking data to prove that transferring genes from one animal to another could convey immunity to disease (Burrell, 1994). This was only discovered when another researcher attempted to duplicate the gene transfer and could not. This skeptical attitude is what makes science basically *self-correcting*.

RESEARCH AND INQUIRY

Research is a continuous process, ranging widely in depth, extension, and utility. "Understanding" and "predicting" are both important aspects of research, and most researchers believe there is a logical progression of discovery, usually starting with open-minded observations, then proceeding to more careful investigation and the formal construction of theories. In other words, we begin with open-minded observations in order to understand the problem in depth, and then proceed to more formal investigations, such as surveys and textual analysis. This form of inquiry should continue until the researcher understands the problem well enough to formulate hypotheses, around which more formal theories can be constructed. But the process is not a single-minded progression in the direction of greater understanding. Sometimes we begin with formal hypotheses without subjecting ourselves to deeper, more intensive analysis, and consequently totally miss the most important parts of the problem. At other times, our testing of formal hypotheses derived from inductive principles shows that the induction was incorrect, and we start over.

However, most of us attack problems by beginning with inductive, open-ended inquiry, followed by tentative hypotheses and then testing these hypotheses. John Dewey's approach to thought still remains a fairly well-accepted method: Begin with exploration and deep analysis of the situation, and proceed to more formal hypotheses and application. Dewey's disciples, however, center on problems as the ultimate rationale for research, and quite often research is more interested in the answer to a theoretical question rather than the solution to a specific social problem.

This book is about research. The goal of science is knowledge, but the term "knowledge" needs additional clarification. Scientific knowledge is quite different from the social knowledge that enables us to get through the day. So what do we mean when we say we "know" something? Obviously, we have reduced uncertainty if we know something. But we have only *reduced* uncertainty, not eliminated it. Sometimes we can eliminate explanations by disproving them, but we do not prove the opposite of statements by disproving a statement. If you review the chapter, you will remember that we know things scientifically if we know them communally, objectively, skeptically, and universally. But to know a "probable" statement universally may seem like a contradiction in terms. One approach to the problem lies in examining the question: "How probable?" We will look at this question in some detail in later chapters.

NOTES

[1] There are many writers in the philosophy of science who feel that the attention paid to "action" theories, or hermeneutical research is largely the result of academic politics (Hanna, 1991). That is, the individuals who have taken this view are reluctant to offend persons in the opposite camp; they attempt to blend approaches so that the implications of their points of view are less offensive.

[2] Taylor actually uses the term "communism" here.

[3] Taylor uses the term "disinterestedness" here.

Chapter Two

The Research Process

In chapter 1 we explored the ways in which communication can be used to solve social problems, and saw that good problem solving depends on having good theories to use for the solutions. Sound theory rests on sound knowledge, and putting the two together is a process that is public, general, skeptical, and objective. It depends on the ability of researchers to be open-minded, to be willing to share their results with others, to be careful about methods, and to go beyond narrow principles to more general ones. These general guidelines help us in doing research. The process itself is quite detailed and involves a great many specific tasks. In this chapter we will examine the very first steps in research: (1) choosing a subject (topic), (2) assessing the kind of questions that need to be addressed, (3) analyzing and refining the problem, and (4) looking for what, if anything, is already known about it.

Preliminary Steps

The first part of any research effort is deciding what to research: Of all the problems in the world, which should occupy our attention? Defining a problem is partially an individual choice, but clearly the social significance of the question should dominate the decision. Suppose you decide to examine the way in which television presents women in demeaning social situations. Then you become aware that television shows often present older persons in the same kind of situations. Television often makes jokes about an older person being forgetful, or cranky, or otherwise unpleasant. Which should you choose—women or older persons? Your choice between these two groups may be only a matter of personal preference. The choice of whether to study verbal aggressiveness in families as opposed to the speech rates of disc jockeys can be guided by the relative social significance of each question.

Research as Discovery

In chapter 1 we noted that we think of communication research as typically employed to *solve problems*—political, practical, and personal. But sometimes we don't know enough about the problem or topic to formulate problems or even specify what we need to know about it. If this is the case, we need to engage in *exploratory* research—that is, to investigate, without preconceptions, what the state of affairs may be in a given problem area. For example, Smythe (1995) explored the ways in which women talked to one another at a fitness facility to see what, if anything, this discourse revealed about women's concerns with the fitness culture. Her research showed a good deal of insight about the way in which women communicate in this given situation, and what they think about "fitness" as a concept. But this kind of investigation may not produce immediate results in solving particular problems—in other words, it may not be practical as we usually think of it. Shouldn't all research be *practical*?

Of course not; research does not have to be practical to be valuable. To discover the existence of a previously unknown phenomenon and explore how it relates to better-known ones is a perfectly reasonable research goal. Many mathematicians are only interested in pure mathematics, describing the analysis of mathematical relationships that may never have any correspondence with events in the "real" world. But curiously, research in pure mathematics often turns out to be practical. When the method of solving simultaneous linear equations was first demonstrated, no possible usage was known. Later on, when scientists investigated the characteristics of electrical circuits, they discovered that the linear equations method applied perfectly to that problem.

We communicate to improve the world in which we find ourselves—our relationships, our work, our families, and our community. The strategy we choose to solve a problem should be based on knowledge of how persons communicate and what the effects of messages are likely to be in different situations. Most individuals learn communication theory by trial and error, by watching others, and by experience. As with the doctor on the *Today* show, those methods are no guarantee that any particular communication theory will be useful or effective. Our individual experience—no matter how extensive—is likely to be provincial and flawed.

Most of us begin with fixed ideas about communicative activity, which we can call commonsense assumptions. For example, most of us believe that the media in the United States are essentially objective and report the news as they see it. However, a person with in-depth knowledge of both large newspapers and the world of finance might notice anomalies that seem to belie this view. Herman and Chomsky (1988) conducted a study which suggested that large newspapers and broadcasters engage in propagandistic activity to support not only their clients (other large corporations) but themselves. Herman and Chomsky discovered these relationships through *qualitative* analysis, that is, an open-minded examination of details and relationships within these organizations. This kind of analysis is an important step in any research.

Qualitative research is not the only form of exploratory research. We also see investigatory research in surveys, content analysis, and factor analysis. We will examine each of these in greater detail later in the book.

Research and Prediction

Sometimes our principal interest is in extending and testing theory, not necessarily in dealing with a day-to-day problem. Let's look at an example. Donohew, Palmgreen, and Duncan (1980) hypothesized that individuals have an optimum level of comfort for information exposure—too much information is as bad as too little. This theory takes the form of an inverted U-shape in its predictions of interest. Donohew, Palmgreen, and Duncan conducted research that showed the hypothesis to be true, and this hypothesis has led to a number of other interesting theoretical findings. It is true that this theory may be of use in designing messages, but the initial purpose of the study was to prove the theory, not design messages. Theory is equally as important in research as application. Both are vital, and both depend on one another.

Research is the process of first discovering and then examining theories formally and objectively. There are many things we need to know about the process before we can apply it to our theories of communication. Let's look at some of the basic elements involved in research.

IN MANY STATES, INDIVIDUALS ACCUSED of a crime are granted *bail,* that is, the privilege of being free, or out of jail, while legal procedures take place. Judges usually grant bail in amounts thought to reflect the character of the accused, the nature of the crime, and the probability of the accused actually showing up for the trial. Actually, accused persons do not put up their own bail but borrow the money from "bail bondsmen" who are little more than usurious loan sharks. The bail bond business is one of the sleaziest aspects of the trial system in many states.

However, sociologists and criminologists conducted research to see what characteristics actually predicted whether or not an accused person would show up for trial. They found that a number of characteristics, such as home ownership, a job, kind of group membership in a community, past criminal record, and other characteristics were excellent predictors of the tendency to be available for trial. Since the research was conducted, many states have replaced the bail procedure with an interview by a professional staff member in the probations office. Accused persons are coded according to a point system, with so many points going for home ownership, other points for education level, and so on. This questionnaire is substituted for the bail procedure and the bail bondsmen have been eliminated in these states. Most importantly, the record of accused persons actually showing up for trial has drastically improved.

Definitions and Operations

Once a general area of interest is chosen, it is vital to get specific definitions of the concepts involved. The typical terms used in describing communication almost always need to be redefined into specific acts that people perform. Going from the general to the specific is the result of *operationalism*, that is, specifying the operations that you will perform to provide an instance of the theoretical term. This is a way to objectify data, in that once the operation is agreed to, the definition is not personal but communal. But it is not an easy task. Usually it requires agreement on a number of predetermined issues. Let's see how this agreement works.

It should be obvious to all of us that there is a global need to save energy. If we work in an energy-conscious organization, we might all agree that we should turn down the air conditioning and only turn it up when the heat reaches the intolerable level. Some persons, however, are more sensitive to heat than others. What is intolerable to one is only pleasantly warm to another. Worse yet, on one day one person may feel too warm and on a succeeding day another may feel too cold, so every day a squabble erupts. One person says "It's too hot," another says "It's warm," and a third says "It's great. Just take off your jacket." The obvious remedy for such a situation is to get a thermometer, have a meeting, and agree on what the ideal temperature should be. But suppose one individual brings a thermometer—and it doesn't correspond to the office thermometer? Most of us would say, "Your thermometer is inaccurate." If the person with the thermometer persisted in defending the instrument, our only strategy would be to find a standard thermometer. How would we do this?

Scientists years ago agreed on standard scales for temperature (Fahrenheit and Celsius), and manufacturers calibrate their products according to these standards. Therefore, when we go to a hardware store and buy a thermometer, we know that the instrument will be fairly accurate. The people in the office can check their thermometer by taking it to an engineering lab or a university physics department to see how accurate it is. Then when someone complains about the heat, the thermometer can provide an external check to see if the problem is real or entirely subjective. But none of this could take place without our *assumptions* concerning the temperature, the scales, and the manufacturers of the thermometer. We also *assume* that there is a relationship between the thermometer reading and the air temperature. Neither of these assumptions is typically questioned, although someone for whom the temperature is uncomfortable might argue or be skeptical, but both are necessary before we can use a thermometer reading. So in a sense, the data regarding temperature contains a theory about thermometers.

Since these assumptions are inherent in the use of thermometer readings, there is a sense in which the data the thermometer yields is partially dependent on theory, or interpretation. You might think that this is stretching a point, but many philosophers of science are concerned about the nature of the assumptions involved in any construction of data statements. Hubner (1985), for example, finds it useful to distinguish between statements which include some observational theory, such as "Celsius scales are better for thermometers," and other statements which do not, such as "It is 27 degrees outside." Some data statements refer to direct perception, but others include assumptions, such as the one about thermometers. But it is important to note that almost all observational definitions include assumptions; in communication, we tend to include more than some other disciplines.

Intersubjectivity refers to the process that scientists generally use to ensure that they are talking about the same thing. It is the process of agreeing on the specific operations that will be representative of a given theoretical term. For example, the term "mass" has a more exact meaning for physicists than it usually does for laypersons. A given volume of lead and a given volume of gold will have different weights. But before we can define weight, we must have an exact standard of comparison to measure the different forces that gravity exerts on objects. Normally we use the term "gram." But what exactly is a gram? To say only that a gram is one one-thousandth of a kilogram is an empty tautology. Many so-called definitions are like that. To know exactly what a gram is, we must be able to know what the operations are that led to its definition. A gram is the gravitational pull exerted on one cubic centimeter of pure water at sea level at zero degrees Celsius. But what exactly is a centimeter? It, of course, is one one-hundredth of a meter. And a meter is one ten-millionth of the distance from the equator to the North Pole. Scientists have long since given up performing these operations to get the standard meter and the standard gram, but if they lost all of their meter sticks and their gram weights, they could recreate the standards because they know exactly what the definitions imply.

This agreement on the part of researchers to use standard units and universal relationships is an intersubjective agreement. This certainly does not mean that our use of these standard definitions for experience is subjective; rather, the opposite is true. Persons must put aside their preconceptions and personal interpretations in order for intersubjectivity to work. What this means, on the most elementary level, is that for theory to have any use at all there must be agreement of some kind about definitions. Sometimes researchers in communication have not been as exact in their use of definitions as have researchers in other disciplines, such as physics. But that doesn't mean that we can't be careful in our use of basic terms to define communicative processes.

OBSERVATIONS IN COMMUNICATION STUDY

Lest our discussion of definitions get too esoteric, consider the following example of the process in communication study. Patricia Kearney and her associates have been studying the ways in which teachers use communication to exert control in the classroom (Kearney, et al., 1984). She was interested in what real teachers did in classroom situations where they needed to alter the behavior of their students. She asked the following question:

> As a teacher, you often try to get your students to do things that they might not want to do. The student usually thinks, and often asks, "Why should I want to do this?" Please give the most common answers you would give to this question (p. 731).

A total of 343 teachers in kindergarten through twelfth grade wrote answers to this question. You can imagine the volume of responses. Three hundred forty-three teachers answering such a question probably generated several thousand different statements. These statements were the raw data in this communication study. How did Kearney and her colleagues make sense of all of these responses? They classified the answers into twenty-two[1] different response categories. Some of these classifications are listed in table 2.1. below.

Table 2.1
Revised Behavior Alteration Techniques and Messages

Technique	Sample Messages
(1) *Immediate Reward from Behavior*	You will enjoy it. It will make you happy. Because it's fun. You'll find it rewarding/interesting. It's a good experience.
(2) *Deferred Reward from Behavior*	It will help you later on in life. It will prepare you for college (or high school, job, etc.). It will prepare you for your achievement tests. It will help you with upcoming assignments.
(3) *Reward from Teacher*	I will give you a reward if you do. I will make it beneficial to you. I will give you a good grade (or recess, extra credit) if you do. I will make you my special assistant.
(4) *Reward from Others*	Others will respect you if you do. Others will be proud of you. Your friends will like you if you do. Your parents will be pleased.
(5) *Self-Esteem*	You will feel good about yourself if you do. You are the best person to do it. You are good at it. You always do such a good job. Because you're capable!
(6) *Punishment from Behavior*	You will lose if you don't. You will be unhappy if you don't. You will be hurt if you don't. It's your loss. You'll feel bad if you don't.
(7) *Punishment from Teacher*	I will punish you if you don't. I will make it miserable for you. I'll give you an "F" if you don't. If you don't do it now, it will be homework tonight.
(8) *Punishment from Others*	No one will like you. Your friends will make fun of you. Your parents will punish you if you don't. Your classmates will reject you.
(9) *Guilt*	If you don't, others will be hurt. You'll make others unhappy if you don't. Others will be punished if you don't.
(10) *Teacher-Student Relationship: Positive*	I will like you better if you do. I will respect you. I will think more highly of you. I will appreciate you more if you do. I will be proud of you.

These items aren't necessarily the exact responses that the teachers gave—for example, a teacher might have said, "You know, if you don't do this, you will really hurt other people, and bring about bad things for the entire class." This kind of response was categorized as "guilt" and was put into category 9, along with all other statements of that type.

Notice that the classification was supplied by Kearney and her co-workers, not by the teachers themselves. Notice also that it is absolutely essential that some sort of sorting and classification take place before these observations make any sense to anybody. The table is titled "Revised Behavior Alteration Techniques," because Kearney and her associates did indeed work with the messages to arrive at some commonality. You can see that no two teachers would list exactly the same response in exactly the same way. If one tried to make sense out of exact listings, it would only be a meaningless list of hundreds of responses. But note carefully that Kearney here illustrates an instance of the *public* dimension of science—she tells us exactly what she did and how she did it. Then she lists the categories in a table so that we can agree or disagree about her data.

The observations in this study are of at least three separate kinds. Kearney first tells us that she worked up this question on a response form and gave it to 343 teachers. Then she notes that the teachers wrote responses that were of twenty-two different types. Following that, she gives us statistical "facts," such as "Response Category 10 (relating to positive aspects of the teacher-student relationship) was reported as being highly used by 44 teachers and less often used by 30 teachers." Then following the analysis, she reports that the reward strategy was perceived as being more effective. These observations are totally different, according to Hubner (1985). Hubner's distinction between statements of basic observation and others that presuppose some interpretation applies to this example. But Hubner's distinction is of less importance than the degree of *objectivity* displayed by these researchers in the creation of the data statements.

What Do We Know?—Reviewing the Literature

If you were interested in the role of communication in behavior management in the classroom, you probably would not repeat Dr. Kearney's research, but you might wish to build on it. There are many ways to discover what is already known about your topic, and obviously we can never exhaust the potential sources of information. But there are two excellent sources that we should all use, and that are available to most of us—the Internet, and more traditional library holdings.

The Internet

What we call the Internet is actually a vast collection of networked computers (Kardas & Milford, 1996). Internet activity is actually quite diverse. The simplest is electronic mail and listservers, and the most complicated is the world wide web. Some special Internet tools available are Telnet, Archie, and Gopher. The World Wide Web is a way of viewing the Internet with the use of HTML (HyperText Markup Language) which makes the Web very fast and powerful.

Gaining information from the Internet can be accomplished in a number of ways. E-mail is often used to ask questions of researchers in a variety of settings. If you are interested in research concerning the effects of advertising on television, you might ask the Television Bureau of Advertising directly about their research. First you need to know what you are after and who to ask. A more useful technique is to use Gopher, a menu-based program that helps you find various resources. You can browse through Gopher looking for specific data on a subject that might interest you. However, you must have special software to use this Internet tool.

The World Wide Web is where most of us will conduct electronic searches for information. The Web has search engines like YAHOO! that scan through the millions of topics available and find lists of websites where information may be found.

For example, a search through WebCrawler (another search engine) using the target word "nonverbal communication" brings up a website called the "Nonverbal Communication Research Page." A variety of options are available on this site, including a course outline used by a professor in California. One option on this site allows you to search the communication journals and when you click on the hypertext link, you see the titles of three major journals published by the International Communication Association, *Human Communication Research* and *Journal of Communication*, in addition to the *Electronic Journal of Communication*. Specific searches of these two journals produce an attenuated list of references on various communication topics.

You can download this information but these searches through journals are attenuated ones and not very exhaustive. Many better lists are available. One can be accessed by going to the site of the National Communication Association. Here we find lists of research, courses and syllabi, conferences, programs, and paper archives.

Learning to use the entire range of the Internet might be a topic for a separate course in itself. An excellent reference is Kardas and Milford's (1996) guide to using the Internet in social science research. This is an outstanding reference and one that would be very useful in every researcher's library.

There are many problems inherent in using the Internet, but the worst one is accuracy. There are no restrictions on putting information on particular websites. A researcher has no idea whether the information has been accurately reported or is imaginary. In the recent fen-phen controversy, one researcher reported that an Internet source had quoted his research backwards; that is, had cited his study as supporting a result opposite to what it actually proved.

Using the Internet to *begin* your research is an excellent idea, but other published resources offer the researcher something that the Internet does not: most published research has been reviewed; that is, independent evaluators have examined the research to verify its validity and to see if it is worth publishing. But even when you find sources listed on the Internet, you will need to go to the library to verify your resource.

Library Research

There are a number of basic information sources in your library that will help you search the research literature. The card catalogue is an excellent place to start. But you can save an enormous amount of time by using the NOTIS Online Public Access Catalog (NOTIS OPAC); it provides access to books and government publications that are available in libraries. For journals, you would wish to consult the *Academic Index*, which provides access to journal and magazine articles published in 1,500 general interest and scholarly periodicals since 1990. Searching NOTIS OPAC for information on most subjects will result in the retrieval of references to both books and government publications (books have Dewey Decimal or Library of Congress Classification numbers assigned to them, while government publications do not). Government publications received by library systems since the mid-1970s are also included in the NOTIS OPAC. In general terms, online information systems usually allow searching of three types of subject terms, subject headings, descriptors, and keywords. Searching by subject headings or descriptors requires that you know something about the subject heading or descriptor system being used. It is probably a good idea to concentrate exclusively on keyword subject searching.

Probably the most efficient way to search the communication literature exclusively would be to use CommSearch, software developed by the National Communication Association. This software comes on its own CD-ROM disk and requires the use of a personal computer and Microsoft Windows. In this software, twenty-four journals are indexed by title, author, and keyword. Some of the journals indexed are:

Argumentation and Advocacy
Communication Education
Communication Monographs
Communication Reports
Communication Quarterly
Communication Studies
Communication Theory
Critical Studies in Mass Communication
Howard Journal of Communication
Human Communication Research
Journalism Quarterly
Journal of Applied Communication Research
Journal of Broadcasting and Electronic Media
Journal of Communication
Journal of the Association for Communication Administration
Philosophy and Rhetoric
Quarterly Journal of Speech
The Southern Communication Journal
Text and Performance Quarterly
Western Journal of Communication
Women's Studies in Communication

Journals with article title and author are listed through 1994. The full text of six NCA journals from 1991 to 1995 are available, and abstracts of the same six journals are also available from 1978 through 1995. These six journals are:

Communication Education
Communication Monographs
Critical Studies in Mass Communication
Journal of Applied Communication Research
The Quarterly Journal of Speech
Text and Performance Quarterly

Searching all these journals is an onerous task. Each publication has about six articles in it; and each is published quarterly. While the *Quarterly Journal of Speech* goes back to 1915, you would probably not go back that far to look for instances of compliance-gaining research. But even so, you might wish to go back forty years, which means that there could be about twenty thousand published articles in communication for you to search. Clearly you can't look at all of them. Soon you will develop a knack for examining journals that have articles that interest you. If you are interested in mass communication, you will tend to look at the *Journal of Communication, Critical Studies in Mass Communication, Communication Research,* or *Journalism Quarterly.* While you can learn to skim, there is no real substitute for careful reading of the reported research.

Textbooks typically are not considered an excellent source for research, because textbook writers generally impose their own point of view. Citing research as it has been filtered through many readings is a bad idea. To see just how bad, let's look at an example. Many persons are convinced that "nonverbal" communication is more powerful than verbal. You can see statements like this in many textbooks; these books cite for their authority a book called *Silent Messages* by Albert Mehrabian (1972). This book in turn cites the actual research reports (Mehrabian & Ferris, 1967; Mehrabian & Wiener, 1967). If we look at these actual studies, we find that there is little evidence for this claim. The studies examined *one-word* "messages" and tested them being presented in different ways. The listeners were specifically instructed to listen for "tone" or "content" in their evaluations. It is easy to impart an affective tone in a one-word "message" but truly hard to convey much content with it (Lapakko, 1997). To overgeneralize from this kind of research is tempting, but shows how little we should take for granted. The best rule is to look at the original research report and see what the researcher reported.

CONSTRUCTING HYPOTHESES

The next step in conducting research is to use your operational definitions, your theory, and your suppositions to construct *hypotheses*. A hypothesis is a conjectural statement describing relationships between concepts. It is constructed in order to give shape and form to your research. Often some causal relationship is implied in your hypothesis, but not necessarily. Typically a hypothesis takes the form: "If this theory is true and I do X, then Y will result." One of the principal functions of a hypothesis is to guide the research design and exemplify the theory in a way that gives the effort meaning.

Let's look at an example. Berger and Jordan (1992) believed that "plans" are cognitive representations in individuals' memories that guide the way we decide what to say in a conversation. If the plan is drawn from a complicated memory, then it will be harder to put a communicative strategy together. If it is drawn from a simple memory, then it will be easier. As Berger and Jordan put it, "people planning to reach goals first search long-term memory for instances in which they have tried to achieve the same or similar goals in the past rather than generate new plans by applying rules each time a new goal is activated" (1992, p. 131). Since Berger and Jordan can't look into people's heads to see what the memories look like, they rely on external manifestations to signal that one memory is more complicated than another. Accordingly, in their study, their third hypothesis read: "Familiarity with goals will be inversely related to the frequency and duration of non-verbalized pausing while plans are discussed" (p. 132). To put it more simply, if an individual involved in a conversation was relying on a less familiar memory, the conversation would have more pauses in it. Subsequently in their research, they found that the hypothesis was confirmed—people working with unfamiliar memories paused more.

Let's next look at some of the characteristics of good hypotheses.

Simple

Good hypotheses concern only one aspect of the research at a time. If you are interested in what prime-time television thinks of handicapped persons, you might hypothesize that "In prime-time television, no main character is in a wheelchair, is visually handicapped, has a hearing loss, or has lost a limb." You can see that this hypothesis is too complicated to test, primarily because it contains too many diverse elements.

Observable

A good hypothesis is observable in that it is related to the theoretical phenomena and actually can be observed. This usually means verification through one of the many senses. Many things that interest us are not observable in the usual sense. The statement "The Gateway Arch in Saint Louis is 192.024 meters high" sounds as though it is observable. If we actually visit the monument and perform the measurement, we will need a ruler that is at least 200 meters long. It would be much easier to look at the blueprints of the arch. We would see that the total monument is made up of smaller parts of known dimensions; the total height could be derived by adding up the parts. Or we could borrow a transit (a surveying instrument) from an engineer and measure the angle produced along a line of known dimensions and look up the angle's dimension from a table of trigonometric functions. It should be clear from this example that the process involved in verification is not really direct, and the nature of the process itself is of great importance. The transit method implies that we believe in trigonometry. Connecting the observation to the theory involves a set of assumptions, so the process is not really direct.

Testable

A good hypothesis is testable; that is, it is possible to actually make the observations involved. Communication apprehension (McCroskey, 1977) is one of the most thoroughly researched of the many communicator characteristics that interest us, but we know little about how it gets started. Suppose we think that this characteristic is caused by family communication patterns. We would hypothesize that "Families that eat dinner together and talk a lot produce children with less apprehension than families that do not." Unfortunately, it is not possible for us to create a "control" group and an "experimental" group, because there is no way to control the behavior of individuals at dinner time. Even if we could do this, the ethical implications of actually trying to create a group of children with communication apprehension are shocking.

HYPOTHESES VS. RESEARCH QUESTIONS

Many researchers distinguish between hypotheses and research questions, reasoning that hypotheses represent a formal testing of a theory and a research question represents a more general exploration of phenomena. As we proceed through the book, we will see instances in which formal hypotheses make little sense. The choice of hypotheses as opposed to research questions is determined largely by the state of theory in the area, the statistical procedure used, and the preferences of the researcher. We will return to this issue at a later time.

SUMMING UP

Research begins with solving problems, either theoretical or practical. One sure guide to deciding whether a problem is worth investigating is to assess the relative "significance" of the problem. In addition, a problem should be interesting to the researcher, that is, to have some personal value or to return some benefit for all the work the research entails. Whatever the problem, the first important step is to operationalize the theoretical terms involved in the research. Operationalization makes a general theoretical term into something specific and observable. Searching the literature of communication is the next step, and computer searches are probably the easiest and most efficient. CommSearch, published by the National Communication Association, is one of the best available databases. At this point hypotheses can be constructed and the research continued.

NOTE

[1] Although Kearney used twenty-two different categories of responses, only ten of them are listed in the interest of space. After the table was created, Kearney performed various analyses on the responses and response categories. She concluded, among other things, that a deferred reward strategy was perceived as one of the most effective techniques for altering student behavior.

PART TWO

Fundamental Skills
in Research

So far in this book, we have examined the nature of communication research and compared some of the reasons why we do research. Some of the preliminary steps in getting research started were also discussed. Now it is time to examine the specific activities of research: the basic skills involved. While it is important for researchers to show commonality, objectivity, skepticism, and openness, they need to possess some other skills, specifically the use of *numbers* and *principles of measurement*. While most of us probably feel that we know all about numbers, we will find that numbers have important differences and that the differences affect the way we conduct research. We also feel that we are familiar with measurement, but when we try to measure the phenomena involved with communication, we are confronted with some special circumstances that need to be examined.

In explanatory research, such as qualitative, survey, and textual research, numbers and measurement may not be quite as important as they are in theory building. Nonetheless, numerical thinking can play in important part in the development of exploratory data. It is true that many qualitative researchers conduct their inquiry without using numbers or measurement, but it is also true that many qualitative researchers do use these basic operations to enhance their observational framework.

Chapter Three

Using Numbers

In chapter 2 we examined the first steps we take in doing research. First we decide on a topic, area, or problem; then we search the literature to see what, if anything, is known about the problem. Following that, we decide whether enough is known about the problem to form hypotheses about it or if we need to discover important aspects of the subject through less directive research. One thing that you may notice as you work your way through this procedure is that ideas of "greater" and "lesser" continue to crop up. Also, we tend to think of ways that individuals are classified into meaningful groups according to the demands of the problem area. While searching the original literature on your topic, you may also notice that almost all the articles on the subject used numbers to designate quantity and groupings. Numbers are an excellent shorthand language that enables the researcher to say much about the observations made in the investigation. In this chapter we will discuss the nature of numbers and look at the reasons we put our observations of communicative behavior in numerical form.

College athletics has long been plagued by charges that coaches and alumni recruit young people to compete for their schools who are not necessarily able to benefit from higher education—in short, that schools recruit athletes who can't pass and who ought not to be in college. To help prevent this kind of abuse, the NCAA (National Collegiate Athletic Association) has ruled that young persons receiving athletic scholarships should have a strong background in high school courses and a certain minimum score on an admissions test, such as the SAT. Obviously, the NCAA assumes that *without* knowledge of the high school background and of the SAT score, the possibility of the student athlete doing well in classwork in college cannot be evaluated. *With* the knowledge, on the other hand, they feel that we can predict success or failure, and feel more *certain*.

Obviously, this "knowledge" that we wish to employ in making admissions decisions is useless unless it has a certain degree of *gener-*

ality, or universalism. In other words, the SAT score and the high school record should be dependable predictors for most students, whether they are athletes, literature majors, or musicians. It should be the same next year as it is this one, and it should apply on the West Coast equally as well as it does in the South. If we are to make any differential decisions about human beings—and we do, on a daily basis—we need to achieve as much generality, or universalism, as we can.

We frequently see exhortations from communication theorists that each human being is unique; that each situation is unique; and that to generalize is dangerous and misleading. Nonetheless, the process of generalization is absolutely necessary for any of us to conduct our day-to-day activities. However uncomfortable we may be with admissions tests for university acceptance, we know that some kind of indicators are necessary as a practical matter.

In other situations, such as the legal system, we see that today the courts are confronted with many instances of torts for which litigation is pending. A "tort" is wrongful conduct that results in harm to someone—negligence or malice is specifically indicated. A "mass tort" is conduct that harms large numbers of persons, such as the use of asbestos or tobacco. Judge Hillel Zobel of the Massachusetts Superior Court has noted that "The characteristic of a mass tort is that, although each injured person's story is of course in some ways unique, all individuals share a common experience: contact with a substance that is thought to have caused injury" (Zobel, 1997, p. 19). Judge Zobel urges that Congress adopt some national guidelines making it easier for trial judges to generalize about particular products, or the state and local courts will be overwhelmed with the amount of litigation.

NUMBERS AND COUNTING

We achieve generality primarily by examining aggregates of individuals. While it is true that each of us is an individual, with individual characteristics, uniqueness does not help us find universal relationships in a practical way. If we are to discover general statements about groups of persons, we need to use descriptions that can be aggregated in a meaningful way, and that implies the use of numbers. The process of describing human characteristics with numbers is relatively complex, and in this chapter we will examine some of the basic principles involved with numbers and their use.

Let's return to the problem of the NCAA and the college athlete. Definition of "success" in college in a way that can be applied to a large number of college students is not easy. Some might call college a success if *any* student learned *anything*. Others might hold that "success" comes with graduation and nothing less. Still others might argue that graduation is not always the most reliable index of college success, because many individuals drop out for reasons not related to academics. However, most would agree that the most common indicator of success for students is grades achieved in courses, or "grade point average." This is an *aggregate* description of grades assigned by professors, and even if the grade in a course in chemistry represents quite a different kind of achievement than a grade in field hockey, the scale is the same. Sometimes the institution differentiates between kinds of courses (many don't count physical education toward the grade point average), but usually grades are aggregated into a single average. We do this because we feel that the average is meaningful in a way that individual grades are not. In other words, the "grade point average" is a concept that we feel is general enough to apply to most students, regardless of background or other mitigating circumstances.

We are so familiar with this process that we forget all of the assumptions and ideas that have gone into it. The first is the idea of "greater" or "lesser." High grades represent greater accomplishment and lower ones stand for lesser. Similarly, the SAT score is also assumed to represent "more" or "less." So in dealing with a specific student, the university might say that the SAT was "good" or "very good," and that they would expect that the student's grade point average would also be "good" or "very good." But words like this are very imprecise. So most educators have decided that, instead of saying "good or bad," "more or less," or "successful or unsuccessful," they will substitute a numerical expression for these qualitative judgments.

They hope that when they do so, the numerical expression will have greater generality than any of the adjectives by themselves. It is important to note that the greater generality can conceal the more individual characteristics of any given student. Two students can have exactly the same grade point average, but if one is a chemistry major, focusing on a premedical curriculum, the average will indicate very different characteristics if the other student is a history major, specializing in the Russian revolution. Everyone who uses numbers should be aware of what numerical language does and doesn't do.

In spite of the shortcomings, using numbers lets us deal with the central concept of predictability. The only way to tell if a researcher has produced a useful measure is to determine if it really reflects "greater" or "lesser" certainty of a result. This is why many researchers believe that science is not possible without the specific quantifiers of numbers. But wouldn't ordinary language do to describe quantities? Ordinary language does contain a number of terms describing quantity, such as many, few, or some. However, although they "sound" like quantities, specifics are missing and misinterpretations can result. For example, if one says there are a lot of people in this room, that statement doesn't tell the reader if there are fifteen or one hundred people present. We are primarily interested in making predictions. Whether these predictions are certain or uncertain is the true key to whether our science is going to be valuable in a practical sense. However we articulate it, the best way to be confident about our predictions is to use a specialized language designed for such tasks—numbers.

Counting is familiar to all of us, but counting to describe the results of communication is not as widespread as it is in describing other activities. Everyone who works in agricultural research knows how important counting can be. When a particular fertilizer or pesticide is used, its success or failure is almost always expressed in terms of "bushels per acre" or some other familiar ratio. A "bushel" is a familiar unit. Unfortunately, we don't seem to have the same convenient units to count the results of a communicative act. While persuasive communication may result in "votes" for someone involved in a political campaign, it is hard to connect voting to any particular communicative decision. For one reason, voting is usually done in secret and is hard to count. Further, it is often influenced by many other factors, such as party labels and personal assessments.

People who pay to put commercial messages on television may hope that the result will be "buying behavior," but few of us dash out to buy a new car after being exposed to a car commercial. Buying a car is a big decision, and money probably has more to do with it than any other factor. But even if we never bought a BMW, it would not make sense to assert that watching a BMW commercial had no effect or made no impression on us. Commercial messages have intermediate effects that might *eventually* lead to buying behavior if the circumstances were right.

Sometimes these effects are referred to as "attitudes" or "intentions." We typically don't contend that a commercial message made "lots" of attitudes, even though that may actually be the case. It is more probable that we will think about a "'stronger" rather than "weaker" attitude as a result of our message. This assessment of strength, just as in counting, depends on an assumption that we can assign a number for the degree of strength of the attitude, and compare that way. This is an absolutely vital assumption, and if this assumption cannot be made, the use of quantitative models in social science is unwarranted. Most of us make that assumption, and spend little time thinking about it. But assigning a number to any human action should only be done with careful thought. Leonard Berkoweitz (1993), in writing about emotion, mentions that it is common for people who are experiencing anger in different degrees to say that they are "annoyed," "angry," or "enraged," depending on the force of the emotion they feel. It would make little sense for us to describe "annoyed" as "ten" and "enraged" as "one hundred" unless we had some other criteria to justify the use of the scale.

Consider the doctor on the *Today* show that we mentioned at the beginning of the book. Suppose he prepares a truly effective, hard-hitting brochure outlining the dangers of smoking and distributes it to each patient that comes into the office. Better yet, he gives it to each patient personally and spends five minutes discussing some of the dangers of heart disease, emphysema, and lung cancer that smoking induces. Next week out at the country club, he mentions his efforts. "How do you know it works?" asks his friend, the pediatrician, getting ready to tee off. "They seemed to like it," mumbles the doctor, slicing into the slough. Most of us would not be happy with his answer. We would want to know what *results* the brochure produced, especially if we were asked to contribute toward the cost of the message.

If information alone is enough to produce an effect, then everyone who read the brochure would quit smoking. But we all know smokers who readily admit that they "know" that cigarettes will kill them, but they smoke anyway. So we can't expect a one-to-one relationship between information and behavior. But suppose we ask if the *proportion* of smokers changed. It might be very likely that someone in the patient pool quit as a result of the brochure. The vital question is: Do enough patients modify their behavior to make the expenditure of time and money on the brochure worth its cost? How much is enough? Five percent? Ten percent? How about if no one quit, but everyone experienced some other kind of effect? We can't answer any of these questions unless we can translate these questions into sensible propositions involving numbers, and to do that, we need some kind of specific procedure that we can agree is both reasonable and descriptive. If we can find these, then we can use numbers in describing them. In other words, the use of numbers makes it possible for us to apply comparisons that we could not otherwise make, and these comparisons help us decide if communicative acts are effective or not. When we make those comparisons, we are testing our theory about communication in a formal way.

KINDS OF NUMBERS

Most people are surprised to learn that numbers can be of several kinds. Let's look at some of these.

Nominal Numbers

As the name implies, some numbers are only names. Your social security number is a good example. There is no inherent value associated with having a social security number of a certain value—i. e., if my number is larger than yours, I am not necessarily better than you, or older, nor should I earn more money. In other words, the number is really a *name* (hence the word *nominal).* Other numbers of that type are your car's license plate number and the number on your volleyball jersey. All these numbers do is distinguish one person or thing from another—they do not imply quantity or degree of importance.

Ordinal Numbers

This kind of number implies a position. For example, apartment number 15 is usually next to number 16, and closer to that number than it is to apartment number 22. Ordinal numbers imply an order, or a system of some kind. Ordinal numbers are formed by putting a suffix such as "th" or "est" after the number (for example, "fifteenth"). But note that an ordinal number doesn't indicate that a given apartment has any other characteristic other than position. A hospital may have a logical system of numbering rooms, but it doesn't imply that room 105 is larger or smaller than room 151. Room 200 may be on another floor, but not necessarily.

Cardinal Numbers

Cardinal numbers are what most of us think of when we use the word "number," in that some quantity is implied. A cardinal number can be thought of as the answer to the question "how many?" If the building in which you work has different numerical prefixes for your office numbers which indicate the floor, you are using cardinal numbers, at least in a crude sense. If your office is 1553 and you are on the fifteenth floor, and if all the offices on the floor below you are numbered beginning with "14," such as 1403, 1467, and so forth, then you have a cardinal number system. Odd as this may seem, the quantity implied in your office number is how many floors there are in your building. There isn't always a one-to-one correspondence between the number system and the floors, but usually the actual number can be derived from the system.

Number theorists tell us that fractions are different from whole numbers, and that integers are different from divisible numbers. Computer designers tell us that numbers are "integer" and "real," and if that isn't enough, mathematicians also tell us that the number system is arbitrary—we could be using a system with a base of twelve, for example. Binary numbers are composed of ones and zeros, and hexadecimal numbers utilize different symbols for twelves, thirteens, and so forth. But it is very important to keep in mind that number systems are not magic—they were invented by humans to do human things. The fact that some numbers or concepts are not "real" only means that they are computational aids, and not that some ethereal quality "out there" exists in "infinity" just because we use such a concept to describe certain numerical progressions.

Let us recapitulate briefly. Science—especially a "human science" like communication—depends on the use of numbers in order to describe aggregations of people or responses. This in turn makes comparisons between different kinds of communicative events possible. However, we need to be especially careful with the number system used, because of the tendency we all have toward subjective evaluation of the concepts we study. The use of terms like "attitude" and "motivation" are typical of concepts that numbers are used to describe.

In the next section, we will look at statistical notation, or the specific systems that are involved in the use of numbers to describe human events.

STATISTICAL NOTATION

When we first see mathematical symbols we tend to be mystified—primarily because they are incomprehensible by themselves. However, the systems used are actually quite simple and make sense when they are examined one element at a time. The systems are necessary because we usually want to deal with *aggregate* data, in other words, groups of numbers. These operations of aggregation and grouping are expressed in mathematical shorthand. In this next section we will look at some of the more important symbols used to express mathematical operations and concepts.

Greek and Roman Letters

The first convention to master is the choice of Greek or Roman letters to stand for numbers. "A" is the Roman letter, and "α" is the Greek equivalent. You will run into "α" quite a lot in statistics, and it is usually used to express the "significance" level, or the degree to which a statistical test could have produced a chance result. The rule in statistics (a "convention," or custom among mathematicians) is that we use Greek symbols to express "parameters" (theoretical terms) and we use Roman letters to express actual observations which may or may not be similar to these parameters. Another way of putting this is that the Greek letters describe ideas or terms that have no "real" existence and the Roman letters describe "actual" observations. This will be explained in greater detail in upcoming chapters.

Subscripts

If you think back to your last algebra class, you will remember that calculations, to be "general," used letters instead of numbers. In other words, "a + b = x" meant that for any two numbers that you had, you would define a third number, "x," which would be the sum of the first two, which you called "a" and "b." In statistics, however, we often wish to refer to a group of numbers, rather than any specific one. The most common letter to define a "set" of numbers is "X." X can denote almost any characteristic of a group of things—the hat size of all the people in your research methods class, or the SAT score of all the entering students at your school. To define the set of X's that we have in mind, we use the following notation:

$$X_i, \quad i = 1, 22$$

This is another way of saying "there are 22 numbers that I am going to call 'X' in this set." Then to pick out any particular person's hat size, or SAT score, we use a subscript, thus: X_{22}, or X_{13}. This means literally "the 22nd X" or "the 13th X."

Arrays

If we have several numbers that we think are important for each member of your research methods class, such as shoe size, height, number of siblings in their family, as well as their SAT score, we could use another subscript. Typically "j" is the next one. So now let's imagine that we have 22 members of your research methods class and you know each one's hat size, shoe size, height, number of brothers and sisters, and SAT score. We have six numbers for each student, or 132 in all. A convenient way of designating these numbers is as follows:

$$X_{ij}, \quad i = 1, 22 \quad j = 1, 6$$

Now we could pick out any one number in this set of 132 numbers simply by using a pair of subscripts. For example, $X_{15.3}$ could mean "Wanda Smith's height." At this point, many persons say, "Why don't you just say that and eliminate all the subscripts?" The answer is that expressing yourself with symbols this way is much more convenient (especially when you get used to it) and that you can express things this way that you couldn't in ordinary English. Another reason is that the symbolic notation in mathematics makes it possible to express concepts more efficiently and more clearly. Look at the following table:

$$
\begin{array}{llllll}
X_{11} & X_{12} & X_{13} \ldots & X_{1i} \ldots & X_{1k} \\
X_{21} & X_{22} & X_{23} \ldots & X_{2i} \ldots & X_{2k} \\
X_{31} & X_{32} & X_{33} \ldots & X_{3i} \ldots & X_{3k} \\
X_{j1} & X_{j2} & X_{j3} \ldots & X_{ji} \ldots & X_{jk} \\
X_{n1} & X_{n2} & X_{n3} \ldots & X_{ni} \ldots & X_{nk}
\end{array}
$$

You can see that by using these subscripts, we can now have a powerful descriptive system—simply by using the subscript, we can designate any position in the table with an economical statement. Another name for scores or numbers laid out this way is **array**.

To see how this works, let's next look at the specific operators used in statistics. An operator is a symbol for a particular operation in arithmetic. The Greek letter *sigma* (Σ) is one of the most familiar of these. It is simply an instruction to add a given set of numbers. Consider the following expression:

$$
\sum_{i=1}^{22} X_i
$$

This is a compact and efficient way of saying: "sum all the X_i's that you have—from 1 to 22." You will note that specific instructions are on the bottom and the top of the sigma sign. This gives you great flexibility. You can say "sum the first 10 X's," or more simply, write it this way:

$$
\sum_{i=1}^{10} X_i
$$

If you would like to have a more general expression, such as "for ANY set of X's" you might use the letter n to stand for the last X in the set (X_n). Then your summation term might look like this:

$$
\sum_{i=1}^{n} X_i
$$

It should be clear that mathematical notation is nothing more than a highly efficient way of expressing a number of mathematical operations. To see how this works, let's take the most simple operation that we are likely to use in statistics, the "average," or the "mean." Here is how this simple calculation is described:

$$\bar{X} = \frac{\sum_{i=1}^{n} X_i}{n} \tag{1}$$

You can see from this statement that a new symbol has been introduced—an X with a line over the top of it, which we call "X-bar" and that its value is equal to the sum of all of the X's divided by the number of X's. "Hey," you might be saying, "That's the mean!" You would be right. You will also notice something new in that expression—a number in parentheses off to the right of the expression. This is to help you find this expression later on, and so that we can refer to the definition of a mean as Expression (1). Many combinations and manipulations can be accomplished using this notation. For example, if you wished to exclude all of the scores under five and those 20 or over, you would write:

$$\bar{X}a = \frac{\sum_{i=6}^{19} X_i}{13}$$

The use of statistical notation is a powerful tool in the analysis and manipulation of numbers.

To make the use of this notation a little more concrete, let's look at a typical example of numbers in communication research. Melanie Booth-Butterfield and Stephen Booth-Butterfield (1990) hypothesized that individuals differ from one another in the ways they are aware of their emotions in communication activities. In other words, some people know when they are upset, and others aren't as aware of it. The researchers devised a scale to measure this awareness, which they called "affective orientation." Table 3.1 presents their test of affective orientation.

Looking more closely at the test, you will notice that Item 7 states "I trust my feelings to guide my behavior." The Booth-Butterfields have assumed that if a respondent marks "1" or "strongly disagree" that this person is quite different from a respondent that marks "4" or "5." Almost everyone else would agree with them. Then if we would take the total score from the scale, we would have a good measure of the importance of emotion in a given individual's communicative behavior.

Let's look at a sample of individuals' scores on the Affect Orientation (AO) scale. Table 3.2 presents some hypothetical values that might have been selected by 39 individuals in responding to the AO scale.

Table 3.1
Affective Orientation Scale

Directions: The following statements refer to the feelings and emotions people have and how people use feelings and emotions to guide their behavior. There are no right or wrong answers. Also realize that emotions and feelings can be positive or negative. A person can feel anger; another can feel love and tenderness. Both cases, however, are emotion. The statements refer to both types, positive and negative.

Strongly Agree	Agree	Uncertain	Disagree	Strongly Disagree
5	4	3	2	1

1. I am very aware of my feelings.
2. I use my feelings to determine what I should do in situations.
3. My feelings and emotions are very important to me.
4. I listen to what my "gut" or "heart" says in many situations.
5. My emotions tell me what to do in many cases.
6. I try not to let my feelings guide my actions.*
7. I trust my feelings to guide my behavior.
8. I don't pay much attention to my emotions most of the time.*
9. My feelings tell me a lot about how to act in a given situation.
10. The intensity of my emotions does not change much from situation to situation.*
11. I use my feelings to determine whether to trust another person.
12. I learn a lot about myself on the basis of my feelings.
13. I am not usually aware of my feelings at any given moment.*
14. Feelings are a valuable source of information.
15. My feelings don't seem to be very intense or strong.*
16. I use feelings to guide me more than most people do.
17. Feelings only interfere with behavior.*
18. I orient to people through my emotions.
19. My emotions have many different levels of intensity; I can be angry, for example, or very angry.
20. I seem to have just a few basic emotions.*

---

* Indicates reverse-coded items

Table 3.2 Affect Orientation Scores

Case	1	2	3	4	5	6	7	8	9	10	11	12	13	14	15	16	17	18	19	20	Total
1	5	4	5	3	5	4	4	4	5	4	4	2	5	3	5	3	4	3	5	3	80
2	5	3	3	3	4	4	2	2	5	3	4	4	4	4	5	3	4	5	3	4	74
3	3	4	4	4	2	2	2	1	3	3	2	3	2	3	4	4	4	3	3	3	59
4	4	5	4	4	4	4	4	5	4	4	4	4	3	5	4	5	4	5	4	5	85
5	5	4	4	4	4	4	3	3	5	4	5	4	4	4	5	5	4	4	4	4	83
6	5	4	3	4	4	4	3	3	4	4	5	4	4	4	5	5	5	5	4	4	83
7	4	4	3	4	3	3	3	5	4	5	4	4	3	4	4	4	5	5	4	5	80
8	4	3	4	3	4	3	4	3	4	3	4	3	4	3	4	3	4	3	4	3	70
9	4	4	4	4	3	2	2	2	5	4	5	3	4	3	5	4	4	4	5	5	76
10	4	4	4	4	5	4	2	3	4	4	5	4	4	5	4	5	4	4	4	5	82
11	4	4	2	4	3	4	1	3	4	4	3	3	3	3	4	4	4	4	5	5	71
12	3	3	2	3	3	3	2	2	3	3	3	3	3	4	3	2	3	3	3	2	56
13	4	4	2	3	3	3	2	2	5	4	4	4	4	4	4	4	4	4	4	4	72
14	4	3	5	3	2	3	5	3	5	3	5	3	5	4	5	3	5	3	5	3	77
15	4	3	2	1	3	3	3	3	5	4	5	5	3	3	4	4	4	3	4	4	70
16	4	3	2	1	2	1	1	1	5	3	3	3	3	3	5	3	4	3	4	3	57
17	3	3	3	3	4	3	3	3	4	4	3	4	3	1	4	3	3	3	3	3	62
18	4	4	3	4	3	2	3	4	3	3	3	4	4	5	5	4	4	4	4	4	74
19	3	3	3	3	3	3	3	3	3	4	4	3	3	2	3	4	4	3	3	4	64
20	3	3	2	3	2	3	2	2	4	3	4	3	4	3	4	2	4	2	4	4	61
21	4	4	4	4	3	3	1	1	4	4	4	5	4	4	5	5	5	4	4	4	76
22	4	2	3	4	3	2	2	4	4	4	3	4	3	4	3	4	3	3	3	3	66
23	4	3	3	3	3	3	2	2	3	3	3	3	3	3	3	3	3	4	3	3	60
24	4	4	3	4	5	5	2	2	5	4	5	4	5	5	5	4	5	4	4	3	82
25	5	4	3	3	5	5	3	3	5	4	5	4	5	4	5	4	4	4	4	4	83
26	4	3	4	4	4	4	4	3	4	3	4	3	5	3	4	3	5	3	4	3	74
27	3	3	3	4	4	2	2	4	4	4	4	4	3	5	3	5	4	4	4	5	74
28	4	4	5	4	4	5	5	4	5	4	5	4	5	5	5	5	5	4	4	5	91
29	4	4	4	5	3	4	3	3	4	3	5	4	3	3	4	4	4	5	3	3	75
30	4	5	5	3	3	1	4	5	5	3	3	3	3	3	4	2	5	5	5	5	76
31	3	3	3	4	2	3	2	4	3	3	2	3	3	4	4	4	4	3	3	3	63
32	4	4	4	3	2	2	2	4	4	4	3	5	4	4	4	4	3	5	3	5	73
33	5	4	5	4	5	5	4	5	5	5	5	5	4	4	5	3	5	4	5	4	91
34	4	3	4	5	4	3	3	5	4	5	4	5	5	5	5	5	4	4	4	4	85
35	5	3	5	5	3	3	2	3	4	4	5	3	5	3	3	3	3	3	4	3	72
36	3	3	2	4	3	2	4	5	4	4	3	5	5	5	4	5	3	4	3	5	76
37	3	3	3	3	2	3	2	4	3	3	3	3	4	3	4	3	4	4	3	4	64
38	2	3	3	3	2	2	3	3	3	3	3	3	3	3	3	4	3	4	4	4	61
39	3	3	3	4	5	4	2	3	3	4	4	4	3	3	3	3	3	4	3	3	67
Total	151	137	133	138	131	124	106	124	154	144	152	144	148	144	161	148	156	148	149	150	2847

The utility of statistical notation is easy to see when the terms refer to actual numbers. There are 39 individuals filling out the questionnaire, and 20 items on the questionnaire. So if we designate any score by "X," then

$$X_{ij}, \quad i = 1,20 \quad j = 1, 39$$

"$X_{7,26}$" represents the score for individual number 26 on item number 7. The following expression,

$$\sum_{j=1}^{39} X_{7j}$$

means the total of the scores for item 7 for all the individuals responding. The next expression,

$$\sum_{i=1}^{20} \sum_{j=1}^{39} X_{ij}$$

represents the total of all the scores in the table.

AGGREGATING NUMBERS

We mentioned that one of the important reasons we use numbers is to describe an aggregation of observations in an economical and efficient way. A few pages ago, we mentioned the *mean*, or average, which is one standard descriptor of an aggregate (or group) of numbers. There we mentioned that the mean was calculated by adding up all the scores and dividing the resulting sum by the number of scores in the collection. The following sections describe some of the aspects involved in aggregating numbers.

Central Tendency

Another term for the mean is a *measure of central tendency*. Other familiar measures of central tendency are the *median* and the *mode*. The median is the midpoint of the distribution; half of the numbers in any distribution will lie above the median, and half will lie below it. The mode is the number that occurs most frequently. So if your collection of scores has no number that is repeated, then there is no mode. But if one number is repeated more often than the others, then it is the mode. Each of these measures of central tendency can be useful, depending on the data set. (We will discuss them in more detail in chapter 8, where we examine the normal curve.) But none of these measures of central tendency are useful without knowing how variable, or scattered, the scores are. To see how this is so, let's look at an example.

Suppose the city council in your town is concerned about the quality of the trees in a particular neighborhood. At great expense, oak trees were planted twenty years ago on several streets throughout the city and they hope that the trees are doing well. North and South Broadway are two such streets. North Broadway is primarily residential, while South Broadway is mixed residential and commercial. The city council is concerned about how the trees are doing, and hopes that no regulation is necessary to preserve the trees. A research group of forestry students makes a random sample of six trees from each street, measures them and presents the results to the city council.

Here are the measurements (in meters) the forestry students have gathered:

	South Broadway	North Broadway
Tree 1	14	11
Tree 2	13	10
Tree 3	7	9
Tree 4	10	8
Tree 5	6	12
Tree 6	10	10

As we look at these two sets of trees, we might wonder which group is doing "best." The average height for each group of trees is 10 meters, so the city council concludes that the two streets are the same. Ten meters is over thirty-nine feet, a good height for a twenty-year-old tree. But the students point out that the two groups of trees vary considerably. The trees on South Broadway deviate a good deal from the mean, and the trees on North Broadway do not. Here are the deviations:

	South Broadway		North Broadway	
	Height	Deviation	Height	Deviation
Tree 1	14	4	11	1
Tree 2	13	3	10	0
Tree 3	7	3	9	1
Tree 4	10	0	8	2
Tree 5	6	4	12	2
Tree 6	10	0	10	0
Totals	60	14	60	6

The South Broadway trees have an *average deviation* of 2.3 meters, and the North Broadway trees have an average deviation of only 1 meter. What causes the difference? We don't know, but we do know that the two groups are different. So just knowing the *mean* of the groups is not enough—we also must know the *variability* in each of them. Another way of saying this is that *knowing a mean is useless unless you know its variance.* Let's look at variability a little more closely.

Variability

Variability can be described in a number of different ways. Range tells us how far apart are the largest and the smallest scores. Average deviation tells us how far, on the average, each score varies from the mean, like the example in the trees given above. But the most important measure of variability is the **variance**, which is the *average of the squared deviations from the mean.* Expression (2) is the definition of *variance*, which is usually expressed by a small sigma squared (σ^2).

$$\sigma^2 = \frac{\sum\limits_{i=1}^{n} (X_i - \bar{X})^2}{n} \qquad (2)$$

The value of σ^2 will be much larger than the average deviation, since each individual difference from the mean is squared.[1] When most of us encounter the idea of variance, it seems unnecessarily complicated to us, but there are excellent reasons for using this measurement. The most important one is that variance is the basis for estimating probability, the foundation of statistical inference. We will explore some of these reasons in a later chapter. But for now, it is important to remember that the variance is the basic unit in calculating the normal curve, which is the foundation of most probability models in statistics. It is the principal unit used in calculating variability.

Let's go back to the data on affect orientation presented earlier. If we were to use expression (2) to calculate the variance, we would proceed as shown in table 3.3.

Notice that the mean of the collection of 39 scores is 73; to determine the deviation we subtract the mean from each score. The first score is 80, and when we subtract 73 from it, we get 7. Squaring seven (the deviation) gets us 49. Adding up all the squared deviations gives us 3319, and dividing it by 39 yields 85.102, the variance of these scores.

The variance is not always the most important measure of variability, however. For one thing, it seems too large, being the result of

Table 3.3 Calculations of the Variance of Responses to the "AO" scale

Respondent	Score	Mean	Deviation	Squared Deviation
1	80	73	7	49
2	74	73	1	1
3	59	73	−14	196
4	87	73	14	196
5	83	73	10	100
6	83	73	10	100
7	80	73	7	49
8	70	73	−3	9
9	76	73	3	9
10	82	73	9	81
11	71	73	−2	4
12	56	73	−17	289
13	72	73	−1	1
14	77	73	4	16
15	70	73	−3	9
16	57	73	−16	256
17	62	73	−11	121
18	74	73	1	1
19	64	73	−9	81
20	61	73	−12	144
21	76	73	3	9
22	66	73	−7	49
23	60	73	−13	169
24	82	73	9	81
25	84	73	11	121
26	74	73	1	1
27	74	73	1	1
28	91	73	18	324
29	75	73	2	4
30	76	73	3	9
31	63	73	−10	100
32	73	73	0	0
33	91	73	18	324
34	85	73	12	144
35	72	73	−1	1
36	76	73	3	9
37	64	73	−9	81
38	61	73	−12	144
39	67	73	−6	36
Totals	2840		0	3319

squaring the deviations from the mean. Another widely used unit of variability is the **standard deviation**. It is simply the square root of the variance. Expression (3) is the formula for standard deviation:

$$s = \sqrt{\frac{\sum_{i=1}^{n} (X_i - \bar{X})^2}{n}} \tag{3}$$

So, for the group of scores in affect orientation, we see that the mean is 73 and the standard deviation is 9.225. We can look at the total score in this collection and see where each individual lies with regard to the mean of that set of scores, the means that other researchers observed, and make some judgments about how these persons might act in given communicative situations.

So a very crude way of assessing the consistency of the scores on affect orientation is to calculate the standard deviation, and see how variable a set of scores might be. In general, we feel that if a measure has a lot of variance, it is much less stable than if it has a smaller amount.

Later on, as you are introduced to statistical notions of greater and greater complexity, you will find the notational system a highly efficient way of expressing relationships in a set of numbers. Immediately, however, you will note the greater economy and ease involved in designating complex relationships.

CAUTIONS ABOUT USING NUMBERS

Before we leave the topic of numbers and their value, we should remind ourselves that many important human concepts cannot be expressed this way. Sometimes we think numbers are the only "modern" form of expression. In other words, it has become trendy to use numbers or number-like expressions where an ordinary English sentence may suffice. Researchers should avoid this kind of "puffery." If your idea demands the use of numbers, use them. If not, avoid it.

Institutions and customs often have demanded we use numbers even though the use of them makes no sense. In 1978, Neil Postman, a well-known expert on technology and professor of media ecology, presented a speech on "The Technical Thesis" at Seton Hall University. He wanted to illustrate how we have become obsessed with numbers and technology.

Everyone must have a favorite and real example of the tyranny of numbers. I have several, the most recent having occurred a couple of months ago. I and several people of reputed intelligence were together in a hotel room, watching a television program called "The Miss Universe Pageant." Now, even in a nontechnicalized culture, a beauty pageant would be, it seems to me, a degrading cultural event. In this one, pure lunacy was added to the degradation by the utilization of computers to measure the measurements, so to speak, of the women involved. Each of the twelve judges was able to assign a precise number to the charm of a woman's smile, the shapeliness of her bosom, the sensuality of her walk, and even to the extent of what was called her "poise." But more than this, as each judge assigned a number, a mother-computer, with legendary speed, calculated the average, which was then dashed on the upper right-hand corner of the TV screen so that the audience could know immediately, that Miss Holland, for example, was a 6.231 on how she looked in a bathing suit, whereas Miss Finland was only a 5.827. Now, as it happened, one of the people with whom I was watching believed, as he put it, that there is no way Miss Finland is a 5.827. He estimated that she is, at a minimum, a 6.3, and maybe as high as a 7.2. Another member of our group took exception to these figures, maintaining strongly that only in a world gone mad is Miss Finland a 5.827, and that she should count herself lucky that she did not get what she deserved, which, as he figured it, was no more than a 3.8.

Postman echoes a sentiment that is very popular today. There is a good deal of truth in what he says—some things (like the Miss Universe contest) probably ought not to use numbers for their evaluations.

What we need to remember is that numbers are very useful in some ways, and not so useful in others. Of course, we would all prefer not to "be just a number." But there are times when numbers are the only way to look at things. If I make one long-distance call per month, I should not pay the same bill that you do if you call your cousin Liam in Ireland every week. We need to look at each circumstance afresh, and see if numerical description is the best way (or even a sensible way). Numbers are truly useful, but obviously they are only useful when used appropriately. In the pages that follow, we will look at many examples of ways in which communication researchers have used numbers. Quite often, these numbers were the only way to handle the issues involved. In other instances, there may have been choices. Each researcher needs to judge.

NOTE

[1] You may have seen expression (2) written using "n-1" instead of "n." The use of "n-1" derives from the process of *estimation*, which is the assessment of a large group based on much smaller samples taken. We will discuss this process in detail later in the book.

Chapter Four

Measurement

In chapter 3 we examined the reasons why we use numbers, and looked at some of the reasons why many researchers feel that numbers are essential for the aggregation of observations and particular kinds of comparisons. Later we will explore why numbers are essential to the use of probability in proof. In this chapter we will look at some of the underlying ideas involved in measurement and some of the ways researchers measure concepts in communication.

When most of us think of measurement, we think of units like feet, inches, and meters—and some of us are accustomed to using less familiar units, such as "column inches" or "cost per thousand." We need to remind ourselves, however, that each of these units of measurement are arbitrary and have been subject to a good deal of change. In the Renaissance, for example, Leonardo DaVinci used a unit of length called a "bracchi," which was a unit of length as long as an arm. It was about 0.583 meters ("Leonardo's Lengths," *New York Times,* 1994). Probably the most common unit used in Renaissance Italy was a unit used by the Romans, the *piede,* or the foot. It was about 11.73 inches. (The metric system came into use after the French Revolution and set an international standard.) Almost every unit of measurement came from some "convention" or custom entered into by practical persons.

The process of measurement is a response to the nature of the world—almost everything differs in some way or another. We describe a house in terms of its square footage, and a road in terms of its length. These may not be the most important aspects of houses and roads, but certainly they are meaningful ones. Similarly, people differ in ways that are measurable. We are familiar with height and weight as basic units in which people differ, but people differ in other ways as well. We have already looked at examples of the way individuals differ in "argumentativeness," as well as other characteristics. Individuals differ in *qualitative* and *quantitative* ways (Ghiselli, Campbell & Zedek, 1981). Qualitative differences appear when we look at categories, such as occupation or geographic location. Quantitative differences are those to which we can assign numbers and use them to describe qualities of more or less; larger or smaller in specific characteristics. For example, we could say "Mark has twenty-three houseplants" (quantitative) or "Mark's exotic houseplants make his house an interesting place" (qualitative). Or we could say "Nancy has three dogs" (quantitative) or "Nancy's dogs are truly beautiful animals" (qualitative).

In studying communication, measurement is less obvious. Generally we measure three very large classes of things—the communication behavior in which individuals engage, the particular characteristics of people themselves (usually in regard to communication), and responses to communication. In the first category, a good deal of the focus is on what people say in particular situations. For instance, we might be interested in what individuals say when their boss tells them that their vacation will be in February rather than May. Our main interest would be in finding patterns in the way these individuals react to a change in their vacation time in order to gain insight into how communication will take place in future, similar situations. In the second category, we are interested in specific differences among individuals in communication behavior. Gender studies, in which we examine the way that women and men differ in communicative behavior, is one example. Other examples are "argumentativeness," and the "apprehension" that individuals feel prior to formal speaking situations. In the third category, we see a greater interest in the results of communication, or people's responses to messages. The doctor on the *Today* show, mentioned previously and throughout this book, would have been mostly concerned with the smoking response, and its diminution. Political communication aims at

---

HOW CAN YOU MEASURE GENDER?   For many years, researchers have been concerned with differences due to gender. The biological distinction of sex is easier to classify, but it is clear that many men and women share similar psychological characteristics—there are "masculine" women and "feminine" men. Sandra Bem set out to discover what, if any, defensible personality traits are associated with *gender* as opposed to biological sex. The result was a list of characteristics that denoted masculinity and femininity. For example, masculinity was defined by words such as "assertive," "dominant," "independent," and "forceful." Femininity was defined by words such as "gentle," "helpful," "warm," "sincere," and "friendly." Researchers found that classifications like "masculine," or "feminine," were not sufficient to describe most persons. Some were both—androgynous. Some were neither—undifferentiated. The BSRI test produces four "sextypes," masculine, feminine, androgynous, or undifferentiated. These "sextypes" differ greatly from biological sex. (Bem,1974)

voting behavior (and sometimes fundraising). Let's look at each of these classifications briefly, along with some examples of how researchers in communication have attempted to assess them.

COMMUNICATIVE BEHAVIOR

Usually when we examine the different ways people communicate, we wonder why they did what they did—or, we wish to explain the differences. We have a variety of choices concerning communicative behavior. We could count the time spent in communicating, the number of words used in an interview, or the intensity of the adjectives someone uses in describing a relationship. Some of these involve a good deal of "coding," or transcribing individual responses into categories.

For example, Ellis and Hamilton (1985) studied the way that different kinds of couples use language. They examined the ways in which couples used particular words that might give some strong indications of the nature of the couples' relationships. This means also that the couples can be said to have different meanings for the words as a consequence. To test their theory, Ellis and Hamilton examined word usage by two different types of couples. Significant differences were found, for example, in the number of times the word "I" was used by independent vs. traditional couples. (To see Ellis and Hamilton's frequencies, see the section "Ellis' Functional View of Language," in chapter 6.) The interest in this kind of measurement stems from the classification of the kinds of couples in the study.

Communicative Characteristics of Individuals

Most of the tests of individuals' communicative characteristics concern a report of some personality or evaluative characteristic related to communicative activity (for example, dominant or submissive; bold or retiring). In the last chapter we looked at such an inventory, "affect orientation." Probably the most common of these used in communication study is the "Personal Report of Communication Apprehension," devised by James McCroskey. This test assesses the emotional reactions of those of us who experience fright when we communicate. Table 4.1 presents a short form of this questionnaire (McCroskey, 1974).

Table 4.1 Short Form of the PRCA

Respondents are instructed to circle the response next to each item that most closely describes how they feel, according to the following scale: 1 = "strongly agree," 2 = "agree," 3 = "undecided or don't know," 4 = "disagree," and 5 = "strongly disagree."

1 2 3 4 5   1. I look forward to expressing myself at meetings.

1 2 3 4 5   2. I am afraid to express myself in a group.

1 2 3 4 5   3. I feel relaxed and comfortable while speaking.

1 2 3 4 5   4. Although I talk fluently with my friends, I am at a loss for words on the platform.

1 2 3 4 5   5. I always avoid speaking in public if possible.

1 2 3 4 5   6. I feel that I am more fluent when talking to people than most persons are.

1 2 3 4 5   7. I like to get involved in group discussions.

1 2 3 4 5   8. I dislike to use my body and voice expressively.

1 2 3 4 5   9. I am afraid to speak up in conversations.

1 2 3 4 5   10. I would enjoy presenting a speech on a local television show.

To score these items for a communication apprehension total, we take items 1, 3, 6, 7 and 10 and add them, calling it "total A." Then we take items 2, 4, 5, 8, and 9 and add them, calling this "total B." Then starting with an arbitrarily chosen number (in this case, 36), we add total A to it and subtract total B from it. You see from the scales chosen that "total B" expresses apprehensive feelings and "total A" expresses positive feelings. So if we wish to know how apprehensive any one individual is, we should counterbalance the negative with the positive. But an easier way to express the apprehension score is given by the following expression:

$$CA = 36 + (X_1 + X_3 + X_6 + X_7 + X_{10}) - (X_2 + X_4 + X_5 + X_8 + X_9)$$

We could simplify the procedure by making all the items unidirectional (constructing the items to be either all positive or all negative), but then we would run the risk of measuring the general "positiveness" or "negativity" of the respondent.

Clearly, the assignment of an "apprehension" score to any one individual doesn't express the "quality" of any individual's experience of apprehension—but it does provide an index that makes it possible for us to make general statements about groups of persons. If we were to try to alleviate apprehension among college students by trying one specific technique (such as praise instead of criticism), we could compare students in sections that were treated this way to students who were not. If we found general differences, we would be more confident of applying the technique to other students. There are many different kinds of questionnaires relating to communication acts and activities. Scales for "self-monitoring," "verbal behavior," and "parasocial interaction" abound (Sypher, Palmgreen, & Rubin, 1994). Other scales measure more specific personality traits, such as "self-esteem," "locus of control," and others.

Responses to Communicative Behavior

In some communicative activities, there is interest in creating, changing, or strengthening someone else's responses (Miller, 1980; Bostrom, 1983). We have long recognized that not every message will produce dramatic responses. Suppose you feel strongly that the government should not allow the sale or possession of assault rifles—military weapons which include large magazines and other features, such as grenade launchers. You design a message for gun owners that states, "Real men don't need assault rifles to be attractive!" and put it in a short speech. You know that if you try it out at the next meeting of your local chapter of NRA you will be booed off the stage. But you still might think the effort worthwhile if one hunter would tell you that you "made him think." This response, however, doesn't meet the requirements of science, in that an element of "publicness" is essential. We can't look at this hunter and know what he is thinking. An intermediate kind of public response is usually chosen to show effectiveness. For instance, instead of asking someone to give money to our cause, we might hand them a bumper sticker instead. Accepting the bumper sticker is a very low level of acceptance and giving money is much higher.

Let's look at another example. In this modern age, sexually transmitted diseases are a clear social danger. The usual approach to controlling such diseases is to urge people to "be responsible" and use some kind of protection in sexual practices, such as condoms. But how would a public health official *prove* that a campaign advocating sexual responsibility had been successful? The critical responses (sexual behavior) are highly private ones, and we wouldn't allow anyone from our county health office into our bedroom to see what we do. In other words, *in many important public problems, the affected behavior itself is impossible to observe directly.* So we are confronted with a dilemma—we must either admit that we don't know how effective the communication attempt is, or find some other way to assess it. The traditional approach to solving this problem has been to use the concept of *attitudes*—cognitive precursors of behavior.

There are a number of approaches to defining attitudes; they are almost always thought of in terms of statements. Going back to our earlier example of assault rifles, we could gather a series of sentences on the subject:

1. It's okay for people to own assault rifles, but I'd never hang around with them.
2. Assault rifles are too expensive for private use.
3. Only an insecure person would want an assault rifle.
4. An individual would be a fool to own an assault rifle because he or she could be sued in case of an accident.
5. The government has the right to regulate your private behavior.
6. A woman would be stupid to marry a guy who owned an assault rifle.

Each statement centers on a particular domain. The first is behavioral, the second economic beliefs, the third evaluative, the fourth legal, the fifth invokes a larger social framework, and the sixth romantic. Yet a general schema—a "superordinate" construct—of negativism about assault rifles underlies all six of the statements. When we can find such a construct we usually call it an "attitude." This basic evaluation of assault rifles and their place in a society probably has behavioral connections in that the presence of certain attitudes raises the probability of behavior in that direction.

An interesting characteristic of attitudes is that typically they are not overtly stated. Many people who agree with some of the statements above would never state baldly, "Anyone who owns an assault rifle is an idiot," even though most of us would think they believe that from the implications of the statements. In other words, we are probably justified in inferring the presence of anti-assault rifle thoughts even though we have no *direct* evidence of it. There is an underlying structure and a series of links among the six statements. The nature of this structure and connections is usually studied in relation to other cognitive structures.

You will recognize that some of these statements are "stronger" than others. But none of them are extremely strong, or extremely weak. We need a wider range. To remedy this, let's add two more statements to the collection of statements about assault rifles:

7. The idea of some pervert owning an assault rifle makes me want to throw up.
8. While it's okay for people to own assault rifles, I feel sort of uneasy about it.

Statement 7 is strong and statement 8 is relatively weak. This gives us a wider range of statements. Anyone who agreed with seven will probably agree with all the rest of the statements, and it would be possible for someone to disagree with one through seven and still agree with eight. "Scaling" statements this way gives us a Thurstone scale if we use independent judges to evaluate the scales (Thurstone, 1959) and a Guttman scale if we use actual responses to scale the items (Guttman, 1944). To prepare a Thurstone scale, the researcher starts with about 100 statements on a given topic; then a group of experts is asked to rank the statements as to strength or weakness. If the items do not clearly reflect one or another, they are discarded. With the Guttman procedure, a large group of scale items is given to a group of respondents. Then each item is compared to the total score. Those that express weak attitudes (such as, statement 8) should be agreed to by everyone; those with strong attitudes (statement 7, for example) would be agreed to by only those scoring strongly on the overall total. Thurstone and Guttman scales are nothing more than ranked sets of statements ranging from mild to extreme. Researchers would use these scales if a high degree of accuracy in scaling is demanded. Their degree of effectiveness depends on how well they are consistently ranked in the same fashion by different groups of persons, one by experts and the other by respondents themselves.

Rensis Likert (1932) proposed another way of measuring attitude: offering respondents an opportunity to agree or disagree with each item and a "mini-scale" to evaluate each item. Likert scales often look like this:

8. The idea of some pervert owning an assault rifle makes me want to throw up.

_____Agree strongly

_____Agree

_____Agree a little

_____Neutral

_____Disagree a little

_____Disagree

_____Disagree strongly

Scoring involves assigning a number to each category, such as a seven for the "strongly agree" category and a one for the "strongly disagree" category (or any other arithmetically consistent scoring scheme). Then if we used all eight statements, we would have a test with a possible total score of 56 for the strongest attitude against assault rifles and 8 for the strongest attitude in favor of assault rifles. Likert scales are popular with researchers because it is almost always possible for a respondent to enter something that makes sense from the respondent's point of view.

One problem from which all attitude measurement suffers is that it is painfully obvious to the respondent what is being measured. So if someone asks you if you really like Beavis and Butthead, you might not be willing to be completely open in your response. If we are interested in measuring a socially undesirable attitude, we might want a measure that is a little more indirect, and that partially masks what is being asked. Osgood, Suci, Tannenbaum (1956) proposed a "meaning-centered" approach to this measurement problem. They found that it is possible to relate concepts to general qualitative reactions expressed by bipolar adjectives. For example, the general term "assault rifles" could be described on series of scales like these:

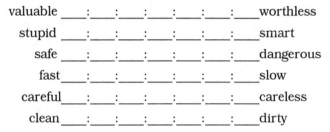

We could use any set of adjectives that we liked—such as good-bad, hot-cold, rough-smooth, and the like. Osgood and his colleagues used a very large pool of adjectives, and discovered that most of them could be said to measure underlying dimensions of evaluation, activity, or potency. However, these dimensions vary depending on the specific behavior that is being assessed.

Contextual Effects

In constructing any sort of measurement device, it is important to remember that the *context* in which it is presented affects the judgement of the *attitude object*, or behavior. If the measurement takes place during other social stimuli (Scwarz & Bless, 1992), it will be affected. The judgment of the ferocity of animals (Herr, Sherman, & Fazio, 1983) and the severity of a sentence given for a crime (Higgins & Lurie, 1983) were shown to be affected by the context in which they were presented. In another study, judgments of the attractiveness of faces depended on whether or not they were presented to the judger together with other more attractive or ugly faces (Wedell, Parducci, and Geiselman, 1987). Usually if the researcher holds the context constant, the judgments will remain fairly equitable, but researchers should always be aware of the possible differences that contexts can make.

In summary, we have examined three main ways in which we assess individual differences in communication—in overt communicative behavior, in individual differences, and in differential responses to communicative stimuli. The examples of assessment presented may have given the idea that researchers start with existing tests of well-known concepts in communication, and that is often the case. But all researchers should start with the definition of the characteristic in mind, and then *operationalize* the characteristic. In operationalizing, the researchers describe the overt ways in which the characteristic would be manifested. Suppose an advertiser hopes that using women as models in a pickup truck magazine ad would generate more interest among women reading the ad. We can't observe directly how interested someone might be by looking at them, so when observing readers, we might record the number of seconds readers took to read an ad. The *operational definition* of interest would then be the number of seconds spent reading the truck ad.

You will notice that in most of the instances presented above, we cannot observe the "behavior" directly; we have utilized paper and pencil tests, which report individuals' memories of behaviors. We usually call such reports *questionnaires,* though many prefer to use the term *tests* to describe them. In the next section, we will examine some of the characteristics of questionnaires in greater detail.

CHARACTERISTICS OF QUESTIONNAIRES

The fundamental purpose of a questionnaire is to elicit the type of response desired by the researcher. For example, if the doctor on the *Today* show used a questionnaire on his patients with the question "How much do you smoke?" we would expect the questionnaire to be useful only if it reflected how much individuals actually smoked. In other words, we hope that people tell the truth—but we never know. As a substitute for direct validation of the questionnaires, we use a variety of techniques, striving for *reliability* and *validity.* We need to discuss each of these in some detail.

Reliability

The basic notion underlying reliability is *consistency.* Individuals who enjoy remodelling and doing their own carpentry work soon learn the adage, "measure three times and cut once." Sad experience has taught them that often the first measurement can be in error. But if all three measurements come out the same, they feel more justified in cutting an expensive piece of wood. We seldom measure three times in communication research, but we often measure twice. When we give the same person the same test twice and compare the results, we call the result *test-retest* reliability.

The measure that is used for consistency evaluations is called correlation. Correlation is a numerical index of the relationship between two sets of scores, which is represented by the symbol R. If there is a strong relationship between the two sets of scores, then R will approach ±1.00. If R is closer to -1.00, then the relationship is negative or inverse (high scores on one variable are associated with low scores on the other variable). Correspondingly, if R is closer to +1.00, then there is a positive or direct relationship (high scores are associated with high scores). However, if there is no relationship at all, the correlation is zero. To calculate R, use the following equation (where N is the number of pairs of scores):

$$R = \frac{N\sum XY - \sum X \sum Y}{\sqrt{\left[N\sum X^2 - (\sum X)^2\right]\left[N\sum Y^2 - (\sum Y)^2\right]}}$$

An example might help to clarify exactly how correlation works using test-retest reliability. The first time a questionnaire was administered, the scores were labeled "X," the second time the questionnaire was administered, the scores were labeled "Y." Listed below are the calculations needed to find the correlation between the X scores and the Y scores.

	X	**Y**	**XY**	**X²**	**Y²**
	6	12	72	36	144
	5	10	50	25	100
	4	8	32	16	64
	3	6	18	9	36
	2	4	8	4	16
	1	2	2	1	4
	0	0	0	0	0
Σ	21	42	182	91	364

To calculate R for the scores above, here's how the simplified equation would look:

$$R = \frac{7(182) - 21(42)}{\sqrt{[7(91) - 21(21)][7(364) - 42(42)]}} = \frac{1274 - 882}{\sqrt{(637 - 441)(2548 - 1764)}}$$

$$\frac{392}{\sqrt{196(784)}} = \frac{392}{392} = +1.00$$

So you can see that the stronger the relationship between the X scores and the Y scores, the more positive the test-retest correlation will be. Of course, these scores were fictitious, we never expect a perfect correlation in social science. Random factors prevent us from having perfect correlations, so when we read communication research, we usually see reliability measures for test-retest correlations ranging from 0.6 to 0.8. Many factors can influence variability in these scores—the time of day, previous experience, mood, and the like.

There are some problems with test-retest reliability. If you had constructed an attitude test about assault rifles as previously discussed, almost everyone you tested would remember having taken the test if you repeated it before anything less than a few weeks had passed. Many researchers try to solve that problem by repeating the measurement only after a long period of time, such as six weeks. The difficulty with this method is that people change their attitudes. If, while the researcher was waiting to retest, a crazed individual used an assault rifle to slaughter a group of children at a fast-food outlet, the whole process would be null and void. Even less prominent events can change attitudes as well.

To solve this problem, many researchers have used *alternate forms* reliability measurement. They design a test that has different versions of the same concept. Such an approach was used in the construction of the Kentucky Comprehensive Listening Test (Bostrom, 1990). Two versions of the same test were prepared and given to the same group of respondents in successive days. The correlation was good enough (0.79) to reason that the test was stable. Similar procedures have been used for other tests. In evaluating research, we should always look for the degree of agreement, usually expressed in correlational terms, for the tests used.

Test-retest procedures are not always possible, however, so other methods have come into use. They are all based on the idea that a test with internal consistency is inherently better than one without. So a very crude way of assessing the consistency of the scores on affect orientation is to calculate the standard deviation, and see how variable a set of scores might be. You might want to go back to chapter 3 and review how the variance and standard deviation are calculated. In general, we feel that if a measure has a lot of variance, it is much less dependable than a measure that doesn't.

Other procedures include *item-total* reliability, *split-half* reliability, *odd-even* reliability, and Cronbach's *alpha.* Each of these has its uses and its own problems.

Item-total reliability is derived by calculating the correlation of each item score with the total score and averaging these correlations. Here each item is compared to the test total (less the item in question). The purpose of this procedure is to examine each item to see if it varies as the other items do. This is most typically used in preliminary stages of a test to see if the test can be improved. If several items in a test have low item-total correlations, then they might be dropped from the test.

Split-half reliability is usually calculated by taking the results of the first half of the test (questionnaire) and comparing it to the second half. If the test is consistent internally, the two halves should be relatively consistent. Sometimes a split-half comparison can be made by choosing the halves randomly, that is, by selecting items through some random procedure, such as flipping a coin or using a table of random numbers. This is usually preferred over a first-half/second-half comparison.

A special form of split-half reliability is odd-even reliability, which correlates the odd items with the even ones. *Odd-even* reliability is just what it sounds like—comparing the odd numbers of the test to the even ones. You can see that this really isn't much different from split-half comparisons. It's just another way of dividing the questionnaire into two parts.

Cronbach's *alpha* approaches reliability quite differently, because it is not based on correlation coefficients. It is important to note that the coefficient alpha is used when a test does not have correct and incorrect answers. If you go back to chapter 3 and examine table 3.2, you will see that each respondent has a score for each item. We could add up all the scores for each respondent, calculate the mean, and calculate the variance for those means. Similarly, we could add up the scores for each item, calculate the mean for each, and then calculate the variance for each item. And then we could add up all the item responses for each person and get the overall mean and variance for that.

Item one had a total of 151, while item 2 had a total of 137. This variability could be calculated using the same formula as the variability in the total scores for each person (see table 4.2). Why would we wish to do this? Remember the way attitude test items were constructed? Some were deliberately made milder or stronger than others. So it might be important to take this variance of items into account. But in addition to item variation and individual variation there is a third source of variation that is a problem for researchers—random happenings.

Table 4.2 Calculations of the Variability of the Affect Orientation Scores

Item	Total	Mean	Deviation	Squared Deviation
1	151	142.4	8.6	73.96
2	137	142.4	−5.4	29.16
3	133	142.4	−9.4	88.36
4	138	142.4	−4.4	19.36
5	131	142.4	−11.8	129.96
6	124	142.4	−18.4	338.56
7	106	142.4	−36.4	1324.96
8	124	142.4	−18.4	338.56
9	159	142.4	16.6	275.56
10	144	142.4	1.6	2.56
11	152	142.4	9.6	92.16
12	144	142.4	1.6	2.56
13	148	142.4	5.6	31.36
14	144	142.4	1.6	2.56
15	161	142.4	18.6	345.96
16	148	142.4	5.6	31.96
17	156	142.4	13.6	184.96
18	148	142.4	5.6	31.36
19	149	142.4	6.6	43.56
20	151	142.4	8.6	73.96
Totals	2840		0	3460

Actually, everyone accepts the fact that there is random variation in tests, usually due to chance factors. The critical issue is the difference between the random factors and the factors that we wish to test, i.e., the affect orientation, and item variation. Kerlinger (1986, p. 411) notes that the proportion of this random variation to the item and individual variations can be used as an estimate of the test's internal reliability. If we compare the variance due to each of these sources, we have a measure of how good we might think our test is.

Kerlinger's formula looks like this:

$$r_{tt} = \frac{V_{ind} - V_e}{V_{ind}} = \frac{1 - V_e}{V_{ind}} \quad (4)$$

To calculate this, Kerlinger recommends performing the same analysis as we would for the analysis of variance (covered in more detail in chapter 10) estimating both the variance for the items and the variance for the individuals. The residual variance is the variance for error (V_e). Kerlinger also notes that this is the same as the alpha coefficient of Cronbach (1951) but is calculated slightly differently.

Validity

After some satisfactory estimate of reliability is achieved, the researcher's next task is to measure *validity*. Validity traditionally has been defined as the ability of the test to measure "what it's supposed to measure." Thus, if someone scores high on a "feminist attitudes" scale, we would expect this person to show some significant behavior consistent with feminism in some other setting. The whole process only has meaning if the behavior measured has the same reliability that the test had. You can see how hard this might be to achieve.

In addition, "significant behavior" is difficult to define. If we constructed a test to measure an attitude about the Confederate flag and achieved satisfactory reliability on our test, then we might cast about to see what kind of behavior might lend credibility to our test. If one of our respondents who responded favorably to the flag also had a bumper sticker with the flag on it, we would feel that our test was a valid one. However, choosing "bumper sticker" behavior as the only validation would be risky. Some persons don't have cars, others don't think bumper stickers are classy, and still others would prefer to keep their opinions to themselves.

Earlier in our book we mentioned that it is typical to classify research into quantitative and qualitative categories. We also mentioned that these distinctions aren't that easy to make. The question of validity is one that blends qualitative and quantitative method. *The choice of a validating criterion is clearly a qualitative decision.* Earlier in this chapter we mentioned that we use attitudes as a research concept because it is often impossible to assess the relevant behavior. But we pretend that behavior is indicated by the attitude test, even if actual validity is impossible to assess. Whether or not the behavior in question is important cannot be determined quantitatively.

Nonetheless, it is vital for us to try our best to assess validity. Some researchers frankly give up and assert that their concepts have *face* validity. To contend that a measure has face validity is just another way of saying the procedure is valid "on its face" without other assessment. Charlie Brown, in the *Peanuts* cartoon, once confronted Lucy, saying "You're not right! You just *sound* right!" Face validity is like that—it sounds right, but that's about all we can say about it. In other words, face validity has no validity.

One excellent way to assess validity is to examine individuals that have already displayed qualities that relate to the characteristic that the researcher wishes to measure. Milton Rokeach, in his landmark study of *The Open and Closed Mind* (1960), hypothesized that the ability to examine incoming data and evaluate argument was an important personality characteristic. Rokeach began his study by examining the general concept of authoritarianism, but found it clearly associated with political attitudes. Instead of measuring general authoritarianism, typical measures had a pronounced bias toward "right-wing" authoritarianism and ignored what Rokeach called the special case of "left-wing authoritarianism" (1960, p. 13). Rokeach felt that authoritarianism ought to be a personality factor, not a political attitude. This led him to attempt to study the structure, not the content of authoritarianism. He designed his approach around cognitive behavior as a determinant of personality structure, measuring this factor in a test commonly called the "dogmatism" test (since it measures the degree to which individuals are "dogmatic"). Rokeach hypothesized that these structures would also be "closed" or "open" depending on the nature of each individual.

After refining his test, his approach to validation was to look for intact groups that might be both politically left and authoritarian. He decided that the Communist party was a likely validating intact group. Finding few Communists in East Lansing, he travelled to Britain and gave his test to an active Communist student group. Rokeach found that the young Communists were indeed both left-wing and authoritarian. This gave his test a validity that other techniques could not have done.

Another problem with validity is that sometimes the concept that was originally defined turns out actually to be many different concepts, not just one. A good example of this is Marwell and Schmitt's (1967) assessment of "compliance-gaining" techniques. These researchers asked individuals to choose what one should do in a situation where interpersonal influence is called for. They asked respondents to imagine a situation where "Dick," a high school student, is not studying enough. What would you do if you were Dick's father?

Marwell and Schmitt felt that the responses generated represented at least sixteen different techniques in compliance-gaining attempts, not just one. As you look at table 4.3, you can see each technique listed after each response.

Ordinary validity assessments are probably not applicable to tests of this type, since you not expect future tests to result in the same responses, because of their inherent differences.

EVALUATING QUESTIONNAIRES

In reading research reports, we always are faced with the problem of evaluation. The principal elements in evaluating the use of questionnaires are the twin concepts of reliability and validity. But there are some other general problems that we should keep in mind while evaluating any research that used questionnaires.

Questionnaires have a number of inherent difficulties. One important problem is that people's memories are faulty. Bradburn, Rips, and Shevell (1987) showed that an individual's memory for events and attitudes is truly flawed, and that questionnaire data may be seriously influenced by these problems. For example, in a study of voting behavior, individuals reported that they had voted for a given presidential candidate (such as Ronald Reagan) while election records showed that they hadn't voted at all! Another problem is interviewer bias. Some interviewers might be more receptive to responses that are consistent with their own beliefs (Feinberg & Tanur, 1990). In other words, if you suspect that some interviewers had a pro-feminist bias, you would insert a question such as "Do you think Clarence Thomas was guilty of the charges brought against him by Anita Hill?" and use these responses as "mini-tests" of bias. Feinberg and Tanur (1990) suggest that a good way to solve the problem of interviewer bias is to select particular responses that might reflect this bias and "build it in" to the questionnaire construction.

But an even more important problem is the way that questions are constructed. In chapter 1, we noted that scientists occasionally let their own feelings get into the construction of tests. We should always be alert to this possibility when we examine questionnaires used by researchers.

Table 4.3   Sixteen Compliance-Gaining Techniques with Examples from Family Situations

1. You offer to increase Dick's allowance if he increases his studying. (promise)
2. You threaten to forbid Dick the use of the car if he does not increase his studying. (threat)
3. You point out to Dick that if he gets good grades he will be able to get into a good college and get a good job. (expertise, positive)
4. You point out to Dick that if he does not get good grades he will not be able to get into a good college or get a good job. (expertise, negative)
5. You try to be as friendly and pleasant as possible to get Dick in the right frame of mind before asking him to study. (liking)
6. You raise Dick's allowance and tell him you now expect him to study. (pre-giving)
7. You forbid Dick the use of the car and tell him he will not be allowed to drive until he studies more. (aversive stimulation)
8. You point out that you have sacrificed and saved to pay for Dick's education and that he owes it to you to get good enough grades to get into a good college. (debt)
9. You tell Dick that it is morally wrong for anyone not to get as good grades as he can and that he should study more. (moral appeal)
10. You tell Dick he will feel proud if he gets himself to study more. (self-feeling, positive)
11. You tell Dick he will feel ashamed of himself if he gets bad grades. (self-feeling, negative)
12. You tell Dick that since he is a mature and intelligent boy he naturally will want to study more and get good grades. (altercasting, positive)
13. You tell Dick that only someone very childish does not study as he should. (altercasting, negative)
14. You tell Dick that you really want very badly for him to get into a good college and that you wish he should study more as a personal favor to you. (altruism)
15. You tell Dick that the whole family will be very proud of him if he gets good grades. (esteem, positive)
16. You tell Dick that the whole family will be very disappointed in him if he gets poor grades. (esteem, negative)

Source: Marwell & Schmitt, 1967, pp. 357-58.

To translate significant observations about communication behaviors into numbers requires a series of operations and assumptions. The first step is to define which aspect of communication is of interest—an individual's communicative behavior, an individual's communication characteristics, or an individual's responses to communication. When the concept is fully defined, the next step is to examine whether or not it is quantifiable, that is, whether it makes sense to think of it as more or less, larger or smaller.

If direct observation of the behavior is possible, it is preferable to self-report of the behavior. However, since direct observation is almost always impossible, researchers use verbal reports, usually in the form of questionnaires. Questionnaires are useful if they are reliable and valid, but aggregation of data is useful only if the variability is known and accounted for.

In the next section we will further explore the basic nature of research as inquiry, focusing on areas where knowledge is less extensive and answers are still open to question.

PART THREE

Generating Knowledge
Research as Discovery

So far in this book, we have examined the nature of theory and data, and examined the process of aggregating data. We have also compared various approaches to the use of numbers. Up until now, we have been using the word *research* as if it had one and only one meaning. In actuality, we use the word in many ways. In this book, we are going to look at two main types of inquiry: research that seeks to *discover* and research that seeks to *confirm*. These two processes are quite different. Discovery occurs in situations where knowledge is minimal (there are probably no situations where knowledge is absent). Confirmation occurs in situations where we wish to extend and validate knowledge.

In many situations, we have little or no knowledge concerning our problem or difficulty. Worse yet, we may have incorrect or misguided ideas about the issue. In this situation, we need to apply Edwin Wilson's (1994) advice: "Data first, then theory." Wilson meant that even educated guesses are founded on observation. There are many kinds of exploratory research. We will begin with qualitative analysis, which explores communicative phenomena from a cultural and value-oriented perspective. Then we will study textual analysis.

While textual analysis can be confirmatory in nature, usually it is exploratory, since the characteristics in the text are not always obvious. The same is true of survey research, but survey and textual research typically employ research questions rather than hypotheses. A research question takes the form "what is it?" and a hypothesis states "I think it is . . ."

After sufficient exploratory research has taken place, we need to then formulate hypotheses about our phenomenon. When we have done so, then we can proceed to confirm our hypotheses in a systematic way.

From this point on, a section on evaluation will be included in each chapter. Evaluation of research is one of the most important parts of communication study, and these sections on evaluation will include general characteristics to look for, possible strengths and weaknesses, and some typical problems.

Chapter Five

Qualitative Research

THE VALUE OF QUALITATIVE RESEARCH

You will recall that in chapter 1 we stated that the purpose of *communication research* is to help solve problems by creating, extending, exploring, and testing *communication theory*. You will also recall that communication theory seeks to predict, explain, and control communicative activities. Thus far, we have been treating research as if its primary purpose is to predict and control, without much emphasis on explanation. Also remember that "explanation" can refer to many things but particularly, for our purposes, is taken to mean that we relate communicative phenomena to larger categories of cultural and social significance. We usually use the word **hermeneutic** to denote this kind of explanation. The most typical method to study hermeneutics is called **qualitative** research, in that one of its purposes is to seek qualities, not necessarily quantities.

Numbers, science, counting, and statistics are all very well, but they have to be applied to people and real events in a meaningful way— they should make sense in some significant way before any formal numerical analysis is applied. Do people do research that doesn't make sense? Sometimes. Not long ago, a group of researchers lurked in the men's rooms of a large organization and covertly observed the behavior of men as they went in and out of these lavatories. Their research concluded that men tended to wash their hands if other men were in the lavatory, but when they were alone (or at least thought they were alone) they often skipped handwashing. Just exactly what social or academic significance this study was supposed to illustrate is not clear. This so-called research illustrates how the manipulations of formal statistics can be meaningless if they are applied to categories and values that may have needed more intense examination.

Studying behavior in men's lavatories is probably not worth any further effort. In other words, the quality of this research is low, in that it doesn't tell us much about the world and ourselves. Qualitative research is devoted to the important questions of the underlying values and social structures in any given communication situation, and what they may or may not mean in our interpretation of them. In some situations, these qualities (or values) are strongly established prior to the research project. In medical institutions, qualities such as "sick" and "well" tend to be fairly clear-cut. In other situations, outcomes or desirability may be more arbitrary.

In addition, the *ways* we classify experience and individuals can be a problem. Medical institutions, for example, are characterized by a structure that is fairly rigid (doctors, patients, nurses, hospitals, etc.). Other kinds of institutions categorize people less rigidly. In some situations there may be qualities that are not immediately apparent. These situations do not permit easy analysis. In addition, categories imposed by organizational structure may be meaningless unless careful observation is made.

Let's look at an example. Ruud (1995) studied the activities in a regional symphony orchestra. Primary participants in this orchestra were divided into the categories of musicians, directors, and management. These categories seem fairly simple and straightforward. But an in-depth analysis of the discourse of the three groups, both within groups and between groups, showed significant differences in the use of communication. These differences were not obvious from the initial classifications. For example, the term "professional" seemed to have different meanings (was used in different ways) in each group. Ruud was able to show how the categories affected decisions and particular orientations concerning the orchestra and its existence. Since the communicative research on this system discovered inherent qualities in the social structure of the orchestra (as well as the surrounding community), it is easy to see why it would be called **qualitative research**.

In communication, as well as social science in general, qualitative research is an important part of the research process. One goal of this approach to research is to address a particular situation as openly as possible, recognizing that the researcher is a participant as well as an observer, and seek relationships or characteristics that might have been overlooked by a less intense method. Anderson (1987) writes that the ideal form of qualitative research is "inductive, eidetic, subjective, contextual, mundane, textual, preservationistic, interactive, and interpretive" (p. 253). While we may not be able to incorporate all of these things into our research, it is clear that the first step in knowledge is to begin with exploration and deep analysis of the situation.

Another description of qualitative research as it might be applied to communication in families is suggested by Janet Yerby. Yerby (1995) suggests that researchers try to "collect and present extended narratives of family members, generate detailed descriptions (i.e., 'thick' descriptions) of particular family interactions, develop research texts with lengthy dialogues extending several pages, include the researcher's process in the construction of what is being explored, and invite subjects, readers, students, and other scholars to generate alternative interpretations" (p. 359).

Yerby is clearly recommending a qualitative approach to the study of families. But more than that, she finds troublesome the quest to isolate "concepts from the family systems literature in order to identify causal relationships in family functioning" (p. 359). She argues that reality is socially constructed and that objectivity in these situations is actually impossible.

Yerby uses as an example a family that includes a recovering alcoholic, which has a particular dynamic that is different from other families. A "thick description" is as valuable in some instances as an objective account of different types of interventionist strategies and a detailed description of how they worked, collected by researchers who have a point to prove.

Whether the researcher proceeds to more formal hypotheses and application is not important. Gathering information, however, is certainly the most rational beginning to any attempt to solve a problem. Generally, qualitative research does not yield generalizations in the same way that other research might produce. Qualitative research is valuable in and of itself.

HOW QUALITATIVE AND QUANTITATIVE RESEARCH DIFFER

Unfortunately, there is a fairly widespread assumption among many communication researchers that qualitative and quantitative research differ, in that qualitative research deals in questions of meaning and understanding (values) and quantitative research deals in scientific principles and absolute generalizations. As we will see when we explore some statistical tests later in the book, quantitative research also takes place in a background of systems of values and understanding. The "significance level" of a statistical test is a qualitative decision that all quantitative researchers have to make, and the basic choice of what kind of problem to investigate—what theories are of interest and of significance—is also highly qualitative. At the same time, almost all qualitative researchers engage in categorization and counting in the same way that quantitative researchers do. So the distinction between the two is largely one of method and approach, not fundamental acceptance of values.

QUALITATIVE RESEARCH SEEKS EXPLANATIONS

Why do qualitative research? The answer is that explanation can be a worthwhile goal in and of itself. Have you ever wondered why astronomers are so interested in the interior of a star that is so far away that the light only gets here forty years after it was generated? This star has very little to do with such practical matters as finding a parking place or getting through school. Yet its composition is of intense interest, in a way that is truly different from the practical matters involved in our day-to-day life. We are interested because of something innate in human beings—we value explanation in and of itself. Many scientists are not afraid to say that theories are of more value than are the possible uses to which they may be put (Brown, 1960). Our desire for knowledge, our wish for explanations, is something we all share and is part of being human.

Natural Explanations

Although it seems paradoxical, the explanation of natural events or scientific findings is sometimes more interesting—and more important—than the happenings themselves. When an event is explained, the perception of the event acquires a richness and a depth that the event alone cannot match. For example, at the beach we are struck by the vastness of the ocean, its relentless advance and retreat, and the regularity of its activity. The waves and the tides are fascinating. But when we realize that the moon, the sun, and even the planet Jupiter control these tidal motions—that what we are watching is the product of gigantic forces at work which extend thousands and millions of miles into space—our simple fascination gives way to awe. The explanation of the event has enriched it immeasurably.

Not all natural phenomena are as compelling as the tides. But most of us want to know *why* things occur as well as *how* they occur. Often we say that we want to know what something "means." This is a question that cannot always be answered but is worth asking nonetheless. So when we say that the tides move because of gravitational forces, we feel that we have supplied the "why" of the tidal motion. But if we ask *why* there is a gravitational force, we are stumped. Physicists tell us that there are four major types of forces in the universe—of which gravity is one—but they don't tell us why there are four, or how it came to be so. So in that case, asking what gravitation "means" may be a waste of time.

Cultural Explanations

It seems very straightforward to say that the tides' action "means" that the moon, the sun, and the planet Jupiter are pulling on the ocean. But there are many other ways in which "meaning" is used in explanations. In our Western culture at Christmastime, for example, many people—religious and nonreligious alike—put up a Christmas tree. Often families have traditional ornaments that commemorate particular events—a graduation or a wedding. Innovations are resisted. The same lights, the same old star, and the same ornaments are used from year to year.

Anyone trying to explain this behavior from a strictly scientific point of view would find it extremely difficult. In fact, the whole idea seems ridiculous. To cut down a tree, bring it indoors (needles and all) and hang a lot of trinkets on it seems bizarre. It is clearly a fire hazard. But this activity is full of meaning for most of us, and we typically say that it is part of our culture, or our traditions, or identity. This kind of explanation is just as complicated as the gravitational forces involved in the tides, but it is clearly different. Think about the way in which you evaluate each event. When you find the perfect Christmas tree, everyone agrees that it's the right size, shape, and has been decorated in a way consistent with your family traditions (or your current version of what you think the tradition ought to be). But you don't get too analytical about it—you simply assess the tree and its "correctness" for the coming season. With the tides, you may simply put a stake out on the beach to see if the tide tables are right. You may be just as impressed with the ocean as you were with the Christmas tree, but you are invoking an entirely different kind of thinking.

Appropriate Explanations for the Situation

So there are at least two kinds of explanation—we have a "tides" type of explanation and a "Christmas tree" type of explanation. One (the tides) is a *natural* explanation and the other (Christmas tree) is a *cultural* explanation. It is easy to see that each came from two different forms of reasoning. Christmas tree decoration is quite subjective (have you ever said, "It needs something—I'm not sure what"?) and the tides are very objective (the ocean doesn't care how you feel).

There are numerous examples of cultural explanation. Of particular interest is the myth. Many ancient myths exist in every society and culture. Our culture in the United States has myths such as George Washington and the cherry tree, alligators in the sewers of New York City, and flying saucers. Linus, in the comic strip *Peanuts* believes strongly that the "Great Pumpkin" returns every Halloween. The fact that myths are entertaining should not lead us to believe that they have no influence. We know that the Pilgrims didn't have turkey dinner on the first Thanksgiving, but we get upset when someone suggests that we have clams alfredo for *our* Thanksgiving dinner. The tradition of the Christmas tree arises from the fact that evergreen trees show "candles" in the spring when new growth appears, and this is a sure sign of better weather to come. Primitive people in Scandinavia felt that bringing the tree indoors and putting an artificial candle on it would *cause* the spring to come. Since the days began to lengthen on December 21, they associated this activity with the sun's behavior, and the tradition has continued.

It is extremely important to know what kind of explanation—natural or cultural—is appropriate for the kind of research we undertake. For example, if we base our decisions about health or social policies on political myths, often perpetuated by the media, we can find ourselves in great difficulty.

QUALITATIVE RESEARCH METHODS

The previous section illustrates some of the problems that occur in looking for explanations. The words we use are part of the difficulty—but there are many more. Communicative activity is especially prone to explanatory difficulties, because both the theories and the behavior they describe are made up of words, which can be construed in so many different ways. What we would like, of course, is a "theory" of communication that would help us understand the process as well as help us work with it to make it better.

Let us next turn to some of the methods we use in qualitative research. They include case studies, field studies, focus groups, and narratives.

Case Studies

A case study emphasizes one individual or group of individuals; the surrounding circumstances and previous events are explored and recorded, not simply one or two communicative behaviors in isolation. Rather than seeking a single score on a questionnaire or some other kind of inventory, studying a "case" involves gathering as much data as possible. In one study, researchers were interested in people who are compulsive talkers (Bostrom et al., 1990). Of course, the important variable was non-stop talking, but the researchers began with selected cases of compulsive talkers and examined much of the social and personal backgrounds of each individual. Here are two of their case studies:

CASE ONE

This "talker" holds a mid-level supervisory position in a large Midwestern corporation. While he has worked at this corporation for over eighteen years, he has remained in his present position for the last twelve of those eighteen years. An intelligent, capable man, he has been passed over for promotion time and time again because of the widespread knowledge of his compulsive talking. He is known to "trap" people in his office and on the telephone, telling them about his wife, children, golf game, etc., ad nauseam. In fact, it has become common practice for co-workers, when they have to talk to him, to preface the conversation with a statement like, "Now I only have a minute I can give you," or "I have to be in a meeting in five minutes, so we have to make this fast."

CASE TWO

Our second "talker" is a middle-aged woman who is the last surviving member of a prominent, wealthy, local family. Single, and with few social outlets, she makes her church the focus of her life. She attends every dinner or special committee meeting, arrives early, and leaves late. Typically she is the first to arrive at a function, and fastens her attention on whomever has the ill luck to be the second arrival. She begins with any topic and switches with skill. If not interrupted, she will talk continually for as long as fifteen or twenty minutes. Individuals cope with her by avoidance, and by attempting to foist her off on other members. Her true position in the church could only be described as that of a social outcast (Bostrom et al., 1990, p. 4).

These two cases showed that the shared characteristic (compulsive talking) had certain similarities, even though the two individuals were quite different in almost every other aspect. These two cases are relatively superficial and contain little in-depth analysis. Other case studies go into much greater detail.

A good example of a detailed case study was conducted by Frentz and Rushing (1993), who examined the film *Jaws* as a case study. You will remember that the great white shark threatens the people on the beach, and eventually a single "hero" emerges to solve the problem. Frentz and Rushing point out how this modern film exemplifies the myth of the frontier hunter who saves the day by killing an animal or a person. They also demonstrated how the frontier myth is used to attack feminine thinking in our culture—the shark is considered a metaphor for some of our other social problems which a frontiersman would solve violently.

Case studies can also analyze political or social events. Pfau, Parrott, and Lindquist (1992) utilized a single campaign for the United States Senate as a case study illustrating the use of "attack" television ads. In this case study, specific details of the political ads were studied, specifically those that attacked the character or background of a candidate. Sometimes case studies can be exhaustive in nature, and the descriptions of the case can run into hundreds of pages of text.

Field Observations

A field study is usually taken to mean research that takes place in the actual place and situation where a particular phenomenon occurs, as opposed to a recording, a written account, or an artificial situation contrived in a research institution. For example, an individual interested in studying how a large group governs itself (parliamentary procedure) might choose to attend a union meeting or a board of education meeting to observe this phenomenon in action.

A widely known example of qualitative research done in the field was conducted in the early 1950s. In a large American city, a "prophetess" (Mrs. Keech) began telling persons that she was in touch with a group of supernatural beings, which she called the "Guardians." These Guardians were travellers in space and time, and they told Mrs. Keech that the world was going to end soon and that a few persons would be saved, primarily Mrs. Keech and her associates. When the prophecy failed, Mrs. Keech and her associates, rather than admitting that they were duped and disbanding the group, instead redoubled their efforts to recruit new members and insisted that minor errors had contributed to the failure of the prophecy. The complete account of the movement and its subsequent effects were told in the book *When Prophecy Fails*, by Leon Festinger, Henry W. Riecken, and Stanley Schacter (1956).

Their method of study was simple. They joined the group. Here is their description of the infiltration process:

> In our very first contact with the central members of the group, their secrecy and their general attitude toward nonbelievers made it clear that a study of the group could not be conducted openly. Our basic problem then was obtaining entree for a sufficient number of observers to provide the needed coverage of members' activities, and keeping at an absolute minimum any influence which these observers might have on the beliefs and actions of members of the group. . . . Our initial contact was Mrs. Keech, whom one of the authors telephoned shortly after the newspaper story about her appeared in late September. He told her his name and said he had called to see if he might talk with her about some of the things she had told the reporter, especially the matter of the predicted flood and flying saucers. (Festinger, Riecken, & Schacter (1956), pp. 234–35)

In spite of the authors' insistence that they were only "listeners" and did not contribute to the central beliefs of the group, it is clear from their description that they had pretended to have "psychic" experiences in order to ingratiate themselves with the group, and that on other occasions they might have reinforced the beliefs of the group by pretending to agree with them.

The study of this group led one of the researchers (Festinger) to formulate a theory called "cognitive dissonance," which generated much interest and provoked a good deal of further research. Although few persons today subscribe to the theory, much of the subsequent research has been interesting and useful.

Narrative

Narrative, as the name implies, is the telling of a story. Often a story illustrates a particular characteristic of an individual, a group, or a corporation. At IBM in the 1960s, employees exhibited extraordinary institutional loyalty and devotion to the CEO, J. B. Watson. At the Lexington typewriter plant, almost every employee could tell the story regarding the day Mr. Watson tried to enter the plant and was turned away by a security guard because he didn't have a proper identification card pinned to his lapel. Rather than berate the guard, Mr. Watson went back to the main office, got the proper ID card, and gave the guard a raise. This story circulated throughout the organization.

Clair, Chapman, and Kunkel (1996) detail the manners in which narrative can have both a practical and a heuristic purpose. In an examination of narratives about rape, consciousness-raising is cited by Clair and others as one of the principal aims of personal narratives of this type.

Narratives can be expressed in formal storytelling or in highly informal settings. Often researchers will want to examine the form of the narrative, including the "actors" in the story, and (like Aesop) to find the "moral" that the story produces. A narrative can function both as an indicator of an organizational culture as well as a persuasive device.

Focus Groups

One technique that is often used to supplement research in political or marketing questions is focus groups. When a political candidate makes a speech in a television commercial, typical polling asks very restricted questions, usually indicating approval and reactions to particular issues. In a focus group, however, the researchers ask general questions and then let respondents say whatever comes into their heads.

Focus groups are in-depth participation by small groups of individuals, usually less than fifteen. The basic idea is that they will be allowed to respond to research issues in their own words, and with their own agendas, rather than responding to questionnaire items preselected by pollsters.

Focus groups can be extremely effective. When the Republicans mounted their campaign for a "Contract with America" a good part of their thinking was derived from focus group activity. Frank Luntz, a leading pollster for the Republican Party in 1994, relied on focus groups almost exclusively to formulate his advice to Republican candidates. In 1994, he accused colleagues of "underutilizing focus groups, because they have a lower profit margin than do telephone surveys" (Kolbert, 1995). The great success of the Republican congressional candidates that year shows, at least in part, that this is an effective method of research.

However, not all professional researchers are fond of focus groups. One real disadvantage is that the focus group may not produce any particular course of action that a decision maker can utilize. Another is that people can respond as a function of a group identity—that is, they can express ideas or opinions that they may not have dreamed of before they attended the focus group. In the example given, James Carville was trying to extract information about prospective political commercials from focus groups. It seems fair to conclude that Carville was not using focus groups in the way that they were intended—i.e., to discover information, not to make decisions. It ought to be clear that qualitative research may not be the best way to test a television commercial.

CAMPAIGN RESEARCH IS LIKE FIRECRACKERS on the Fourth of July, it can be nice, it can be entertaining, it can blow up in your face, and you've got to be a pyrotechnician to fool with it. You've got ten or twelve people in a focus group, and one likes a welfare spot, another one likes an economy spot, one more likes an attack spot. They grade them. One gets a 7.5, and one gets a 7.3. Well, gee, let's do the one with the 7.5. It becomes the tyranny of the focus group. But groups change, we're all over the place and we're out of [a] message all the time. That's why I have a sign on the War room wall (referring to the sign that says "It's the economy, stupid!").

If they make a rule outlawing focus groups, I would be happy. (Matalin & Carville, 1992, p. 356)

ADVANTAGES OF QUALITATIVE METHODS

There are advantages to using qualitative methods. One is that sometimes ordinary research only skims the surface of the responses we get from other human beings. Another is that it allows the researcher to interpret data in a way that quantitative research does not. Research and science have strong value implications, many of which we don't always think about. Let's look briefly at each of these.

Depth

Family planning seems like such a logical thing for those of us in the Western culture that we typically feel that other societies ought to solve the problem in the same way we do. The Chinese government recognizes that population is one of their worst national difficulties and has implemented a "one-child" policy nationwide. This may seem to be a logical solution to a national problem which would gain instant acceptance, but in China the policy has had disastrous results.

We would have difficulty understanding this problem until we examine rural life in China. Unlike the United States and many Western countries, China has no social security system. Chinese therefore feel that children are their key to a comfortable and secure retirement. A Chinese farmer knows that if he has sons, at least one of them will take care of him in his old age. The survival rate among children in rural China is lower than in other countries, and to insure that one family has one grown son might entail the bearing of four or five children. There seems to be little that government propaganda can do to alleviate this situation. An in-depth study might reveal ways of attacking this problem.

Many "rational" explanations for communicative behavior simply don't get into our theories and our questionnaires. You may remember from the previous chapter that occasionally individuals give socially acceptable answers (not necessarily the correct answers) to surveys and tests. Quite often a deeper analysis will reveal the "real" reasons why individuals act the way that they do.

While it may be hard to accept, many large organizations have a preconceived position about social phenomena. The television industry has sponsored research about the effects of violence in the media, but most of it is highly suspect. Sometimes the problem is so bad that communication theorists have characterized some research as "administrative" research (Melody & Mansell, 1983). When the health care industry discusses problems about access to health care, they always assert that the individuals want access to health *insurance*. Actually, people want access to health care, and could care less whether an insurance company or a government agency pays for it. In most of these instances, researchers supported by a government agency or a large health care company are certainly not going to be open minded about how the research turns out.

Interpretation

The impact of research can be enormous. Sometimes the attempt to separate data from interpretation results in making the data appear trivial or uninteresting. Walt Whitman's poem "When I Beheld the Learned Astronomer" describes such a situation. The poem describes a lecture on astronomy, presented by a "learned astronomer," full of charts, graphs, and proofs. Apparently the room is hot, and the poet is uncomfortable.

> Till rising and gliding out I wandered off to myself
> In the mystical moist night air
> And from time to time
> Looked up in perfect silence at the stars.

Many persons have interpreted Whitman's poem as a rejection of science, since the astronomer with his charts and graphs (data statements) simply couldn't compare with the experience of looking at the stars (appreciating the stars). Whitman probably meant for the poem to be taken this way. But what many of these interpretations overlook is that the astronomer probably also is moved by the experience of looking at stars and may have began his career in astronomy by look-ing "in perfect silence at the stars."

EVALUATING QUALITATIVE RESEARCH

Those of us who begin with an idea of scientific research as a dis-passionate, objective process often have difficulty in seeing the point of doing qualitative research. But the researcher's attitudes, or point of view, is a strong influence in any research. It's a well documented char-acteristic of human beings that most of us tend to see what we're looking for, and as a consequence, data are often influenced by our point of view. Qualitative research is especially vulnerable to this kind of distortion, and when we evaluate it, we should be especially aware of it.

How does qualitative research work? If we set out to judge whether a specific television commercial was "in good taste" or "in poor taste," the content of the commercial would probably influence different per-sons differently. Some commercials for beer, for example, may be seen by males as being in good taste—or at least, perfectly appropriate. (After all, what's wrong with a picnic complete with six-packs and the scantily clad Swedish bikini team?) Most women, however, tend to have a differ-ent view. So our first step in evaluating qualitative research is to assess the effects, if any, of the gender of the researcher.

One way to remove the element of bias from the data-gathering process would be to frankly acknowledge it and make some adjust-ments. If researchers are interested in assessing the beer commercials, they may select a group consisting of an equal number of males and females to view the commercials. Then they might report input from the group's responses. This is a crude example, but it shows how the pro-cess works. The attempt to remove personal bias is called objectifying data, and appears in much qualitative research.

There are many special problems with building objective state-ments out of qualitative observations, but most proponents of qualitative method feel that it is well worth the trouble. Confusing fact and value has historically created terrible problems. Hitler convinced the German people that Blacks, gypsies, homosexuals, and Jews were not really human in the Aryan sense, and that they were the equivalent of apes or other animals (*untermenschen*). The attribution of subhu-man characteristics to other persons is a value judgment masquerading as a factual one. The result was the Holocaust.

Today the AIDS epidemic is one of the most serious public health problems facing the world. Yet our government's efforts to deal with it have been hampered by the intrusion of value issues, such as the characterization of AIDS as a "gay disease" and private condemnation of alternate lifestyles. One official in the Reagan administration went so far as to propose that people with AIDS be placed in concentration camps.

Confusing qualitative issues with factual ones is an obvious problem, and many researchers feel that sharp separation is the answer. We can see this issue (health vs. puritanism) in drug-related issues, in the abortion debate, and in the whole health care problem confronting the United States. No one can argue that Jews and Muslims should provide scientific evidence that the eating of pork is unhealthy, nor should Catholics be asked to prove that confession leads to better mental health and more wholesome relationships. But if a religious group seeks to impose their view on the rest of society (as they do in some instances) we would probably ask them to recast their arguments from values arguments to facts. We have separate belief systems in this country, and we have agreed that values are a matter for the individual, not the state.

Chapter Six

Studying Texts

In the last chapter, we examined qualitative research, in which we study a situation in depth to find extensive reports or narratives about behavior or situations. In this research, the investigator looks at every aspect of the situation, its context, and the participants in order to make discoveries about how people communicate. Also, qualitative researchers seek to discover what the activity may mean in a larger context of human affairs and value systems. In this chapter, we will examine one particular aspect of communication: the message. Most often this form of analysis is called **textual research**; it examines the language used by an individual, a couple, a group, or a large organization. In conducting this research, the investigator first must obtain transcripts or recordings of the text itself. This may come from direct recording, or from discovering texts in another source. After that, the researcher must see what sense can be made from the way the texts are drafted and presented.

What can we learn from the way individuals use language? Sometimes surprising things can emerge from a careful analysis of the way words are used and arranged. We are all familiar with the modern issue of political correctness, and its emphasis on the language that people use. The value of this movement hinges on an assumption that we may well display hidden prejudices or attitudes in the language we use. If someone says "We can tell that he will be a good group participant if he listens to the opinions of others," it is a good assumption that the speaker doesn't think about women in groups or can't imagine a woman being a good group participant. Similarly, sexist terms ("babe," "chick," and so on) betray specific kinds of sexist attitudes.

Clearly, the words people use tell us a great deal about the users and the situation. Many times political figures believe that the right word is more important than the right message (Kolbert, 1995). Obviously, if this is true, then the wrong word can tell other people things we may not wish them to know. Consider the following dialogue:

DOUG: The committee recommended the disestablishment of the current assessment of pedagogical emphasis on diversity. This necessitates the dilation of the surveillance step involved in the pedagogical planning problem.
LEWIS: Does this mean I don't have to turn in my syllabus early?
DOUG: Yes.
LEWIS: Great.

At the beginning of this interchange, Doug could simply have said "We're going to forget about syllabi this year," and the "message" would have been the same. In fact, that may have been what he meant. But apparently he wanted to sound more important than that and chose other words. Communicators often wish to make their language sound more lofty, more plain, more obscure, and sometimes more clear. Analysis of texts can tell us a good deal about the users, both individuals and institutions. The most traditional analysis of texts is called content analysis. We associate content analysis with the media, but it has been used extensively in other situations. Other forms of textual analysis are conversational analysis and stylistic analysis. Let us look at all of these in turn.

CONTENT ANALYSIS

Content analysis began as an objective technique for analyzing newspapers (Krippendorf, 1980). One big advantage of this kind of research is that copies of newspapers' contents are readily available. Each newspaper keeps a "morgue" in which everything printed is saved. Some major newspapers are kept in libraries or museums. Many newspapers are also now available on the Internet. Early techniques used in content analysis were simple: examining editorials, "slanted" news, and general quantities of coverage as an index to editorial position or bias in the news.

Berelson (1952) defined content analysis as the "objective, systematic, and quantitative description of the manifest content of communication" (p. 18). The basic questions to be answered were of the type: "Is the *Chicago Tribune* as right-wing as everyone says it is?" or "Does *U.S. News and World Report* ever report anything good about the Democrats?" Then a researcher would analyze the *content* of every day's news in the publication and make a judgment about whether it leaned a particular direction, or if it was fair, or balanced. It has been very common in recent years to contend that the media have a bias toward the left. If this were true, then content analysis would be the best way to discover such bias.

Newspapers aren't the only examples of texts available for analysis. Most government agencies keep copies of meetings, modelling themselves on the reporting of Parliamentary debates in Great Britain and the recording of the proceedings in the U.S. Congress. Complete transcripts of congressional testimony are available through C-SPAN, and presidential texts are available through the Internet (http://www.whitehouse.gov). Many other interesting materials are available through various archives on the Internet. Table 6.1 is a partial list of such sites, accessed through the Archie network (Kardas & Milford, 1996, p. 56). Other political and social rhetoric is available for study. Initially, researchers simply expanded the techniques used in content analysis to include all other kinds of text.

WHAT CAN BE INFERRED FROM WORD CHOICE IN THE MEDIA? Many times specific publications have a strong bias for or against a public figure, but display that bias in subtle ways. *Time* magazine usually claims to be objective and neutral, but close examination displays bias. Where this bias appears is in contrasting treatment of public figures. Researchers examined the way *Time* used language in describing three different presidents: Harry Truman, Dwight Eisenhower, and John Kennedy. The word characteristics examined were attribution bias (Truman "snapped"), adjective bias (Eisenhower's "warm" welcome), and others. They found extreme negative bias in the treatment of Truman, extreme positive bias in the treatment of Eisenhower, and a balanced treatment for Kennedy. (Merrill, 1965)

The most simple method of answering these questions is a quantitative assessment of the amount of attention or content a given individual or institution devotes to a subject. In political analyses, a newspaper might have printed one hundred column inches of text to Republicans, 66 column inches to Democrats, and three for various third-party groups. A television station's news content is usually measured in time units, such as minutes and seconds. However, just a mention of a particular candidate or issue is often counted. Much media criticism is like this. A simple frequency count of leading characters in situation comedies often reveals differing roles allocated to women, men, and minorities.

An example of this kind of analysis was done by Herman and Chomsky (1988), who examined the coverage by the *New York Times* of the Salvadorean election in 1984. The U.S. government had taken a par-

Table 6.1 Addresses of Archie Servers Worldwide

Server	IP Address	Country
archie.au	139.130.4.6	Australia
archie.edvz.uni-linz.ac.at	140.78.3.8	Austria
archie.univie.ac.at	131.130.1.23	Austria
archie.uqam.ca	132.208.250.10	Canada
archie.funet.fi	128.214.6.102	Finland
archie.univ-rennesl.fr	129.20.128.38	France
archie.th-darmstadt.de	130.83.128.118	Germany
archie.ac.il	132.65.16.18	Israel
archie.unipi.it	131.114.21.10	Italy
archie.wide.ad.jp	133.4.3.6	Japan
archie.hana.nm.kr	128.134.1.1	Korea
archie.sogang.ac.kr	163.239.1.11	Korea
archie.uninett.no	128.134.1.1	Norway
archie.rediris.es	130.206.1.2	Spain
archie.luth.se	130.240.12.30	Sweden
archie.switch.ch	130.59.1.40	Switzerland
archie.ncu.edu.tw	192.83.166.12	Taiwan
archie.doc.ic.ac.uk	146.169.11.3	United Kingdom
archie.hensa.ac.uk	129.12.21.25	United Kingdom
archie.unl.edu	129.93.1.14	USA (NE)
archie.internic.net	198.49.45.10	USA (NJ)
archie.rutgers.edu	128.6.18.15	UASA (NJ)
archie.ans.net	147.225.1.10	USA (NY)
archie.sura.net	128.167.254.179	USA (MD).

ticular point of view about these elections: The rebels would disrupt the elections, the elections would be basically corrupt, and so forth. Herman and Chomsky found 62 articles that supported U.S. government policies, and only 20 that did not.

This sort of counting is usually called *frequency indexing*. It is not necessarily confined to counting articles—sometimes a content analysis will count words. If a newspaper uses a particular word or phrase a lot, then we might conclude that there is a good deal of interest in the concept. If the newspaper *Pravda* (the official newspaper of Russia and the old Soviet Union) used the word "peace" 20 times in each 1000 words in 1997, and only 3 times each 1000 words in 1957, a researcher would be justified in concluding that Russian interest in peace had changed in the forty-year interval. Exactly what led to the change is not answered by simple frequency indices.

The most common use of a frequency index is to search for sources of bias. Herman and Chomsky used a different sort of index— that of sources used—to examine the objectivity of the *MacNeill-Lehrer Newshour* on public television. They found that the largest majority (54 percent, excluding journalists) of those who were asked to present their opinions on public television were government officials or former government officials. The next largest group (15.7, excluding journalists) were the employees of a conservative "think tank" (an institution funded by conservative organizations and espousing conservative causes). In most cases, the frequency indices speak for themselves, but in this case, Herman and Chomsky (1988, p. 25) chose to factor out the journalists from their sample (see table 6.2). In other words, they didn't think the journalists were countable, for some reason.

While Herman and Chomsky seem to present a convincing case, it is important to examine what the numbers involved might mean. If the question is whether or not the news has a right-wing slant, it would be most important to examine the stated opinions of both the government officials and former government officials to see what positions they actually took on the program. In addition, it might be useful to analyze the general positions of the journalists invited. In other words, just the work experience held by the participants might not support Herman and Chomsky's contentions. In addition, the dates selected for analysis should be justified.

While it may be more typical to see content analyses that examine specific language use by various aspects of the media, content analysis can also be used to analyze the responses of a large group of individuals. Reuben (1993) conducted such a study, examining the language of 3,868 patients at six health care institutions. Reuben asked patients to

Table 6.2
Experts on "Terrorism" and "Defense" Appearing on the *MacNeill-Lehrer*
***News Hour*, January 14, 1985 to January 27, 1986**

Category of Expert	Number	%	Number Excluding Journalists	% Excluding Journalists
Government official	24	20	24	27
Former Government Official	24	20	24	27
Conservative Think Tank	14	11.7	14	15.7
Academic	12	10	12	13.5
Journalist	31	25.8	-	-
Consultant	3	3.5	3	3.4
Foreign Government Official	5	4.2	5	5.6
Other	7	5.8	7	7.8
Totals	120	100	89	100

recall their most memorable encounters at these institutions. He divided the resulting responses into (1) clinical/technical facets of health care, (2) institutional policies and procedures, (3) facilities and accommodations, (4) personal treatment and/or caregiver interaction, (5) quality of information given, and (6) miscellaneous responses. Reuben concluded that interpersonal communication was one of the most central aspects of institutional health care.

While frequency counts of the kinds mentioned are usually quite interesting and revealing, there are many other ways of examining texts. Let us now turn to another form of textual analysis, in which the character of the style is studied.

STYLISTIC ANALYSIS

Stylistic analysis is another form of textual analysis. There are a number of ways to define "style," and sometimes they can be as interesting as any way of looking at text. For example, Tamara Carbone

(1975) defined style as "listenability," "human interest," "vocabulary diversity," "realism," and "verifiability." She wanted to discover how these elements of style influenced listeners' evaluation of sources. Here is how she defined each of these:

Listenability was defined by the number of words per sentence, the average number of simple sentences, and an "easy listening" formula score, which is derived from the count of polysyllabic words. This sounds like a complicated definition, but it is definitely operational. You might go back to the beginning of the chapter and look at Doug's first statement. It is very low in listenability. Here's another example—the statement "Empirical investigations indicate that telecommunication is inextricably tied up with the incidence of violent behavior among younger persons" is clearly a statement of low listenability.

Human Interest was defined by the average number of personal words and the average number of personal sentences. For example, saying "*Your* kid can learn violence from TV. What are *you* going to do about it?" has lots of human interest.

Vocabulary Diversity was defined as the "type-token" ratio, which is calculated by dividing the number of "types" (the number of different words used) by the number of "tokens" (the total number of words used). Thus, in the sentence "George is George's best friend and George's worst friend," there are six types: George, is, best, friend, and, worst. There are nine tokens. The type-token ratio is 6:9 or 1:1.5.

Realism was conceptualized by using a technique called the "r" count, which is the lack of abstractness, as measured by the average number of verifiable statements.

Verifiability was defined as the average number of clear empirical sentences. This means that the words in the sentence had clear perceptual meaning.

Another excellent example of stylistic analysis is found in Roderick Hart's (1976) study of the public utterances of Richard Nixon. Nixon was a controversial and unique public figure, and Hart wondered if some of his public character would show up in the way Nixon expressed himself. Hart studied seventy-nine speeches of Nixon and examined the following indices:

Power factor: Some words have significant force, such as "God." The power factor is calculated by multiplying the number of power terms times the number of occurrences of each, and dividing by ten.

Absolute Verbs: Includes all forms of the verb "to be." Indicates a placing of individuals into absolute categories.

Collectives: Nouns like "brotherhood, community, and family" that indicate groups of persons rather than individuals.

Leveling terms: Terms like "all" that tend to put separate elements into one category.

Type-token Ratio: Measures lexical diversity by counting the number of individual words and the gross number of words offered (see Carbone's definition, above).

Self References: Words like "I" and phrases like "it seems to me" draw attention to the self in a way that others do not.

Qualifications: Constructions which convey a sense of nonimmediacy between speaker and message, and distance the source from its statements.

Hart then compared these indices to other speeches by individuals in the same time periods and in similar circumstances. He found that in six of the seven indices Nixon differed significantly, and concluded that Nixon's rhetoric was not characterized by "verbal absolutism" in the way he initially thought it might. Here the combination of lexical methods and the use of the computer for the large sorting task produced interesting findings based on these particular speeches. A new program is now available for the computer analysis of texts. Roderick Hart has written a special program called DICTION 4.0 which analyzes texts for a number of qualities, such as certainty, activity, optimism, realism, and commonality.

These forms of textual analyses have used texts already in the public record, since they are typically expressions of public figures and have drawn inferences about particular situations and historical periods. Another form of textual analysis includes the manner in which individuals express themselves in interpersonal situations. These researchers have called this conversational analysis.

CONVERSATIONAL ANALYSIS

The basic premise of conversational analysis is that often the communicative purpose of individuals in actual conversations shows unintended motives or feelings. An important technique of this analysis is the recording of conversations in natural contexts. In this way, conversational analysis takes on many of the characteristics of qualitative research, specifically that of letting the respondents generate messages in an unstructured environment. However, most of us don't carry tape recorders around with us; usually these "unstructured" analyses take place in a relatively formal environment with a videotape camera running.

What can one discover from relatively unstructured interaction? Here is an example of one such interaction cited by Anita Pomerantz (1990):

EXCERPT:

[The referent is L's new bride.]

A: She's a fox!

L: Yeh, she's a pretty girl.

A: Oh, she's *gorg. . . . eous*!

Pomerantz notes that L. doesn't agree quite as strongly as we might think, and that this represents an instance of "less than full agreement" in the interaction (p. 233). In other words, we would expect L. to be really enthusiastic, and he isn't. What's going on? Perhaps he is dissatisfied in his marriage. Actually all we know is his response isn't enthusiastic, and the rest is pure interpretation. The data are used in this case to establish the existence of the "less than full agreement" type of response, but we really can't be sure that there is a relationship of this pattern to other events, such as a "cooling" of the relationship, or other difficulties.

A name for a certain type of conversational analysis is discourse analysis (Jacobs, 1994). Jacobs says we should look for the universal, rather than the typical, or normative. Traditional normative analysis doesn't express the meaning inherent in people's use of language, and further study is needed in each instance to discern what is intended. For example, Jacobs has listed a number of phrases which could be used to hint about the possible exit of a couple from a party:

Let's go home.

I want to leave.

What time is it?

This sure is boring.

Don't you have to be up early tomorrow?

Are you going to have another drink?

Do you think the Millers would give you a ride home?

You look ready to party all night.

Did you get a chance to talk to everyone you wanted to?

Is it starting to rain?

It looks like it has stopped raining. (Jacobs, 1994, p. 204)

What Jacobs does not tell us is what "regularities" can be observed for each of these instances of parallel structure. The usual method in this type of research is to offer a sample of text as an "exemplification" of a process.

The principal reason they are termed "exemplifications" is that they typically don't go farther than the establishment of the existence of a particular interaction in human relationships. Capella (1990) points out that the existence of particular interactions, such as the "less than full agreement" response, is interesting, but it tells us little about other factors that may have caused it or be related to it. For example, conversations that may not appear flirtatious may well bring about attraction between two people (Capella & Palmer, 1992).

It is certainly possible to conduct research that looks at a particular characteristic of analysis. For example, Vangelisti, Knapp, and Daly (1990) studied "conversational narcissism," a characteristic which is manifested when the conversational participant talks about himself or herself constantly. Here is an example of one of the conversations in that study:

A: So, how was your day?

B. Not bad. Just the regular routine. How was yours?

A: Pretty good. A lot of busy-work today. I can't believe how much busy-work I have to do sometimes. More than anyone else I know at the office. I swear, if I wasn't there to take care of some of this stuff, the place would fall apart.

B: Yeah, I know what you mean. I feel that way too sometimes. But now you can relax and . . .

A: (interrupting) I feel that way ALL the time. It's crazy. People just don't take time to do things themselves and then I end up doing it for them. It's not that I mind helping people out, but people always take advantage of a good thing when they got it. You know?

B: Yeah, I think that kind of thing happens to everyone once in a while.

A: Not like it does to me. I'm reliable, everyone knows that, so they all let their work stack up and then they dump it on me. I think I'm too nice sometimes.

B: You certainly are. (pause) Well, what do you want to do tonight? You want to go to dinner? What do you think?

A: Yeah, Yeah . . . but I just don't understand why people aren't as committed as I am. I work hard—so should they. Maybe it's because I've been so successful in the past. You know, it just takes hard work.

B: Honey . . .

It seems obvious that "A" in the conversation is highly narcissistic. The researchers asked respondents to compare these individuals to "normal" conversationalists, and found that the narcissistic conversers were consistently evaluated as less socially desirable. Knowing this basic connection can lead to many interesting conclusions about conversational narcissism.

After one studies a text, the next question that arises is what to make of it. In Hart's analysis of Nixon's speech, the results can't be generalized to anything but Nixon's character. What other kinds of general principles can be deduced from textual analysis? Vangelisti, Knapp, and Daly studied a number of possibilities about narcissicism in a general sense. What other characteristics about communication can be discovered in a textual analysis?

MAKING INFERENCES BASED ON ANALYSES OF TEXTS

One way to study the effects of a form of text would be to compare the text in question with other texts, and then look for ways in which they differ. In the analysis of Nixon mentioned above, Hart was interested to see if Nixon was really different from other public figures at the time. You remember that Hart took samples of the texts that Nixon used and compared them with samples of other public statements. His method was an exploratory comparison, looking for specific ways in which Nixon might have been different. Once this analysis was complete, Hart drew interesting conclusions about the way Nixon expressed himself.

Hart's analysis tells a great deal about Nixon, an important public figure. But if you wished to discover principles of language that were true of people in general, you would need to broaden the scope of the method; that is, proceed in a more general way. This was the technique Carbone used when she studied style. You will recall that Carbone examined various stylistic characteristics of language. In order to see what effects these different characteristics had, she examined what effect the different characteristics of style produced in evaluations of credibility. She defined credibility as qualification-expertness, safety-trustworthiness, and power-dynamism. She found some very dramatic differences. High scores in listenability, human interest, vocabulary diversity, realism, and verifiability all made for a more credible message. Language choice, she concludes, then makes for evaluations of a credible communicator. Therefore a researcher who discovered stylistic differences in texts (at least of the type Carbone studied) would be justified in concluding that the person or organization that used these tests would be considered more credible than one that did not.

Unfortunately, Carbone did not analyze what happens when one element of style is good and another is bad. A text could be highly listenable but might also contain a low type-token ratio. Texts like this appear fairly often in "real life." But her study does show a strong connection between aspects of style and the believability of a persuasive message. Let's look next at some of the general characteristics of language for clues as to what we might find in given samples of texts.

Theories of Language

The centrality of language to almost everything that we consider to be important in communication means that we have to be aware of the nature of language and how it is used in most everyday situations. Although Jacobs notes that normative principles of language are probably not useful in what he terms "discourse analysis," he uses normative principles to discover what he believes is not normative (1994, pp. 208–11). In other words, we can't really know if a given text is unusual or different if we don't know what the "norm" is. Let's look at what many experts in language tell us is important in looking at language use.

Physiological Linkages with Language. A great deal of what we think is important about language is purely inferential and is based on a great many assumptions. But one area in which more and more is being discovered is the area of brain behavior and communication. For example, researchers have discovered that there is a "lateral asymmetry" in the ways words are processed, and that the side of the brain that is involved may be crucial to the decoding of the message. Specifically, we can see that the left side of the brain may be more heavily involved in processing messages with affective content than the right side.

Brain behavior is difficult to study, but some strides are being made. Recently Damasio and Damasio (1992) have examined much of the available information concerning language and brain behavior and have found excellent evidence (in a crude sense) for the hypothesis that specific areas control specific language functions. Unfortunately, most of this evidence comes from the study of persons with brain damage. Obviously, we cannot experiment on people to see what intervention in brain cells will do to specific language functions. In addition, researchers in genetics have discovered evidence that language and human genetic structures are related—i.e., people with different genes tend to use different language (Cavalli-Sforza, 1991).

Pinker (1994) has recently presented a strong case for a model of language that has strong neurological connections—a "hardwired" model. His basic contention is that human beings have evolved specific neurological characteristics that have created language. Most of Pinker's arguments stress the importance of grammar, or structure. One of the important implications of Pinker's point of view is that animals—even the great apes—simply do not qualify as language users because of the lack of grammatical structure in the symbolic activity that they use. In addition, Pinker's point about grammar points more strongly toward an evolutionary model in the origins of language. Linguistic origins, of course, are a fascinating question.

Some linguists are convinced that all human language arose from one original language (Ross, 1991). This is certainly an interesting idea, but you can see that it would be hard to prove. Research (Renfrew, 1994) has discovered that, in anthropological terms, there are significant relationships between linguistic families in the world and our differing genetic structures—pointing the way toward a physically determined evolution of language. Many linguists now believe that all modern languages originated from a single prehistoric language called Proto-Indo-European. Some even go farther back, connecting Uralic and Proto-Indo-European into a group called Nostratic. Theories about the origin of language are quite interesting but of course are highly conjectural.[1]

Associationist Theories. How does language work? First of all, language has two principal aspects—overt verbal behavior and covert inner experience. The inner components are stored and consist of our vocabularies and knowledge of rules, grammar, and usage. The outer components consist of the actual behavior that each of us performs while using language. Language has many functions, each of which are highly specialized. In order to understand the role that language plays in communication, it might be helpful to examine some of them in detail.

How do we use symbols in communication? Many would say that the creation of symbolic associations is the principal means of communication and the most powerful. For example, if a message links energy saving with "patriotism," it will certainly be much more effective than a message linking energy saving to a more mundane concept like "saving money." Many successful advertisers believe that the right word (especially in the naming of a product) is more important than any other factor in merchandising. Sometimes this concern with names seems a little silly. Tubbs (1978) reports an interesting discussion of the problems that General Motors executives had in implementing a decision to manufacture and market a small Cadillac. In many of their minds, the terms "small" and "Cadillac" simply couldn't go together!

The Theory of Signs

One of the important early theoretical analyses of language was *Signs, Language, and Behavior* by Charles Morris (1946). In this book, Morris focused on what he called "the theory of signs," since he felt that significance (or signing) was the principal function that language performs for us. In other words, Morris examined language principally from a functional point of view, distinguishing among different things that language does. According to Morris, signs have perceptive, evaluative and prescriptive functions. This would mean that the very first step some researcher would take in studying a given text would be to classify which of these functions was being studied. To understand which function a sign has at which time is crucial to the understanding of the nature of language. Morris felt that his approach would provide some much-needed precision to the way in which we think about language.

Perceptive Function. The perceptive function is served by those signs which denote classes of stimuli, or "percepts." When we merely identify someone by his or her name, when we designate a street by a street sign, and when the social security administration assigns us a number, we are utilizing the perceptive function of language. This enables us to relay the sense of the object without the object itself being present. You will remember that early languages contained actual pictures of objects as their symbol systems. The letter "A" evolved from a picture of an ox, since it was originally derived from the abstraction of the sound "ah" from the word for ox. Egyptian hieroglyphics and Chinese ideographs (picture writing) all shared this characteristic. This function of language is best performed when it is most specific, and worst when it is highly abstract.

The semantic aspect of language is the most common. Linking a specific percept to a word is the semantic process. Consider what happens when we pick up the telephone and order a pizza from the corner pizzeria. We have a picture in our mind of many different types of pizza topping and what we like. But our knowledge of the various types of pizza topping would be of little use to us if we were not be able to accompany this knowledge with words like "anchovies," "green pepper," and "pepperoni." This perceptive function may be one of the most important functions that language has in our day-to-day use. When we associate a percept with a word, we can say the word has semantic meaning. Semantic meaning, therefore, is what a word "means" when there is a clear percept associated with it.

Once we have established the percept-language links, we can advance to form concepts. A concept is a class of percepts, like "tree." We have stored percepts that are images of fir trees, birch trees, and Christmas trees. But we can use the term "tree" without having to deal with each individual percept. As concepts get more abstract, the less specific they are, the more difficult it is to extract the semantic meaning from them. In recent years it has become popular to use the term category rather than concept, but the idea is the same. Regardless, it is certainly one of the root processes involved in symbolization.

Evaluative Function. We use the perceptive function to inform others, and to store information ourselves. Obviously, accuracy and specificity are prized when we have these intentions. However, Morris' second function, the evaluative function, is quite different from the perceptive. Here we react to a word in a positive or negative emotional manner. Currently many large corporations are tying the word "quality" to products and services to gain positive affect. Whether the word has any relationship to our actual experience is irrelevant. Sometimes the word may acquire its meaning through experience, but at other times the word itself suffices. We may never have met a person who called himself a "communist," but most of us have a strong emotional response to the word regardless of our experience.

The distinguished speech scientist, Wendell Johnson, was fond of regaling his students with a particularly interesting example of the link between symbols and affect. According to Dr. Johnson, he once attended a party where the host was serving rattlesnake meat as an hors d'oeuvre. Guests were trying this delicacy somewhat tentatively. One woman, however, found the snack particularly delicious and ate several. Dr. Johnson found that she had not been told what the source of the meat on the snack was. On hearing that she had been eating rattlesnake, she promptly threw up. The physiological reaction of her stomach to the meat was acceptable, but the mental reaction of her mind to the meat was strongly unacceptable. In other words, the word made her sick, not the rattlesnake meat itself.

When we have emotional associations with words of this kind, we can say that the word has pragmatic meaning. Pragmatic meaning, in other words, is the meaning that accrues when a word is connected with a particular evaluation. Most of the evaluations you and I make are not as extreme as the rattlesnake example. However, we need to be aware of the possibilities in the evaluative functions of language. Persuaders especially will seek the use of words to trigger emotional responses.

Prescriptive Function. One way of looking at the prescriptive function is to think of it as the relationships between words themselves. Sometimes these are simple associations, and sometimes they involve very complicated rules, such as grammar and mathematical functions. These are usually called syntactic statements. We feel that five and six make eleven because our arithmetical system prescribes that it does. We are not used to thinking of a grammatical rule as a prescription in this way. Morris' view is that our moral prescriptions are usually expressed in "logical" relationships, such as in the following statement: "No married man should act that way." The implication is that "that way" (whatever it was) and "married" are incompatible and, therefore, wrong.

The theory of signs offers us an excellent method of analyzing the way that words work, especially in the diagnosis of what a word means. Meaning is different if the words are being used in prescriptive, evaluative, or perceptive functions. Since communication often involves values, perception, and logic, these three functions are extremely important to keep in mind as we look at the way language contributes to the communicative process.

Ellis' Functional View of Language

One example of the study of language from a functional point of view is the way that Ellis (1992) studied the particular contexts of language. He used the term "pragmatic" to describe the way specific individuals in a subculture use language. This particular usage is most visible in unique subcultures but obviously is present in almost all uses of language. Here is an example of the specific usage Ellis presented:

Gene: Nice work.

Jesse: Thanks. Got it done not too long ago.

Gene: Not at some chop shop, eh.

Jesse: Naw, a custom studio.

Gene: Nice, the guy was an artist.

Jesse: Yeah, I'm thinkin' 'bout gettin some new ink.

Gene: Where you gonna put it?

Jesse: Don't know yet, but I've got some clean spots.

Gene: Looking good. See ya.

This dialogue originated between what Ellis calls "tattoo enthusiasts" (1992, p. 8). Without knowing that tattoos were the subject of the discourse, the dialogue would be incomprehensible. This context-oriented usage is most visible in subcultures but obviously is present in almost all uses of language. Ellis distinguishes these codes from syntactic codes and shows how a complete understanding of these is necessary before the complete understanding of the communicative process is possible. Ellis' use of the term "pragmatic" is quite similar to the way that Morris used the word.

In another analysis of language, Ellis and Hamilton (1985) studied differences in syntactic and pragmatic codes in discourse used by different couple types: "traditionals" and "independents" (for more information on couple types, see Fitzpatrick & Indvik, 1982). They thought that the way in which we use particular words might give us some strong indications of the nature of the relationships in which we find ourselves. This means that we also can be said to have different meanings for the words as a consequence. Table 6.3 shows how the word usage in the different couple types were compared. You can see that the couples were indeed quite different in the way that they used language. Ellis and Hamilton go on to draw conclusions about how language interacts with the nature of relationships to make real discoveries about the communicative behavior of individuals.

Table 6.3
Frequencies of Word Usage by Couple Type

	Independent Couples	Traditional Couples
"I-words"	1.04	0.80
Uncommon Adjectives	1.97	1.48
Nouns	2.83	2.23
Disfluencies	0.89	0.59
Personal Pronouns less "I's"	1.89	2.24
Personal Pronouns per total output	0.13	0.16
"I's" per Personal Pronouns	0.26	0.21

EVALUATING TEXTUAL RESEARCH

Analysis of texts is an interesting and productive form of research. Content analysis began with quantitative studies of newpaper content, but has been applied to many other forms of texts in which a permanent record of the text exists. Analysis of the language used in interpersonal interactions has followed a different tradition.

The principal question in examining conversational analysis is whether or not this form of research is essentially qualitative, or whether it can extend its findings to larger groups and issues. While many researchers in this area feel that exemplification alone is sufficient justification for this kind of study, it is certainly true that others have gone ahead to look for more general relationships.

Textual analysis can help us decide exactly what communication can do in a given situation and shed light on relationships between communication and other events. Let us next turn to another form of exploratory analysis, survey research.

NOTE

[1] Some of the theories about the origin of language are quite entertaining. One is the "bow-wow theory" which states that early words may have been formed by imitating the sounds of the objects that they signified. Thus, the origin of the name "bow-wow" theory, since early humans might have used the term "bow-wow" or "roof" for dogs, and "splash" for dropping stuff in water. The "pooh-pooh" theory states that early humans may have made emotional interjections, such as "faugh!" when disgusted, "ooh" when unhappy and "ow" when hurt. We still ask children if they have an "ow-ow" when we mean a skinned knee. The "Yo-he-ho" theory states that in early civilization workers had to coordinate their efforts to pull on a rope, or roll a big rock somewhere. Ritual chants may have been used to coordinate efforts to work together. The "la-la" theory assumes that primitive humans learned to sing before they learned to talk and that the singing somehow got translated into words.

Chapter Seven

Survey Research

We have examined qualitative research, in which we study communicative events in depth, generating extensive reports or narratives about behavior or situations; and we have examined textual research, in which we analyze the structure and content of the language to discover characteristics of individuals and organizations. Both of these types of research concern highly individual situations and events. Sometimes (as in the case of textual research) they concern a single individual. Now we are ready to examine another very important category of research. Here we are interested in the characteristics of a large group of persons and wish to discover the truth or falsity of more general statements or theories. We call this **survey research**, which involves a particular **population** and typically makes use of a formal set of questions, which we call a **questionnaire**.

There are many kinds of surveys, but in general, two main types stand out. Sometimes decision makers in large organizations need to get some sort of feedback about their goods or services in order to improve the way these goods and services are provided. We see these surveys in restaurants, hotel rooms and supermarkets. The other type of survey is one in which we wish to make some judgments about the population as a whole. We might call these *inferential surveys*. Let's look at both of these in turn.

SURVEYS AS FEEDBACK

We live in a culture where most of our goods and services are delivered to us by very large organizations, usually corporations, or universities, or government. These huge organizations did not simply "happen" but have come about because of the growth of our technological knowledge, our increasing population, and our ability to travel and trade. These organizations do our banking for us, provide our groceries, organize our educational experiences and bring us entertainment.

107

Patterns of trade and commerce have been a part of human history since before the Sumerians, but typically a strong central ruler authorized and profited from commerce. Organizations as we know them today began with the guilds of the Middle Ages. These guilds represented an attempt to upgrade the quality of workmanship, improve the skill of the workers, and develop trade ethics. The guilds were probably the foundation of parliamentary decision making as we know it today (Giesbrecht, 1972, pp. 40–41).

In these guilds, merchants and artisans usually dealt directly with their clientele. But as commerce developed, the artisans began to develop specific structure in a system we would now describe as the master-journeyman-apprentice system. The master was responsible for the overall operation of the shop, the journeymen did the skilled labor, and the apprentices did the unskilled work. Any customer or client had access to the master, since he was always in the shop. In addition, the shop usually served as dwelling for the master, as well as an apprentice or two. If the business was successful, expansion often took place and one or two more journeymen might be added. But if this expansion extended to another location in another village, then a "line" of responsibility had to be developed, and the two shops were "connected" by the fact of their common ownership. The concept of ownership of private property was a fundamental aspect of this development, in that it made it possible for a shoemaker to buy or own both a tailor shop and a hatter's shop and therefore become a clothing "company."

Larger organizations emerged when merchants and traders in northern Europe formed an extended group called the *hansa*. Principally formed in northern Germany, these hansas provided international protection for trading, secured cooperation from kings and princes, and formed basic organizational rules (Schildhauer, 1985, pp. 17–18). The emergence of rulebooks is an important step in organizational development, in that it made it possible for traders to exercise control at a distance through rules.

As groups grew larger and more complex, individual clients were no longer able to have direct access to the owner, since the owner might well be in another part of the city or country. Problems had to be relayed through a successive layer of managers whose function was limited by the book of rules. Decisions obviously become more difficult and interaction with decision makers more formal. This tendency reached its high point in U.S. corporations in the 1950s. In a period of worldwide expansion of manufacturing and commerce, the main problem of management was a lack of planning and control. In the 1950s, corporate leaders were mostly returned veterans of World War II who were comfortable with rules, planning, and structure. Robert Reich (1992) notes that during these times, corporations became preoccupied with organizational charts and exact planning (p. 51). One inevitable result of this tendency was a increasing dependence on bureaucracy.

An insensitivity to the needs and wishes of the client is a universal characteristic of these large bureaucracies, and recently many managers have attempted to solve this problem by using customer surveys. Let's look at a common example.

The planning and design of freeways around our cities depend heavily on ideas about how the freeways should be used. This in turn depends on how drivers actually will behave when roads are built. A traffic engineer may be concerned about individuals in cities using the interstate freeway system as a commuting route. The crucial knowledge is whether drivers are planning long trips or short ones. If most drivers are taking short trips at particular times of day, then planners can urge the building of more lanes close to the city and better access ramps. If more people are taking longer trips from city to city, then other options should be considered. Engineers often place sensing devices on the off-ramps and keep track of traffic in this fashion. But these devices are expensive, require lots of maintenance, and sometimes fail just when you want them to work. So an alternate method is the *traffic survey,* in which researchers sample many drivers on a given route to see what their destinations are. The sample, if carefully drawn, tells the engineers a lot about the general population of drivers, which in turn helps in making decisions about the number or types of freeways needed in the future.

Surveys are used everywhere. Retailers mail surveys to purchasers of major items, hoping to gain information about the effectiveness of advertising, the demeanor of salespersons, and convenience of the stores. Political parties use specific kinds of surveys, often called polls. Hospitals use surveys to get some indication of the activities of the hospital staff, the quality of the treatment, and sometimes even the quality of the food! Surveys are an important way of gaining information from a large group of people that simply wouldn't be feasible using direct qualitative methods.

Here's an example of the kind of questions used in a typical feedback survey—this one used by the Ford Motor Company. After a customer has had a car or truck serviced at a Ford dealership, the company mails surveys to the customers. The questions they ask provide information about how the dealership and individuals working there performed the services needed (Service Survey, 1997).

7. **Did the dealership follow up with you after your service visit to see whether you were satisfied?**
   ❏ Yes   ❏ No

8. **Was your vehicle ready when promised (if promised a time)?**
   ❏ Yes   ❏ No

No inferences about other individuals or groups are made. The survey is strictly an internal communication providing "back channel" access to Ford management. The questions selected and the items covered reflect particular company policy. We might ask if these surveys are really research as we have been defining it, or a management tool. No definitive answer is available, but these surveys are common and we certainly need to be aware of them. We also need to be clear about the purpose of surveys, and when we look at inferential surveys in the next section, we can see how different the two surveys are.

INFERENTIAL SURVEYS: ASSESSING LARGER GROUPS

When communication researchers use the term "surveys" they almost always refer to an assessment of a large group. The basic technique is to use a survey as a **sample**, that is, to select a small group to represent the large group. A small group is manageable, and it is simply too cumbersome to survey everyone in the large group. Public opinion polls are good examples of inferential surveys. In a national election, millions and millions of individuals vote, and to survey them all would be impossible. So researchers use samples, hoping that the sample will bear close resemblance to the larger group. For example, Mary Anne Fitzpatrick has done extensive research into the way couples behave toward one another. The couples that Fitzpatrick surveyed seemed to arrange themselves into couple types: traditional, independent, and separate. She looked at three broad dimensions of behavior: interdependence, ideology, and conflict (Fitzpatrick, 1991). Recall our earlier discussion in chapter 6 about types of language used by different couple types. Figure 7.1 shows some of the questions she used in her survey. In these questions, we have presented the high, medium and low responses in a manner that indicates the particular couple type that they represent. In the actual questionnaire, the types (identified at the top of the page) would not be indicated.[1]

Figure 7.1

INTERDEPENDENCE	TRAD	IND	SEP
1. We tell each other how much we love or care about each other.	high	med	low
2. My partner reassures and comforts me when I am feeling low.	high	med	low
3. I have my private work space.	low	med	high
4. I feel free to interrupt my partner when he or she is concentrating on something if he or she is in my presence.	high	high	low
IDEOLOGY			
5. Our wedding ceremony is (will be) important to us.	high	low	med
6. Our society needs to regain faith in the law and in our institutions.	high	low	med
7. In close relationships, there should be no constraints or restrictions on individual freedoms.	low	high	med
8. The ideal relationship is one marked with novelty, humor, and spontaneity.	low	high	med
CONFLICT			
9. If I can avoid arguing about some problem it will disappear.	med	low	high
10. We are likely to argue in front of friends or in public places.	low	med	high
11. It is better to hide one's true feelings to avoid hurting one's partner.	med	low	high
12. In our relationship we feel it is better to engage in conflicts than to avoid them.	med	low	high

---

Whether or not the sample can indeed represent the larger group is dependent on the way in which the sample is chosen. In the next section we will look at some of these methods.

Sampling Methods

The first step in sampling is to decide what is to be sampled. In other words, we must first decide from what large group the sample will be drawn. The nature of the group is determined by our task, or our communication theory, or how general we want our conclusions to be.

It is also necessary to decide what characteristics of the group become of interest to us. The large group is called a **population**. Examples of populations are "middle-aged adults who go to the grocery store at least once a week" or "women between the ages of 18 and 25 who watch television at least four hours per week" and so on. After the population is defined, then a **sample** can be drawn from that population only and not from some other group. For example, if we are interested in the attitudes of long-term members of the Communication Workers of America (a labor union representing workers in the communication industry) we would not include any teamsters in our sample.

The reliability of the inference that your sample is similar to the population depends on the **representativeness** of the sample. No sample will be *exactly* representative of the population. By chance, a sampler might draw a sample that contained more men than it did women. Or a sample might end up with a majority of younger persons in it. These variations will occur, no matter how carefully the sample is drawn.

There are many ways in which a sample can be drawn. In communication research, we see samplers use words such as "random," "quota," "purposive," "judgment," and "unbiased" to describe samples. In this chapter, we will discuss four main types: **random, systematic, stratified,** and **convenience** samples. Each of these has its advantages and disadvantages.

Random Samples.   The most powerful way to insure that a sample is not biased is to remove any suspicion of bias about the selection of respondents. Most of the time, we are unconscious of our prejudices, so the method of random selection ensures that these biases will not be a factor. When you hear someone speak of a scientific sample, you know that they are referring to a random sample, drawn scientifically. In mathematics, the word "random" has a special meaning:

> Random refers to a set of numbers in which no number has a better chance of being chosen than any other number.

In Monopoly, the moves are determined by throwing dice, a random process. We wouldn't play bridge with someone who dealt the cards in such a way that they got all the high cards—we assume at the onset of the game that the hands were dealt according to *chance*. Similarly, a researcher wants to avoid any accusations of "stacking the deck."

We usually use some artificial device to determine randomness. Sometimes flipping a coin can serve as a randomization for situations in which there are only two choices. For example, in drawing a sample you might wish to randomize the sex of the sample. You might flip a coin and when it turned up heads, choose a woman for a respondent. Coin flips are common in constructing tests in which you choose between true items and false items. Other random devices used are card decks, dice, and spinning pointers. But the most common source of randomness is an artificially constructed **table of random numbers**, such as the one included in appendix A.

There are a number of steps involved in using a random number table to draw a sample. To use the table in appendix A, first you need to assign a number to each member of the population. Then you select the first three numbers from the table (appendix A). Putting the first three numbers together makes 104, so the first person randomly chosen is "person 104." The next three numbers are 8, 0, and 1. You then choose person number 801. You continue this way until you have as many respondents in your sample as you had planned.

Systematic Samples. You can see that strictly random samples are not always going to be easy to come by. In addition, the process may not be worth the intensive labor involved. Statisticians have evolved a number of shortcuts which serve well as random samples. One technique is to use numbers already in existence, such as social security numbers. Many times researchers use a technique called **systematic sampling**. This means that, after defining some population (such as all the students in a given university), you would use a random number to start (like 104, from the table) and then choose students at a given interval. For example, if there are 10,000 students in the university and you wished to choose a sample of 500, you would make a random start and choose every twentieth student.

A telephone directory is a common source of names for a systematic sample, but you need to keep in mind that it is not always ideal. For example, in 1936, the *Literary Digest* predicted that Alf Landon of Kansas, the Republican candidate for president, would beat Franklin D. Roosevelt. The magazine sampled names from lists of telephone subscribers and automobile owners for its sampling frame, but they failed to take into account that, at the time, those with telephones and automobiles were probably more affluent than those without. Roosevelt not only won, he won in a landslide. Today, although we may not have the same problems associated with telephone directories as the *Literary Digest* did, we should be aware of the possibility of drawing an unrepresentative sample.

Stratified Samples. Sometimes it is extremely important to know if a given characteristic appears evenly throughout the sample. A stratified sample is a sample in which a given characteristic of the general population is repeated in the sample. If the researcher is examining the attitudes of the general population toward social security, then distribution by age categories will be very important. Older persons typically have very different attitudes about social security than do younger ones. If a sample of 1,000 is drawn, the researchers may want to be sure that age groups are evenly represented. If the categories are 18–25, 25–35, 35–50, 50–70, and over 70, these five categories should each have about 200 respondents each.[2] So the researchers might ask the respondent's age early in the sample. After they had a sufficient number of 18–25-year-olds, they can simply drop all the subsequent respondents in that age group. Many times the phrase "quota sample" is applied to this technique, since the researcher thinks of having a quota for each category.

Convenience Samples. Sometimes it is simply not possible to conduct a true random sample because of the cost. A national telephone survey performed by one of the major research organizations may cost as much as $500 per interview. Should the researcher decide to draw a face-to-face sample from all of the population of the United States, it should be obvious that travel and communication costs would be prohibitive. A convenience sample is one in which the requirements of randomness are sacrificed to save time, money, and/or effort. This is a sample in which the procedure is based on the physical and organizational proximity of the respondents. Most studies that use undergraduates as a population are of this type.

Sometimes convenience samples work well, but at other times there may be a bias due to geography or other intervening factors. For example, Bostrom, Humphrey and Roloff (1981) were interested in how likely individuals were to help other individuals in trouble, and specifically if gender played a role. The researchers decided to make telephone calls to individuals with requests for help. Ideally they should have called individuals around the world, or at least in the United States. However, they confined their sample to adults listed in the telephone book in Lexington, Kentucky. They found that women helped both women and men in trouble but that men didn't help men, only women. The fact that this was a local phenomenon was illustrated when researchers at the University of New Mexico repeated the study and found that New Mexican men helped men—a different finding than the study in Kentucky (Goss, 1986).

Sample Size

How big should your sample be? It depends, of course, on how much error you can tolerate. Error is expressed by the idea of standard error. If you refer to chapter 3 and look at formula (3), you will see how standard error (or standard deviation) is defined for a group of numbers. The standard error of a proportion is different, though the concept is the same. It is defined as:

$$s = \sqrt{\frac{PQ}{n-1}} \qquad (4)$$

In this expression, "s" is the standard error of the proportion, "P" is the proportion produced by the survey (number of people responding in a given way divided by the number of people in the sample), "Q" is (1 - P), and "n" is the number of respondents in the sample.

An example might help. Suppose your survey asked the question "Will Jack Kemp be the Republican candidate in 2000?" If you drew a sample of 1,001 likely voters to answer the question and your sample had 461 respondents that answered "yes," you would conclude that 46 percent think Kemp will win the Republican nomination. The next step is to calculate the standard error of this proportion by the formula. You will find the margin of error inherent in your sample.

Start out with the proportion (P) which is 0.46. Then we can calculate Q (1 - P), or 0.54. We know that n is 1,001, so (n - 1) is 1,000. The result of 0.46 times 0.54 is 0.2484 and the result of 0.2484 divided by 1,000 is 0.0002484. The square root of 0.0002484 is 0.0158. So the standard error of the proportion 0.46, based on a sample of 1,001, is 0.0158.

What good is it to know the standard error of the proportion? In the next chapter, we will discuss more fully the statistical concept of the normal curve, which is a theoretical picture of probabilities involved in random choices. The standard error is one of the important aspects of this curve. For now it is useful for us to remember the number 1.96, which is the number of standard errors on either side of the mean that includes 95 percent of the sample cases. So if you multiply 1.96 times 0.0158, you get 0.031, which is the 95 percent **confidence interval** of your observed proportion. So you are 95 percent confident that the population's proportion is somewhere between 0.43 (0.46 minus 0.03) and 0.49 (0.46 plus 0.03). This is based on the assumption that the sample was randomly drawn and that no statistical anomalies are present. In the next chapter we will discuss the normal curve in greater detail, and you will see how this confidence interval is derived.

The size of your sample should be based on the formula for standard error, and what you think the proportion in the population is. It will also be based on how certain the answer needs to be. Stephan and McCarthy (1958) constructed the following table as a general guideline for choosing sample size.

Table 7.1
Approximate Sample Size Required to Detect a Systematic Error 90 Percent of the Time When a One-way Test is Used at the .025 Level of Significance

	True Value of P in the Population			
	0.50	0.40 or 0.60	0.80 or 0.20	0.90 or 0.10
Amount of Systematic Error				
0.01	26,000	25,000	17,000	9,400
0.02	6,800	6,300	4,200	2,400
0.03	1,100	1,000	670	380
(Stephan & McCarthy, 1958, p. 145)				

You can see that when a sample gets larger than 1,000 the error doesn't get proportionally smaller. In other words, a sample larger than 1,000 produces little more in accuracy.

DESIGNING QUESTIONNAIRES

Questionnaires are the key to survey research. The design of the questionnaire is more important than the nature of the sample or the statistical analysis employed. Remember that in chapter 1 we noted that sometimes scientists let their predispositions influence the way they gather data. In this section we will show you how to avoid this type of pitfall in designing a questionnaire. Let's look at an example of a poll taken by the Roper organization about the Nazi participation in the Holocaust. In 1992, the Roper organization asked the following question in a national survey:

> Does it seem possible or does it seem impossible to you that the Nazi extermination of the Jews never happened?

The answers that were given were: Impossible—65%; Possible—22%; and Not sure—12% ("Poll on doubt," 1994). This poll seems to indicate that one out of five Americans had doubt about whether or not the Jews really did suffer in World War II. However, after much criticism, the Roper organization admitted that the question could have been flawed. Individuals might well have believed that the Holocaust happened but at the same time, because of the way the question was worded, reported that "it seems impossible." The following year, a new question was formulated:

> Does it seem possible to you that the Nazi extermination of the Jews never happened, or do you feel certain that it happened?

This time the answers were: Certain it happened—91%; Not sure—8%; Possible it never happened—1%. You can see that the form of the question made all the difference in the world. Clearly, the sensitive nature of the subject matter also made a difference.

Before considering the design of a questionnaire, it might be useful to review the general principles of measurement mentioned in chapter 2. Basically a questionnaire is designed to be simpler, to be given to larger groups, and usually for some specific purpose. There are a number of general principles that should be followed in designing a questionnaire (Fowler, 1993). First, the questionnaire ought to be self-explanatory. Second, the questions should not be open-ended, and a limited number of questions should be asked. Instructions should be simple and clear.

Let's look at some guidelines to use when constructing questionnaires.

Avoid Questions with Obvious Answers

Your items should not have obvious answers. In the following example, a pharmacy wants to know how likely a customer would be to ask a pharmacist for advice. How well would the following item address the pharmacy's concerns?

If you have a minor medical problem, who do you think you would be most likely to consult for information?
___ pharmacist   ___ neighbor
___ physician   ___ registered nurse
___ medical reference

Few people are going to have a medical reference, no one will ask a neighbor, and of the three professional sources, almost everyone would answer "physician." This item has an obvious answer. Now look at another item:

> **If you have a minor medical problem, would you consider asking a pharmacist for information?**
>
> ☐ **Yes** ☐ **No**

This item is simpler, gets at the issue, and might be answered either way. Even if you responded "yes" to this question, you still might have responded "physician" or "registered nurse" as an answer to the first question. Of course, if you weren't interested in pharmacists as a source of information, it wouldn't matter. Since you are, the question could be crucial.

Use Clarity

Your item should not confuse the respondent. Too much information in the item can be truly confusing. Look at the following item, a questionnaire sent out to WLAK listeners:

> **Station WLAK broadcasts fourteen hours of classical, semi-classical, and modern serious music every Sunday. Do you think that's too much, about right, not enough, or REALLY not enough of this kind of music?**

Compare it to:

> **How do you like WLAK's Sunday schedule?**

Make Them Simple

Your items ought to measure one thing only. You don't want your respondents to give answers based on only one part of the question:

> **Madeleine Albright, the Secretary of State, is the first woman to ever hold that position. Do you think that her gender would be a problem in dealing with the Arab world, which is a male-dominated culture, or a problem with leaders in the Far East?**

This item could be rewritten as:

> **Madeleine Albright, the Secretary of State, is the first woman to ever hold that position. Do you think that her gender would**

be a problem in dealing with the Arab world, which is a male-dominated culture?

Respondents Must be Qualified to Answer

Another problem with survey items is that individuals don't always remember what they did, and sometimes they don't tell the truth about their behavior. In one survey, names were drawn from voting records, and those who had NOT voted were included. The respondents were asked who they had voted for, and they blithely supplied the names of candidates even if they hadn't actually voted (Bradburn, Rips, & Shevell, 1987). Keep in mind that individuals may provide false data about themselves to avoid casting themselves in a bad light.

Avoid Biased Items

Many words we use carry intrinsic bias. A question that begins "Don't you agree with the President of the United States that . . ." will draw a very different response than one that begins "How do you feel about the Clinton administration's policy that . . ." A word like "welfare" will be evaluated differently than "aid to single mothers." An item that asks "Should the United States carry out its obligations in Bosnia?" will be answered quite differently than an item that asks "Should U.S. soldiers in Bosnia be called home before Christmas?"

ADMINISTERING QUESTIONNAIRES

There are a number of ways to administer questionnaires. They can be mailed, read on the telephone, or administered a variety of other ways. Mail surveys are certainly convenient, but the response rate is poor and there is no way of telling what sources of bias can intervene. Researchers often guarantee money as an incentive to get respondents to mail the survey back in, but the rates are still low.

Just stopping people on the street is probably not a good idea. Sociologist Harry Edwards relates that he stopped 150 people on the streets of New York City at the height of a recent mayoral election (in which Rudolph Giuliani won) and asked "Who do you think is going to win?" Thirty-four people mentioned one candidate or another, but most of the others answered "the Mets" (Kohn, 1992, p. 80).

Calling people on the telephone is better, but you are obviously limited to evening hours, since most people work in the daytime. Random digit dialing is a method of getting randomly selected telephone numbers, but there are still a number of people with unlisted numbers or who don't answer the telephone. In addition, you are limited as to time. Ten or fifteen minutes is a long telephone conversation, and you need to remember that people might well be watching their favorite basketball team when you call them!

Other methods include visiting the malls and confronting every fifth or sixth person to ask them, for example, what they think of Yeltsin's leadership in the Kremlin. One time researchers set up stands in the supermarket and handed out little pieces of pizza with questions about the next schoolboard election. These examples may sound contrived, but they actually happened! However, schools and daycare centers make good places to gain access to people in their homes. At school, researchers can send a questionnaire home with the third graders and trust to luck that the third grader gives it (and the return envelope) to their mother or father. Return rates using this method usually run less than 50 percent, and with this method your sample will not include adults without children.

There are so many problems associated with questionnaires, most students wonder why they are so widely used. The truth is, sometimes there really isn't any alternative to polling, and most of us realize that some information is better than no information at all. Useful data can be generated using questionnaires and sampling techniques.

EVALUATING SURVEY RESEARCH

As we review survey research, we can see that our evaluation of any survey begins with an assessment of the purpose of the survey. If the study has been conducted simply to act as feedback within a large organization, then we need to spend little time evaluating it. Inferential surveys, however, depend on a number of factors that should bear close scrutiny. The relationship between the sample and the population is the crucial characteristic. Good survey research stays as close to random sampling as possible. Our evaluation of surveys should certainly include an assessment of the way the sample was drawn, together with the response rate.

When deviations from the ideal occur, we need to examine the reasons for such and evaluate them on their merits. However, even if a sample has been drawn with a geographic or demographic bias, it is important to ask if this bias is actually relevant. Much university research is done with college students as a sample base. For many kinds of questions we might recognize that this bias is irrelevant, that is, in many instances college students are quite similar to a more general population.

If the survey asks about health risks such as prostate cancer or Alzheimer's disease, it would be clear that college students would not be very appropriate for a sample group. Common sense can go a long way in our evaluation of samples.

A second and fundamental evaluation occurs when we look at the confidence limits of the survey. Most pollsters report a "margin of error" factor, but typically we should be skeptical of these. Calculating standard error is easy when the number of respondents and the proportions reported are known. The basis the polling agency uses for reporting margin of error may well be less stringent than someone else might need.

If it is possible to see the actual questions the surveyors used, then we can check for the usual characteristics: obvious answers, clarity, simplicity, and bias. These evaluations are obviously qualitative ones and should be done.

It is common for many practitioners in the media to solicit responses from viewers and readers and to call these "surveys." During a high-profile criminal trial, television stations often supply "900" numbers for viewers to call in their judgments of guilt or innocence. These activities are truly not surveys, primarily because each person who calls has a preconceived notion about the outcome. The utility of this collection of data is confined to promotional activity at the station.

NOTES

[1] Fitzpatrick makes no claims about systematic sampling and inferences about larger populations. We will look at some the problems involved in systematic sampling later in the chapter.

[2] In other instances, the researchers might want the sample to reflect the proportions of these age groups that are actually present in the population. Whatever rationale is used, the technique is the same.

PART FOUR

Confirmatory Research
Testing and Extending Theories

In the last three chapters we examined research that has an exploratory flavor: qualitative research places an emphasis on investigation into cultures and individuals in depth; textual research examines a sample of language and seeks to discover what, if anything, can be learned from it; and survey research looks into what the characteristics of a large group of people might be. These forms of research are not *necessarily* atheoretical, but they typically begin without any particular theoretical orientation.[1] However, one central concern of these three forms of research is the *explanation* of the phenomena discovered, and developing these explanations into *theories of communication*. The next logical step in research is to test these theories, with an eye toward developing them and extending them.

The development and extension of theoretical statements is essential before we can think about using theories. In chapter 4 when we discussed measurement, we examined how researchers explore reliability and validity to extend the usefulness of the measurement procedure. The same process underlies confirming theories and extending them. In a sense, this research can be said to be searching for reliability about our communication theories.

---

[1] One exception occurs in survey research when a particular hypothesis is tested in a survey. We will deal with this exception later in the book.

Chapter Eight

Normality, Variance, and Chance
Reasoning and Research

THE INTERACTION OF RESEARCH AND THEORY

Just how theories and research interact may not be clear. First remember that theories are collections of statements, some of which are based on observations and others which are derived from logical extensions of other theories. When a statement is based on observation, it is not a simple description of a factual occurrence, such as "George put the cello in the closet." Observations usually involve events which are connected to one another, primarily in a causal way. When we are conducting research based on a certain theory, we are investigating two things about the statement: whether it is true or not, and how general it is. Theories based on untrue statements are pretty useless! There are many criteria for truth, but the most important one in this context is "correspondence," or semantic truth. We want to know if the statement corresponds to events in the outside world. Secondly, we wish to know whether the observations in the statement are typical, and if we are justified in making general statements about them.

Let's begin with an example, a well-known statement from persuasion theory: "When a message is attributed to a source with high credibility, that message will have greater effect than a message attributed to a source with low credibility." Since this is a foundational statement of many theories of persuasion, it is really important for us to know if it is true or not. Testing this statement is a research task. How could we do this?

First we **operationalize** (decide which procedures or operations will be most useful in our analysis) the key concepts—*credibility* and *effect*, usually in terms of observations that we make of the sources and receivers. If the source was the doctor on the *Today* show (see chapter 1), then you could ask his patients questions such as "Does this doctor know what he's talking about?" and "Do you think he has your best interests in mind?" and construct a credibility scale. Then you could

125

observe the behavior of the patients, noting who stopped smoking, who cut down, and who simply went on as before. Again, you would want to construct some sort of index of effects, such as a proportion of quitters, or gross amount of cigarettes consumed, for instance. But once you arrive at your operational definitions and perform your experimental manipulation, you need to take the next step and *connect* the two events. In short, you need to *prove* that the credibility was the probable cause of the effect, and not something else. You can only do this by finding a low-credible doctor who delivers the same message. Then, to demonstrate that credibility works, you need to show that there is a difference between the results obtained by the one with high credibility and those of the one with low credibility.

Unfortunately, working with human beings is a chancy affair at best, and it is quite possible for a reasonable, well informed person to get a warning from a low-credible doctor and subsequently stop smoking. Also, many of us get messages from high-credible doctors and ignore them. These variations may be due to personal problems, the peace process in the Middle East, the current pollen count, or sunspots. Many times we haven't any idea what causes them. You will remember from the previous chapter that we usually refer to uncontrolled, capricious events of this kind as *random* events and say that they are caused by *chance*.

Let's say that we do everything correctly, operationalize our concepts, and observe the relationships between credibility and subsequent healthful behavior. Given the nature of capricious human behavior, a skeptic could easily say that we "lucked out" this time because the relationship occurred, but that next time we may not find the same relationship by using the same test. What we would like is proof that our observed relationship between credibility and behavior was not chance. The only way we can do that is to know something about chance.

To say that an event is caused by chance is a poor way to put it, but researchers say it all the time. What they mean is that the event is not caused by anything—or that if it is caused by something, we haven't a clue what it is. In other words, the events are purely random. Random events are also known as "uncertain" or "chaotic" and are generally considered the enemy of science and good theory.

Science has as its goal the reduction of uncertainty.

Actually, we would like to completely eliminate uncertainty if possible. We know that isn't possible, so we usually settle for a reduction. It follows then, if the aim of science is the reduction of uncertainty, that we need to be able to measure the degree of uncertainty in any set of observations. In other words, we can't say that we reduced uncertainty unless we know how uncertain something is. This implies a scale in which an event is totally uncertain on one end, or completely caused and certain on the other end. How can such a scale be constructed?

Randomness

The most "uncertain" that anything can be is "random," or totally without order of any kind. In the last chapter we spoke of a random sample, but here we wish to note that randomness occurs in a great many situations. The weather is an excellent example. We know that weather for the next few days can be predicted with some accuracy (usually less than 50 percent), but when we look forward more than a week, it is totally unpredictable. Random movements of the jet stream, ocean currents, and the earth's rotation all play an important part in what our weather will be in the future. Many meterologists are fond of saying that when they get better data and larger computers, their accuracy will improve. This may be true, but essentially the process is a random one and may ultimately defy prediction. So if a weather forecaster (or a stock market forecaster, or a fashion forecaster) makes predictions that are no better than chance, we would feel that the forecasts were not all that valid. It is vitally important to know when something is truly random, or if it just seems to be. That implies that we need to know *how much* randomness is present in any given system.

Scientists obviously look at randomness as the enemy—chaos is always bad in their minds. However, we could never expect to know everything there is to know. Our knowledge ranges somewhere between total randomness and total predictability. A really important question, in any set of observations, is "how random is it?" We can answer the question of how random only if we have some measure of randomness. How can we do that?

An event is random *if and only if* its occurrence is totally independent of previous events. Imagine a track made to fit a steel ball of about an inch in diameter. A ball can roll down the track without deviation because its sides hold the ball in place. For contrast, make a short stretch of track (about an inch and a half) without sides, and place a steel peg in the middle of the track. A rolling ball will hit the peg and fall off the track—either on the right or left side. Whether or not the ball goes right or left is a random event. We can manufacture machines to create random events *in theory*, but true randomness can only be assessed after we try them out. Hidden biases can appear in the most unlikely places.[1]

Now imagine a large board with many layers of steel pegs set into it, so that a ball dropped from the top of it and rolling down it will encounter not one, but dozens of pegs. If the ball goes either to the right or left *randomly* at each choice point, the balls will collect at the bottom in a strange set of categories. The process is repeated until the ball gets to the bottom of the rack. This is a way of demonstrating what happens when a *binomial* choice occurs over and over again. In mathematics this physical process is described by a mathematical expression called *binomial expansion.*

The Binomial Expansion

Think back to your high school algebra class for a moment. If your memory is good, then the expression

$$(a + b)^n$$

will come back to you and you'll remember that this is the basic algebraic expression of the binomial expansion.[2] The value of n determines how complicated the expression will be. If $n = 2$, then:

$$(a + b)^2 = a^2 + 2ab + b^2$$

As n gets larger and larger, the intermediate values in the expressions also get more complex. If the value of n was as great as 8, then the expression would read:

$$(a + b)^8 = a^8 + 8a^7b + 28(a^6b^2) + 56(a^5b^3)$$

$$+ 70(a^4b^4) + 56(a^3b^5) + 28(a^2b^6) + 8(ab^7) + b^8$$

Now, remember the example of the ball rolling down the board and hitting pegs—going right or left as chance decreed? If "right" is one of the values in the expansion, and "left" is another, we would assume that the probability of each would be 0.5, or one-half. It is equally probable that the ball will go either direction, so 50 percent of the time it goes right and 50 percent of the time it goes left. Now let's change "a" to "p" and "b" to "q."

The binomial expansion of $n=8$ when $p=0.5$ and $q=0.5$ is given in table 8.1. If we take the values of the intermediate terms from table 8.1 and place them in a histogram, we would get a shape like the one in figure 8.2. If you think these values are beginning to look familiar, you would be correct—they are becoming closer and closer approximations to the normal curve.

Table 8.1
Expansion of Binomial (p + q)ⁿ, Where p = q = 0.5 and n = 8, to Illustrate the Normal Frequency Distribution

p^8	1(0.00390625)	0.00390625
$8p^7\,q$	8(0.0078125)(0.5)	0.03125000
$28p^6\,q^2$	28(0.015625)(0.25)	0.10937500
$56p^5\,q^3$	56(0.03125)(0.125)	0.21875000
$70p^4\,q^4$	70(0.0625)(0.0625)	0.27343750
$56p^3\,q^5$	56(0.125)(0.03125)	0.21875000
$28p^2\,q^6$	28(0.25)(0.015625)	0.10937500
$8p\,q^7$	8(0.5)(0.0078125)	0.03125000
q^8	1(0.00390625)	0.00390625
Total		1.00000000

Source: Hays, W. M. (1973), *Statistics for the Social Sciences* (New York: Holt, Rinehart, & Winston).

Figure 8.1   Histogram that Illustrates the Normal Frequency Distribution

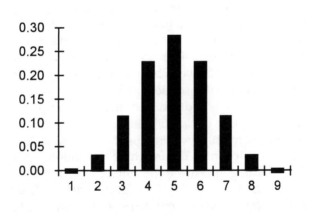

Let us look at another way of approaching the measure of randomness. Imagine a "forest" with trees two meters apart. Then imagine birds in the one central tree, all clustered in one place. What would happen if the birds were agitated a succession of times, all dispersing in random directions? At first, we might think successive dispersal would just create a mess, but when it is examined analytically, specific characteristics emerge. The successive dispersals make a regular pattern among the birds. You see that these frequencies tend toward a familiar shape.

Some people may recognize that if these frequencies were graphed in histograms they would tend toward a shape we call the normal curve. If we progressively increase the value of n the intervals will be smoother, and when n = infinity, the junctions between the categories will disappear and the resulting shape will form a curve.

The Normal Curve

The normal curve is the best estimate of the expansion of the binomial distribution where q=0.5, p=0.5 and n=infinity.

In actual practice, a normal distribution is a good approximation when $n > 10$.

A recent popular book used the term "bell curve" to describe this familiar distribution (Hernstein & Murray, 1994). These authors attribute almost everything good that happens to people as a result of "intelligence" and conclude that since the distribution of intelligence (as they define it) is curved, the distribution of rewards in life, such as promotion, good salary, and so forth, will also be curved. Hernstein and Murray state that: "It makes sense that most things will be arranged in bell-shaped curves" (p. 557). Actually, this wide generalization may make no sense to you at all. However, it makes lots of sense to describe *random events* this way. Consider the random behavior of the steel balls dropped down through a large board encountering dozens of pegs; The binomial expansion will produce the same randomness. In other words, the normal curve is a diagram of the way completely random events would occur. This is one of the common uses of this familiar statistic: It shows how something would look if it were actually random.

What good is it to know if something is random? Actually, not much. But if something appears to be random, we know that it's not something systematic or caused by some other external agent. In other words, if we know that a group of numbers or observations fit a normal distribution, then we know it wasn't caused by invisible rays from outer space. If we visit the home office of the International Widget Manufacturing Company and measure everyone's shoe size, we will probably see that the resultant numbers are random and fit into a normal distribution. We have used the word distribution to describe how a group of numbers is distributed, that is, what characteristics the collection has. We still don't know much about the people that work for Widget, but we do know that in this respect, they aren't unusual. To actually obtain useful information about distributions, we need to know more.

There are two vital dimensions to a normal distribution. You will remember (from chapter 3) how we calculate the **mean**, or average of the scores. This is the first important dimension of the normal curve.

$$\bar{X} = \frac{\sum_{i=1}^{n} X_i}{n} \tag{1}$$

The second important dimension of the normal curve is the **variance**. The formula for calculating the variance is given here:

$$\sigma^2 = \frac{\sum_{i=1}^{n} (X_i - \bar{X})^2}{n} \tag{2a}$$

Also remember that the **standard deviation** is the square root of the variance.

Standard Error

If you compare expression (2a) to expression (2) in chapter 3, you will see that in one instance we used n and in the other, we used $n-1$. What's going on? Think back to the previous chapter and recall the difference between population and sample. Testing a sample of the population is a method of estimating what the characteristics of the population might be. To do this, we need to have at least two or three other things in our vocabulary. One difference between sample and population is simply the terms used. We use the term **parameter** when we speak of the population, and the term **statistic** when we speak of the sample. The mean of the population is termed "mu" (μ) and the variance of the population is "sigma squared" (σ^2). The mean of the sample is "X-bar" ($\bar{X}$) and the variance of the sample is "s squared" (s^2). But since the function of the sample is to estimate characteristics of the population, the process is a little more complicated. On the average, if we draw a number of samples of scores from a large population, the variances of these samples would be a bit too small. Most mathematical statisticians recommend that enlarging the estimate by reducing the value of n to $n-1$ is the best way to correct for this bias (Ghiselli, Campbell, & Zedek, 1981, p. 47). Throughout the rest of the book, we will use $n-1$, and the terms *standard error* and *standard deviation* will be interchangeable from now on.[2]

The normal distribution has a number of interesting characteristics. The mean ($\overline{X}$) determines where the center of the curve will be, and the standard error determines the basic width of the curve. Look at figure 8.2.

Figure 8.2   The Normal Curve

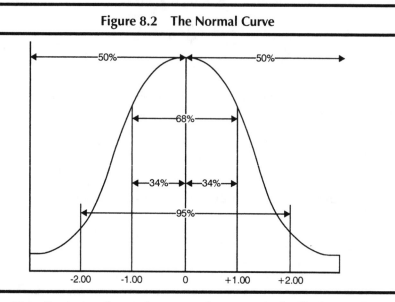

This illustrates the perfect normal curve, which all of us realize is only a figment of a statistician's imagination. The curve is defined by the mean ($\overline{X}$) and the standard error (s^2). The mean tells us where the center of the curve will be, and the standard error tells us how wide or "fat" the particular curve will be. Figure 8.3 shows us three different normal curves, one with a large standard error, one with a moderate one, and one with a small one. The interesting thing about distributions is that they are all different. When a normal distribution has a small standard error we say it is **mesokurtic** and if it has a large standard error, we say it is **platykurtic**.

Let us return to the perfect curve for a moment. You can see that the curve determines an *area*, much like other geometric figures do. This area can be divided in many different ways, but the most useful technique is to move along the baseline and draw perpendicular lines up to where the line intersects the curve. Any line like this will divide the curve into areas to the left of it and to the right of it. If you look back to figure 8.2, you will see that a line is drawn at the position of the mean, which *bisects* the area. In other words, 50 percent of the area of the curve is on the left side, and 50 percent of the area is on the right side.

Figure 8.3   Three Examples of a Normal Curve

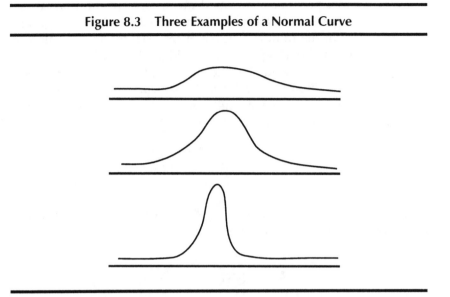

The line to the right of the mean is erected at one standard error along the baseline. One interesting thing that we know about normal curves is that this area (one standard error from the mean) is 34 percent of the total area of the curve. This is true of all normal distributions. One standard error from the mean in the other direction has the same area, so it is correct to say that 68 percent of all the numbers in a distribution lie within an area defined by plus or minus one standard error.

z Scores

One of the most important aspects of the normal curve is the statistic we call the **z score.** This score is an arithmetical transformation of the "raw" score into standard deviation units. To see how z scores are obtained, let us go back to table 3.2 and look at the scores for affect orientation. Here we see that the mean of the collection of 39 scores is 73, and the variance is 87.342. Remember that we calculated the variance by adding up all the squared deviations ($\Sigma \, [X_i \, \text{-} \overline{X}]^2$), which gives us 3319, and divided that by 38 (or n - 1), which yields 87.342. The square root of this number is 9.35, so the standard deviation of this collection of scores is 9.35. The mean is 73, and so one standard deviation upward from the mean is 82.35 (or 73 + 9.35). Two standard deviations above the mean is 91.7.

However, we need a standardized way to present these scores so that we can compare research results from one scale to another. You will note that none of the numbers in the affect orientation collection of scores is a decimal. So the conversion would be: The mean z score is 0, and as we go up, we add standard deviation units for each score. Each increment is 1 / 9.35 in size, or 0.107. This means that the z score for 74 is +0.107, for 75 is +0.214, and so forth. You can also simply plug in the numbers in the formula for z scores, which is:

$$z = \frac{X - \bar{X}}{s}$$

(5)

where s is the standard deviation (9.225), $\bar{X}$ is the mean (73) and x is any score. If we use 68 for x, we get

$$z = \frac{68 - 73}{9.35} = -0.53$$

It might help to formulate a linear scale to show how this is done. The top number is the raw score, and the bottom number is the z score, or standardized score:[4]

67	68	69	70	71	72	73	74	75	76	77	78	79
-.64	-.53	-.43	-.32	-.21	-.10	0	.10	.21	.32	.43	.53	.64

Standardized scores are extremely useful, in that most measures we use in the social sciences contain different raw score units. A few (IQ is an example) are constructed in such a way that the scales are already standardized in form. IQ tests have a mean of 100 and a standard deviation of 10, so their form is already (by definition) standardized. But consider one kind of research assessment that has had wide use in communication—listening scores. The Kentucky Comprehensive Listening Test has five subtests—short-term listening (STL), short-term listening with rehearsal (STL-R), interpretive listening (INT), lecture listening, (LECT) and listening when there are distractions (DIST) (Bostrom, 1990). Each of these has its own mean and standard error. This test has been given to a very large group of respondents, and the proportions of correct and incorrect answers was different for each scale. The STL mean for this group of respondents (20,000) was 8 (out of 12), STL-R mean was 9 (out of 12), INT was 5 (out of 10), LECT was 8 (out of 14) and DIST was 8 (out of 12). Suppose a student took the entire test and had a "profile" like this:

STL	10
STL-R	9
INT	8
LECT	7
DIST	9

It would be difficult to glean a great deal of information from these scores, other than simple percentages and number of items correct. But if we "standardized" the scores and added them to our table, we would have a good deal more information. Now our table looks like this:

Scale	Raw Score	Standard Score
STL	10	1.5
STL-R	9	0.5
INT	8	1.2
LECT	7	-0.5
DIST	9	0.5

In other words, the standard scores give us a much better picture of the general position of each respondent that took the test. Whether or not the standard score is positive or negative tells us whether the score is above or below the mean of the entire collection, and the value of the standard score gives a good picture of how extreme the score differs from the mean. We could use this same procedure in any comparison of communication measurements.

HYPOTHESIS TESTING AND THE NORMAL CURVE

The most interesting characteristic of the normal curve is that the areas under the curve are quite different at different positions along the number line. In other words, there are different numbers of people (or scores) at different places in the distribution. Remember that 34 percent of the collection of scores lie one standard deviation above the mean. This also means that 34 percent lie one standard deviation below the mean. So 68 percent lie between +1 and -1 standard deviation: most of the population. But we know even more than that. We know *exactly* how many can be expected to be at any one point above or below the mean.

We can get these values from appendix B. This table is titled "Areas under the Normal Curve." This table is constructed to be as compact as possible, so it is not as easy to read as we might like. A little practice will help. Let's pick a z score at random for an example—how about 0.52? We go down the left-hand column and find "0.5" and then go over the top row till we find "0.02," and this gives us 0.52. The value in this cell is 0.1985. This means that a z score of 0.52 is going to define 19.85 percent of the total volume of the curve. Let's try another one—1.26 (remember that we just picked 0.52 and 1.26 randomly). We go down the left hand column and find 1.2. Then on that row, we go over till we find the 0.06 column. The value is 0.3962. That means that the area between the mean and a standard deviation of 1.26, is 39.26 percent of the total. Now how can we use this for hypothesis testing?

Testing hypotheses with the normal curve begins with a general idea, such as "College students are in poorer physical condition than they used to be." That's not very specific. A more specific hypothesis might be "Students at Wildemere College are heavier in proportion to their height today than they were twenty years ago." Now we have to operationalize the term "heavier in proportion to their height," and assign each student a number (after weighing and measuring them, of course). If a student is 20 percent heavier than he or she should be according to the weight tables, we will assign this student a 20. Now if we know what the numbers were for Wildemere College twenty years ago, we can test the hypothesis that they are fatter today. Let's say that we know that the Wildemere student bodies were slightly overweight twenty years ago, and that the campus average was 8 percent heavier than what they should have been on the weight tables. We would therefore test the hypothesis that today's average is 8. We line up everyone, measure them, and weigh them. We get a campus average of 16. In addition to that, we get a standard error of 3.2. Now what?

First let's try to explain the finding of a mean of 16 in terms of chance. This would result in a statement like "Well, I believe strongly that today's average is really 8. This finding at Wildemere College is totally due to chance." This is not really a hypothesis—it is actually a *null* hypothesis. But those of us that think today's college student is heavier say, "Wait. It could be due to chance. *But if it were, how big a chance would it be? How unlikely a chance is it?*" So we convert the finding of 16 to z units; 16 minus 8 is 8, and 8 divided by 3.2 is 2.5; so there is a 2.5 standard error discrepancy between 16 and 8. Look in appendix B; 2.5 is a value of 0.4938, or 49.38 percent. In other words, IF the true mean is 8, then over 49 percent of the samples taken would be less than 16. But there's more. If we consider the statistical argument fully (that the Wildemere College result is totally due to chance) then we would have to accept that it could be *lower* than 8, as well as higher than 8. So if the result came about because of chance, that chance would have occurred only once out of 98.76 times. That isn't very often. Another way of putting it is in decimal form: 1/98.76 is 0.010125.

All this means is that if Wildemere College students are like they are because of chance (and we have to accept that possibility), then the chance is about 1 in 100. Do you believe that this truly unlikely event happened? In other words, if Wildemere College students got to be like they are because of chance ONLY, it would have happened only once in a hundred college samples. Most of us wouldn't think so, and so we agree that we must *reject the null hypothesis*.

This, in a nutshell, is the way all statistical arguments are formulated. In chapter 2 we looked at some of the characteristics of good hypotheses. Let's look over them again as they apply to the Wildemere College hypothesis. Good hypotheses are simple, observable, and testable.

Simple

Good hypotheses concern only one aspect of the research at a time. In the study about Wildemere College, we wouldn't have analyzed shoe size as well as height and weight. Nor would we have included statements like "Since today's college students are worthless and don't exercise . . ." and so forth.

Observable

A good hypothesis is observable in that it is related to some observational system and can actually be measured. In our example above, we constructed an index of a ratio between weight and height, both of which are easily measurable. Our observations should be relatively simple and have some relative significance to other factors that we think are important.

Testable

A good hypothesis is testable; that is, it is possible to actually make the observations involved. Notice that the value for college students twenty years ago was available in this example. If that figure is not available, then the hypothesis is not testable. Many statements made today about drug use and the incidence of violent crime are not testable, simply because these indices have not been kept for a long period of time.

Hypotheses vs. Research Questions

You may remember that in chapter 2 we distinguished between hypotheses and research questions, reasoning that hypotheses represent a formal testing of a theory and a research question represents a more general exploration of phenomena. The choice of hypotheses as opposed to a research question is largely determined by the state of theory in the area, the statistical procedure used, and the preferences of the researcher.

CALCULATIONS ON THE COMPUTER

You may have noticed a lot of calculations in this chapter, and there are more to come in the rest of the book. A hand calculator is invaluable for these little problems. But when we get to larger collections of data, like the scores on affect orientation we used in this chapter, even the use of a hand calculator involves a lot of work. Fortunately, there are some shortcuts. One is to have someone else do it for you! But if you are not fortunate enough to have a roommate who just loves to work problems, then a more reasonable answer is to use the computer. In most research, there are two major options: using a desktop machine (a PC), or using a mainframe. You may be using your PC for word processing, but with a little adjustment it can work statistical problems for you. The mainframe computer is what we would use if we had really large data sets, or if the data were already stored on a central unit.

Microsoft Excel and the PC

There are many statistical applications available for personal computers. Here we will describe one of the most common, called Excel. If your personal computer has Windows, then it may already have Excel on it. Excel is part of Microsoft's package called Office, which you may have to load separately, if it's not already on your computer.

Here's how to use Microsoft Excel to calculate the standard deviation: (1) Activate Windows. (2) Click on Microsoft Excel. You will see a data sheet that looks like an accounting ledger. (3) Enter the scores from table 4.3 in this data sheet. (4) Click on the Tools menu and then click on Data Analysis. (5) Move down to Descriptive Statistics. (6) Enter the range of your numbers. In this case it is A1:A39. This means that your numbers are in column A, numbers 1 through 39. (7) Make sure the box for Summary Statistics at the bottom of the dialog box has a checkmark in it. (8) Click OK and the program does your work for you! The output is in figure 8.4. You can see that the program gives you more output than you really need.

Mainframe Computers and SAS

If you have a truly large data set, or if the data set is stored on one of these big machines, you will need to use a different kind of program. We will use the Statistical Analysis System (SAS) here, since it is commonly

Figure 8.4   Output in Microsoft Excel for Descriptive Statistics

Column1	
Mean	73.02564
Standard Error	1.496504
Median	74
Mode	74
Standard Deviation	9.345664
Sample Variance	87.34143
Kurtosis	-0.74159
Skewness	-0.00946
Range	35
Minimum	56
Maximum	91
Sum	2848
Count	39
Largest(1)	91
Smallest(1)	56
Confidence Level(95.0%)	3.029514

available and easy.[5] See figure 8.5 (on the next page) for a printout of an SAS job that will do the same things Excel did. This is a "batch" job, and you will need to check with your local computing center to see how to submit this listing and where to get your output. These differ from installation to installation and may take some getting used to.

Figure 8.5 SAS Batch Job

```
//A EXEC SAS
DATA AFFECT;
INPUT AFFECT;
CARDS;
80
74
59
87
83
83
80
70
76
82
71
56
72
77
70
57
62
74
64
61
76
66
60
82
84
74
74
91
75
76
63
73
91
85
72
76
64
61
67
PROC MEANS;
PROC PRINT;
TITLE EXAMPLE;
/*
```

EVALUATING RESEARCH USING THE NORMAL CURVE

Statistical reasoning is ubiquitous; that is, it is everywhere. This form of reasoning depends on comparing our observations to what the same observations might have been if they had been determined by chance, rather than what we suspect caused them. To do this, we need a model of chance, and that model is called the normal curve. Its main dimensions are the mean and the variance, and when we know these we can make inferences about the general characteristics of the population. We can use the normal curve to test a hypothesis that a given set of observations does or does not fit into a given theoretical framework, or that a particular idea is or is not true.

Typical research into "normality" depends on an assumption that chance has been the principal determinant in arranging whatever variable is being studied. Pioneering researchers in the measurement of intelligence made this assumption, and many still do. The fact that height, weight, hat size and even shoe size measurements fit the normal curve quite well is certainly not a compelling indicator that other human characteristics are also arranged this way. But many researchers have thought so and therefore have forced their measurements into normal parameters. When evaluating this research, we should ask if the normal curve was determined by the nature of the data or superimposed by the researchers.

Research in communication would profit from using ideas of randomness in the measurement of information. *Information* is usually defined as the absence of entropy, or predictability. Information is based on choices between two equally likely events and is therefore measured in numbers based on the logarithm of the number 2. Information is such a basic characteristic in communication that it is surprising that so few researchers employ this concept in their theories.

NOTES

[1] In the 1950s, a small group of engineering students from a California university went to Las Vegas and carefully observed the behavior of balls rolling around on the roulette tables. They were looking for tables that had a consistent bias toward red or black, and a bias large enough to offset the "0" and "00" categories on the betting board. They did indeed identify a few tables and began to bet. In casinos, consistently winning attracts the attention of the management, and the students were told to beat it. Undaunted, the students recruited new faces to go in and beat

the tables. The casinos got wise, and for a time closed each table and randomly substituted new parts each night until the bias disappeared.

[2] Standard deviation is based on raw score measures, while standard error refers to measures other than raw data and is called the standard error of something, for example, standard error of estimate. We will use the two terms interchangeably.

[3] The binomial expansion is the foundation of many important concepts in probability, notably "Pascal's triangle" (Hart, 1947, pp. 153–60).

[4] The numbers in the bottom line are rounded off to the nearest hundredth.

[5] Another widely used system is the Statistical Package for the Social Sciences, or SPSS. Both SAS and SPSS have versions for your PC, if you have lots of disk space and around $100 for the software.

Chapter Nine

Comparisons, Statistical Logic, Significance and Error

In the previous chapter, we took the first step toward the examination of hypotheses in terms of chance models. This form of thinking assumes that an excellent way to prove a hypothesis is to attempt to disprove it, and the best way to do that is to test whether a given outcome could be attributed to chance. The normal curve is a description of how chance outcomes are distributed in any population, and the z statistic and the mean of the distribution are the two main determiners of this curve. So when we engaged in "hypothesis testing" using the z statistic, we tested the hypothesis by comparing the sample we drew to the hypothesized value. Since one z is the equivalent to one standard deviation, we tested the hypotheses by looking at the dimensions of the normal curve and inspecting to see if the sample is close to the hypothesized value. If the distance was so great that it represented an event sufficiently rare, then we could say that the difference we observed could not have occurred by chance.

If you think about it for a moment, you might observe that when we used the term "hypothesis testing" we were actually referring to one specific kind of hypothesis, that an observed value was different from a given theoretical (hypothesized) value. Actually the general term "hypothesis testing" could be applied to many other types of questions, and the nature of our study or our experiment will determine what the nature of these hypotheses might be. In this chapter, as well as the chapters that follow, we will look at a number of these questions. The principal source of hypotheses is the logical process we call *induction*. Before we proceed to testing hypotheses, it would be useful to examine how we arrive at hypotheses in the first place.

INDUCTION

There are many important uses of qualitative research, but one essential use is to serve as a base for constructing more general statements about communicative activity.

Suppose we are convinced that many persons in an introductory public speaking class seem to be frightened while they speak. As we observe the students in the class, we see that some of them exhibit trembling in their hands while they speak, and some do not. We assume that trembling hands is a symptom of fright, and we want to explore other aspects of the phenomenon. So we devise a test that gives students in the class an opportunity to volunteer for their speeches. We observe that those who don't volunteer usually show trembling hands when they speak, and those who do volunteer never have trembling hands. We conclude that the existence of fright "causes" both trembling and unwillingness to volunteer and say, "Every time someone shows an external symptom of fright (trembling hands) they will be reluctant to perform in public." We have *induced* this principle from our observations.

In another situation, we observe that every time high credible sources present messages to an audience, they are more effective than low credible sources. We have induced another principle from data. Then we see that persons who watch more television than the average watcher are more fearful of their safety than those who watch little. We induce that television produces a "scary world" in people's minds. Each time we induce something, we keep track of future predictions and find out that it works every time. All of our predictions come true—the person with the trembling hands refuses to volunteer, the high credible sources produce attitude change, and the frequent television watchers are reluctant to go out at night. We begin to think that this business of induction is pretty good stuff. Three times we tried it, and three times it worked. So we *induce* that induction works.

Can we do this? Unfortunately not! We are trying to prove a general principle of induction that depends on a general theory of induction to make it valid. This logical confusion is the reason why most philosophers of science tell us that induction cannot be justified on logical grounds alone (Hempel, 1965). For us to accept induction we must partition our logic into levels, and must assume *metalogic* (logic about logic) that may be different (or the same) as the logic that we are attempting to study.

Early Positivists

The early positivists felt that for inductions to be valid, they should be couched in the same truth-statements as data statements. In other words, any inductive statement should be *operational* in the same sense that the data statements were; that is, verified by controlled observation. This principle was introduced as a corrective measure for truth-statements that were justified on logical grounds alone, such as statements about an ideal metaphysical world.

All this means is that we can't *formally prove* that the sun is going to rise tomorrow morning, because there is no way to prove formally that the inductive principle works all the time. Actually, we can predict not only that the sun will rise, but exactly when and in what direction. This enables us to plant our gardens in particularly sunny places and to build solar houses so that the sun will produce the maximum benefit in the winter months. It makes no sense to ignore solar tables because they can't be formally proven. What this shows us is that although logical proof has its values, it certainly has its limitations as well.

Opponents of the inductive principle go even farther. They point out that no particular number of empirical tests guarantee certainty and cite this as grounds for dismissal of the entire approach. The views of both the positivist and the opposition would seem to be rather extreme.

Logical Empiricism

One approach evolving from positivism was Carnap's (1953) logical empiricism, which also accepts that universal statements can never be verified and relies on confirmation from the accumulation of empirical tests. This accumulation does not constitute *exact proof*, but instead focuses on proof *with an acceptable level of probability*. When these are taken as a whole, they point to a general explanation. So when we see that trembling hands lead to low volunteering rates and that negative comments also lead to trembling hands, and we couple these observations with many other observations of physiological symptoms and communication behavior, we are justified in accepting a conclusion that reinforcement leads to volunteering in a probabalistic sense. This is generally termed the *inductive-statistical* model. The big question, of course, is what constitutes an acceptable level of probability—in other words, how often should we make a prediction and wait until it comes true before we believe the relationship to be a real one?

So what do researchers do? Clearly, they must get beyond the mere collection of observations. Hardly anything could be more boring than a collection of unrelated statements of empirical "facts." This is why Anderson adds all the other functions of qualitative research to the inductive function—more is needed. Going from the state of data collection to the construction of a theory may be what is desired, but it should be clear that theory construction is not an empirical activity. Theory construction *based on* empirical activity is another matter. In this group of theorists, *testing* based on empirical activity is an important part. We will discuss this activity further.

A theory is an interrelated set of propositions, and the propositions are usually derived from data in one way or another. So there are a number of "next steps," depending on the nature of the data. If the data in the collection are strictly empirical in nature, then the theory that most naturally follows is an objectivist account. If the data include more than empirical observation—if they contain theoretical assumptions embedded in them—then the theory produced will most likely be a qualitative one.

If a physician wants to perform an operation because she has deduced the presence of a tumor indicated by a particular symptom, the patient will want the physician to have used a large database and be very sure. The patient will also want to be sure that the doctor's logic is good. If the question is not so important, one can use a smaller number of cases and less stringent deductions. Statisticians use probability estimates, which include characteristics such as the size of the effects as well as the number of cases, to assess a numerical value to the induction.

It might help to look at a specific communication example. Diane Christophel undertook a study of the ways in which "teacher immediacy" affected learning on the part of the students. Immediacy is defined as "the degree of physical and/or psychological closeness between people" (Christophel, 1990). Teachers achieve this immediacy by their nonverbal and verbal behaviors. Christophel's "fundamental theoretic assumption" was: *Students who are more highly motivated (aroused) are likely to learn more than those who are not.* She expressed this in "lawlike form" as the model stated above. Then she tested the degree to which teacher immediacy produced a motivated state, and the degree to which this state produced more learning. In other words, she *derived* part of her prediction from a lawlike statement. Her test of the prediction worked out the way that she predicted—high teacher immediacy did produce both higher motivation and more learning.

The strict interpretation that a proposition must be rejected as soon as it encounters a single falsifying instance would render this model inappropriate for the study of human communication. It is highly unlikely that invariant laws of a universal nature will ever be found in this area of study. Critics of covering law approaches often cite this interpretation as grounds for rejection without giving evidence that they are aware of other interpretations.

Reductionism

Many object to induction because it is based on reductionism, that is, a search for the simplest account of reality. Most theories in the physical sciences, for example, are highly objective and have the additional characteristic of being quantitative and therefore subject to mathematical analysis. They also may be the most general. But emulating physics is certainly not the best way to proceed in our study of human beings—in fact, it has proved disastrous. So many dramatic discoveries came from the development of physical theories that many behavioral scientists (Hull, 1943) took these theories as their model and proposed highly quantifiable statements as behavioral theories.

The biological sciences generally take a very different approach to theory. Statistical laws replace absolutes; classification is much more important, and experimentation is not as prominent as a method. Contingencies are stressed, with a real interest in interactive principles rather than absolutes. Where physical scientists generalize to the entire universe, biological scientists confine themselves to our earth.

Compared to both of these, the behavioral (social) sciences are truly different. The physical sciences explain, predict, and control physical events; the biological sciences explain, predict, and control the activities of plants and animals, and the "social" sciences explain, predict, and control the activities of human beings. Most of these sciences have a significant relationship with one another, usually that of subsumption. Edward O. Wilson (1994) noted that the laws of physics are the basis for chemistry; the laws of chemistry are the basis for biology, and the laws of biology are the basis for social science. We might go on and add that laws of social science form the basis for communication theory.

These hierarchies sometimes lead us to think that they work in both directions, not with the "subsumption" principle that seems so obvious. In other words, communication theory will not contain statements that affect the laws of physics, no matter how much any theorist might wish to include levitation as a basic principle. Strong findings involving the reinforcement principle and our physiological nature have caused a substantial group of social scientists to go into denial. The implications of reinforcement phenomena, for example, involve a powerful explanation for the manipulation of behavior that goes on in corporations, universities, and churches. Rather than examine the nature of this manipulation for what it is—behavioral control—many have chosen to deny its existence and continue to believe in "folk psychology." A substantial number of social scientists have denied the subsumption principle and steadfastly deny a biological basis for human action. Rorty, for example, recently advised us to avoid "reductionism—the idea that biology can somehow overrule culture" (1996, p. 41). This is a very typical view. Rather than recognizing their own biases in favor of nonmaterialistic knowledge systems, these social scientists deny the possibility of objective analysis of human behavior and its physical and biological foundations. A common argument is that science is "only" a belief system and is "rhetorical" in nature (Rorty, 1987). While some could use this as a justification for qualitative research, others might well see it as a drawback.

TESTING HYPOTHESES WITH THE *T* TEST

Once a set of principles has been derived and seems to make sense, researchers will want to test them as carefully as possible. As we have just discovered, we can't prove that hypotheses are true by induction. On the other hand, we definitely can disprove them if they are false. Logicians might argue whether proving that something is not false is the same as saying that it is true, but standard research practice involves testing hypotheses by casting them into negative form, as if the hypotheses were not true. So we will begin by examining the "hypothesis of no difference," a statement which asks if different groups of numbers are significantly different from one another. Here we don't have a previously established value for the hypothesis, we only wonder if one group is different from another. To see how this might work in actual practice, let's look at an example.

Suppose we wish to improve the reasoning ability of individuals enrolled in a basic public speaking course. We have observed that our courses have an assignment toward the end of the semester that calls for students to construct and deliver a reasoned argument on a public issue. But instead of documented evidence and support, the students have been using astrological charts, letters from Elvis, and scenes from *Star Wars* as part of their argument. Logic also seems to be missing from the students' arguments. To solve the problem, we devise a unit of study in critical thinking, including material on evidence, Toulmin's model of claims and warrants based on this evidence. We try this unit in our classes, and student performance seems to get better. However, before we ask that everyone in the department use this assignment, we would like to have a little more support for our idea. The other public speaking teachers agree that we should test our unit. We divide the classes into two groups: One half uses the traditional syllabus, and the other half uses a syllabus with our critical thinking unit in it. Then at the end of the semester we compare the two groups. First, we have an independent group of evaluators grade all the outlines of the argumentative speech assignment, and we ask the students to evaluate their experience in the course. What we want to know is if the groups are different, and if we can show it statistically. The usual statistical technique that is done to make this comparison is called the "*t* test."

Let's look at an example of a *t* test in communication research. Nancy Buerkel-Rothfuss and Pamela Gray studied the criteria that graduate institutions use for selecting prospective graduate students. They were interested in the differences between communication programs and noncommunication programs, and they sent a questionnaire to department chairpersons at a number of schools. Table 9.1 is an abbreviation of the original table found in Buerkel-Rothfuss and Gray (1990). The numbers in the columns represent the average responses of the decision makers, with a "2" representing a response stating that they did indeed use the criteria and a "0" indicating that they did not. The numbers in the third column are the "*t* tests" which indicate whether the difference between the communication department and the noncommunication department was significant.

Table 9.1

Variables	Communication	Noncommunication	*t*
GPA	2.0	1.8	2.6**
Recommendations	2.0	1.8	2.2*
GRE	1.3	1.2	0.6
Teaching Course	0.4	0.4	-0.04
General Requirement	1.5	1.2	2.1
Teaching Experience	0.5	0.8	-1.9
Reputation of UG Degree	0.7	0.7	0.0
Interviews	1.1	0.6	2.2

In the column labelled "*t*" you notice a number, either positive or negative, and an asterisk following it. The authors of the study mention that two asterisks mean that the difference was significant at the 0.01 level and one asterisk means that it was significant at the 0.05 level. What does all this data mean? How did they come up with it?

We should start with a brief explanation of what "*t*" is. Simply put, it is a chance distribution (similar to the normal curve) formed by comparing the means of two different groups and adjusting them according to their standard deviations. The distribution formed is similar to a normal distribution but is slightly different. The method of calculation is quite different. First, you must compute the standard error for each collection of scores. Then, using the numbers in each collection and the means for each collection, you have all you need to complete the formula. Here's how you calculate t:

$$t = \frac{\bar{X}_1 - \bar{X}_2}{\sqrt{\frac{n_1 s_1^2 + n_2 s_2^2}{n_1 + n_2 - 2}\left(\frac{1}{n_1} + \frac{1}{n_2}\right)}} \qquad (5)$$

. The formula looks formidable but really isn't, if you take it step by step. First subtract one mean from another; then plug the number of cases and the standard error from each sample into the formula, and do the arithmetic. Let's try an example. Suppose the collection of affect orientation scores in table 3.2 were randomly sampled from all the communication majors at your school. You think that communication people are a little more sensitive than the students in the College of Engineering, so you persuade a friend in engineering to get a random sample of engineers to take the test. Your friend returns with 30 questionnaires, and, on scoring everything, you find that the engineers had a mean of 67.7 and the communication majors had a mean of 73.0. Aha! We thought so. But remember the chance hypothesis? What we need to do is see if this difference could be ascribed to chance rather than to the academic department where the students were enrolled. So we do a "t" test.

The standard error of the engineers' scores was 10.04, and recall from chapter 8 that the standard error for the communication students' scores was 9.35, that so we enter these into the formula for "t":

$$t = \frac{73 - 67.7}{\sqrt{\frac{39(9.35)^2 + 30(10.04)^2}{39 + 3 - 2}\left(\frac{1}{39} + \frac{1}{30}\right)}}$$

Let's do each calculation separately. The result of 73 - 67.7 is 5.3; 39 x $(9.35)^2$ is 3409.48; 30 x $(10.04)^2$ is 3024.05; 39 + 30 - 2 is 67; 1/39 is 0.026, 1/30 is 0.033. Now the formula is simpler. We can make it even simpler still. The result of 3409.48 plus 3024.05 is 6433.53; 0.026 and 0.033 are 0.059; 6433.53/67 is 96.02; and 96.02 times 0.059 is 5.66. The square root of 5.66 is 2.38, and when you divide 5.3 by 2.38 you get 2.23. Therefore, in this particular comparison, t is equal to 2.23.

$$t = \frac{5.3}{\sqrt{\frac{3409.48 + 3024.05}{67}(0.026 + 0.033)}}$$

The next step is to try to figure out what this particular value means. If you recall the logic behind the normal curve, you will remember that the chance estimates were different depending on how many individual cases were in the sample. If you look back at table 7.1, you will see that the estimates change, depending on how many persons were sampled. A similar logic holds in all tests of chance based on the normal curve (the t and the F statistics are both based on the mathematical characteristics of the normal curve, sometimes called the basic *parameter*. Therefore, these tests are often called *parametric* statistics). Each of these tests also has a characteristic similar to the number of individuals sampled, but not quite. Just to make things confusing, statisticians call this characteristic *degrees of freedom*.

Degrees of Freedom

For the t test, the degrees of freedom are equal to ($n_1 + n_2$ - 2). In other words, you take the number sampled in the first group, add it to the number sampled in the second group, and subtract 2 from it. In the worked example, this works out to 39 + 30 - 2, or 67. Next we look at the table of t values in appendix C. The left-hand column is degrees of freedom, starting with 1, 2 and so forth. Go down this column toward the bottom and you will see the numbers 40, 60, and 120. These intervals are this large because there is very little difference in the chance values when the degrees of freedom are this large. Our problem gave us 67 for our value, so we look at the tabled value for 60. Starting at 60, we move to the right, and see 1.296 in the first column, 1.671 in the second, 2.000 in the third, 2.390 in the fourth, and so on. Our t value was 2.23, so it lies between 2.000 and 2.390. We choose the lowest value, 2.000, and go up to the top of the table. Here we see two numbers, one for a "one-tailed test" and the other for a "two-tailed test."

One-Tail or Two-Tail?

What is a one-tail test? First, let's go back to the normal curve. Remember that the middle of the normal curve was where the highest percentage of the scores were found. Now we need to look at the outer edges or tails of the normal curve. These tails represent the region of rejection, the proportion of the normal curve in which the null hypothesis is rejected. A one-tail test predicts that the results will fall on only one side of the normal curve—either the positive side or the negative side. The two-tail test is less stringent than the one-tail test because it doesn't predict a direction at all. You will generally use a two-tail test when you have little information about the research area. However, we would use the one-tail test if, for example, we thought the engineering majors' scores would be lower than the communication majors' scores.

On the other hand, we may have set out simply to see if the scores were *different*, either lower or higher. If that's the case, then we would consider a difference in either direction an interesting outcome. Here we would opt for the two-tail test. Clearly the logic of the problem determines the logic of the significance test. If you remember the formula for calculating t, you will recall that the means are subtracted from one another to form the numerator of the fraction. Which value is subtracted from which determines whether the overall value is positive or negative: if you subtract the larger number from the smaller number, the outcome will be negative; if you subtract the smaller number from the larger number, then the outcome will be positive.

Once you have made your decision, then you can choose which of the values in Appendix C that you use. If you opted for the one-tailed test, a t value of over 2.000 is significant at the .025 level. This means that the difference might have been due to chance instead of due to the difference in majors; but if it was, it would have happened only once out of fifty occurrences.

STATISTICAL LOGIC

Now that we have mastered how to calculate the t test, we need to examine some of the underlying principles and assumptions that make it useful for us. We have already discussed the nature of statistics as a probabilistic argument, and the quality of that argument stands or falls on whether or not we can accept these assumptions. These assumptions are important ones in relation to the rest of the statistical tests discussed in the book. Let's begin with the idea of statistical significance.

Significance

Statisticians speak of the outcome of an experiment or a survey as being significant. What does this mean?

> An outcome is significant if the finding is sufficiently rare to lead us to believe that it would not have occurred by chance.

Obviously the term "sufficiently rare" is the key. Social scientists generally feel that if you get a t value that indicates a chance of 1 out of 20, this is sufficiently rare. To indicate this chance they use the phrase "**significant** at the 0.05 level." Researchers in many other fields, such as biology and agriculture, normally use a more stringent test, typically the 0.01 level. It is typical in research to set the significance level prior to the start of the study. If you decide at the outset that you wish the significance level to be 0.01 (1 chance out of 100), you wouldn't readjust it when you get a finding that is less than that, say 0.03 or 0.05.

Error

Even if we set a high significance level, sometimes unlikely things will happen and the one rare instance might occur at the time that we do our study. When this happens, we have committed an **error**, that is, we got a significant finding by chance. Statisticians often speak of a "significant finding" as an instance of the statistic "falling into the rejection area," which is another way of saying the same thing. (Keep in mind that the hypothesis tested is *null*, that is, we are testing a hypothesis of no difference. If we reject this hypothesis, we assume that there is a difference.) In other words, our theory works. If we set our significance level at 0.01, the chance of getting a spurious result is one in 100. So if we do 100 experiments or studies, one of them will result in a "significant" finding that isn't really true. We call this a "Type I" error. The chance of making a Type I error is usually called α (alpha), and when you read in a study that $\alpha = 0.01$, then you know that a Type I error could have occurred; but if it did, it was only once in 100.

Another type of error occurs when we fail to achieve significance on our statistical test, but our hypothesis is correct nonetheless. This is a Type II error. The probability of making a Type II error is usually designated as β (beta). The probability of β is harder to calculate, because it depends on our knowing what the "true" value of the hypothesis is, and on the number of cases (degrees of freedom) in the analysis. Here's how it would look in a table:

	The null hypothesis is true	The null hypothesis is false
Test indicates that the null hypothesis is true	No Error committed	Type II Error committed
Test indicates that the null hypothesis is false	Type I Error committed	No Error committed

We use the idea of Type II error in calculating the power of a statistical test.

WHAT HAPPENS IF YOU'RE WRONG? The consequences of a statistical test being right or wrong is clearly a *qualitative* decision. To see how this might be so, let's compare a statistical test to a blood test. Supposing we think we might have AIDS. A blood test would be called for. The null hypothesis would be "I do not have AIDS." If the test indicates that the hypothesis is true, then we would be quite relieved. And if the hypothesis is *really* true, then all is well. But there is a chance that the test is wrong. If it tells us that we actually have AIDS when we really don't, we would have been the victim of a Type I error. The consequences of this error are anxiety, retesting, more medication, and the like. If we set *alpha* at .01 (one time in a hundred) we might then think that this is a reasonable chance—one person in a hundred would be subjected to this anxiety. On the other hand, if the null hypothesis is false, and we actually do have AIDS, we would hope that the test would tell us so, so that we could begin treatment, and alter out sexual behavior. But if we really do have AIDS and the test tells us we don't, we will be the victims of a Type II error. Here the consequences are disastrous. Without treatment illness and death are certain, and transmission of the disease is an even more disastrous consequence. So the consequences of a Type II error in each case is different, and can only be discussed in qualitative terms.

Power

Some people think that *power* is more important than any other aspect of research. Significance was related to the probability of making a Type I error (α), and power is also related to the probability of making a Type II error (β). Power is defined as $1 - \beta$, or gamma (γ). Usually power is a function of the number of cases in the sample and the hypothesized distance between the theoretical means. You may remember in chapter 7 that we discussed the question of sample size. The answer will depend on the variance (pooled, in the case of the t test), and what you think the proportion in the population is. It will also be based on how certain the answer needs to be. Stephan and McCarthy's table (table 7.1) in chapter 7 gives you an idea of how power varies.

Qualitative Aspects of Statistical Decisions

You may remember that in chapter 1, we indicated that "qualitative" and "quantitative" are only conventional terms, and that almost everything we do has a qualitative dimension to it. Now it is time to examine some of the qualitative aspects to statistical decisions. You will recall that the α level differs from to discipline to discipline; that the social sciences typically use the 0.05 level and that other kinds of inquiry use the 0.01 level. The only way to decide what level to choose is to compare the consequences of being wrong. If you are being tested for AIDS, for example, and if you actually do have AIDS, it would be disastrous if your test turned out to show that you didn't. These kinds of consequences can only be assessed by looking at how we plan to make use of the knowledge we discover in the research.

If you took your car to a car dealership to get your oil changed, and the service manager called you later in the day to tell you that they thought your fuel pump was exhibiting symptoms that meant it was wearing out, you might have just told him to replace it. But on the other hand, if you had data available that showed a statistical connection between the symptom (it makes a funny noise) and the actual incidence of pump wear, you might evaluate more rationally. If this data had been analyzed at the 0.05 level, there would be a one in twenty chance of the study being incorrect. If, on the other hand, it had been conducted at the 0.001 level, there would be only a one in a thousand chance of it being wrong. What are the consequences of being wrong? If you only drive around the neighborhood, you belong to AAA and can get road service, and you don't mind the inconvenience, you might take the chance. But if you're driving to Alaska on the Alcan highway, a breakdown would be really serious, especially if there were bears around.

Most of us don't go into the probabilities involved in our decisions well enough. Medical care is the prime area where we need good decisions. If a doctor tells you that you have a lump in your breast and recommends that you have surgery to remove it, the first question that you would ask (if you were thinking clearly) is what would happen if you decided against surgery. Surgery is expensive, dangerous, and painful. Sometimes people have cysts that resemble a cancer, and a surgeon might wish to be conservative and remove it regardless. However, when the consequences of ruling out surgery—of being wrong—include the death of the patient, then the qualitative elements in the decision are quite different.

THE T TEST AND THE COMPUTER

If you thought the calculations in this chapter were onerous, you may wish to use the computer to do the work for you, just as you did in the previous chapter. Let's start with the PC.

Excel and the *t* Test

First you must get into Windows, and then activate Excel. If you saved the file with the affect orientation data from chapter 8 on it, then you should open that file. The first column will have your data in it, and you will need to add the data from the engineers in the example above (see figure 9.1; type in both columns of numbers).

When you're finished with that, click on the Tools menu and then click on Data Analysis. This will bring up a menu that includes many options. Scroll down and click on "*t* test Two-Sample Assuming Unequal Variances." You will then see a screen that asks you to put in the ranges for your data. You will notice that in the example, titles were inserted in the A1 and B1 cells, and the numbers started with the A2 and the B2 columns. So for the first one, you put in A2:A40. For the second one, you put in B2:B31. Then click OK. You should get an answer that looks like figure 9.2. If everything is correct, you should get the same answer for the problem that we did earlier in the chapter. You will notice that Excel calculates the α level for us (in Excel it is labeled "P(T<=t) one-tail") and gives an exact value of 0.014545. When we did the problem by hand, we could only place the α level between certain values. This is one distinct advantage of the computer. Excel (among other computer programs) has an algorithm (a built-in section that makes calculations) that computes the exact probability of any value of the test result. We probably don't really need them, but sometimes it's nice to have them. Now let's look at how the mainframe would do the same problem using SAS.

Doing a *t* Test on the Mainframe

You remember that with Excel, the first step was to enter the data. This is the case with the mainframe, except the data are entered differently. In chapter 8, figure 8.5 shows 39 numbers in a list after the CARDS; statement. For our current problem we have to enter the 30 numbers from the "engineers" sample. But we have to do more than that—we have to tell SAS which number belongs in which group. If you look at figure 9.3, you will see that we added the word COM after the first 39 numbers. Then when we added the 30 numbers from the engineers, we appended the word ENG after them.

We have complicated the process a bit. We must now tell SAS what these words mean. We do this in an INPUT statement. The statement looks like this:

INPUT AFFECT GROUP $;

Figure 9.1   Input in Microsoft Excel for *t* Test

Communication	Engineering
80	84
74	79
59	69
87	75
83	62
83	56
80	71
70	72
76	65
82	52
71	67
56	58
72	69
77	60
70	69
57	57
62	51
74	64
64	71
61	53
76	60
66	88
60	73
82	81
84	66
74	56
74	86
91	72
75	71
76	75
63	
73	
91	
85	
72	
76	
64	
61	
67	

Figure 9.2   Output in Microsoft Excel for *t* Test

t-Test: Two-Sample Assuming Unequal Variances		
	Variable 1	Variable 2
Mean	73.02564	67.73333
Variance	87.34143	100.892
Observations	39	30
Hypothesized Mean Difference	0	
df	60	
t Stat	2.235891	
P(T<=t) one-tail	0.014545	
t Critical one-tail	1.670649	
P(T<=t) two-tail	0.02909	
t Critical two-tail	2.000297	

INPUT tells SAS what kind of statement it is, AFFECT tells it that the first thing it reads will be the value for affect, and GROUP $ tells SAS that the next thing it reads will be the name of the group in which the number belongs. If SAS sees a $ after the name, it will designate that character as an alphanumeric variable (that is, not a number but a name—see nominal numbers in chapter 3). After the data are read into the program, we have asked SAS to sort the data into two groups, COM and ENG. Then, after we ask it for the means of these groups, we say:

PROC TTEST;
CLASSES GROUP;

This tells SAS to do a *t* test on our data. Notice that all SAS statements have to end with a semicolon. This is because this program is written in a computing language called PL-1, and this language insists on semicolons. So don't leave them out.

Figure 9.3
SAS Job to Calculate "*t*"

```
//A EXEC SAS
DATA AFFECT;
INPUT AFFECT GROUP $;
CARDS;
80 COM
74 COM
59 COM
87 COM
83 COM
83 COM
80 COM
70 COM
76 COM
82 COM
71 COM
56 COM
72 COM
77 COM
70 COM
57 COM
62 COM
74 COM
64 COM
61 COM
76 COM
66 COM
60 COM
82 COM
```

```
84 COM
74 COM
74 COM
91 COM
75 COM
76 COM
63 COM
73 COM
91 COM
85 COM
72 COM
76 COM
64 COM
61 COM
67 COM
84 ENG
79 ENG
69 ENG
75 ENG
62 ENG
56 ENG
71 ENG
72 ENG
65 ENG
52 ENG
67 ENG
58 ENG
69 ENG
60 ENG
69 ENG
57 ENG
51 ENG
64 ENG
71 ENG
53 ENG
60 ENG
88 ENG
73 ENG
81 ENG
66 ENG
56 ENG
86 ENG
72 ENG
71 ENG
75 ENG
PROC SORT; BY GROUP;
PROC MEANS; BY GROUP;
PROC TTEST;
CLASS GROUP;
TITLE EXAMPLE;
/*
```

The results of the *t* test are presented in figure 9.4. Notice that SAS gives you slightly different answers. If you remember the output from Excel, you will notice there that you could have asked for a test based on equal variances. SAS just gives you answers to both types of *t* tests, whether you want them or not. If you think the variances are equal, you can compute this different *t* test, but the answers are so similar that it makes little sense to do so if it will require a lot of hand calculation. This decision, like the significance level decision, is a qualitative one.

Figure 9.4   Output of SAS Job to Calculate "*t*"

TTEST PROCEDURE

Variable: AFFECT

GROUP	N	Mean	Std Dev	Std Error	Minimum	Maximum
COM	39	73.02564103	9.34566373	1.49650388	56.00000000	91.00000000
ENG	30	67.73333333	10.04449869	1.83386617	51.00000000	88.00000000

Variances	T	DF	Prob>|T|
Unequal	2.2359	60.1	0.0291
Equal	2.2573	67.0	0.0273

For H0: Variances are equal, F' = 1.16   DF = (29,38)   Prob>F' = 0.6691

EVALUATING RESEARCH WITH *T* TESTS

Examining research that begins with a hypothesis clearly involves evaluating that hypothesis; more than that we would wish to evaluate the inductive process that brought about the hypothesis. Both qualitative and quantitative processes are involved in induction, and much of the evaluation will follow the guidelines suggested in chapter 5. Typical aspects of evaluating descriptions should be employed. Specifically, we should look for specificity in language and adequacy of description.

Once the hypothesis is formulated, the basic comparisons involved in testing the hypothesis should be examined. Exactly what operations have been performed to exemplify the hypothesis should be carefully analyzed.

Working with the t test gives us a chance to examine much of the basic logic involved in statistical testing. The formula for calculating the test looks complicated but is simple, once it is broken down into mathematical operations. Statistical reasoning takes the form "it is possible that this outcome was due to chance, and if it was, the chance would be . . ." This, of course, argues by exclusion. Important elements involved in using this kind of argument are the significance levels and the power of the test. What these levels should be is a qualitative decision, not a quantitative one.

Chapter Ten

More than Two Groups
Analysis of Variance

In the previous chapter we examined the t test, which seeks to discover whether or not two groups have different means. This can be a useful statistical procedure and serves as a good way to familiarize ourselves with basic statistical concepts, such as significance, power, and the like. More formally, we might say that the t statistic tests the hypothesis that one mean is different from another ($\overline{X}_1 \neq \overline{X}_2$). The test has one significant drawback, however. If we wish to add a third element to our comparison, we have problems in the logic of the comparison.

THE DIFFERENCE BETWEEN THE T TEST AND THE ANALYSIS OF VARIANCE

Remember our example from the previous chapter? In that example, we compared the affect orientation scores of two groups of students, communication majors and engineering majors. But suppose we extend our interest to the affect orientation of a group of computer science majors? We could simply take a sample of this group and then compare them to our other groups, doing a t test for each one. But now we would have a number of t tests, one for communication majors versus engineering majors, one for communication majors versus computer science majors, and one for computer science majors versus communication majors. What's the problem?

The problem lies in our statistical logic. Remember the argument "This difference could be due to chance. But if it is, the chance would only be one out of twenty." If we do the comparisons mentioned above, we will have not one but three t tests. If we do one test and reason that we get a significant result, we are saying that the outcome could have been due to chance only once in twenty tries. But if we do three, then a significant result might appear three times out of twenty times, or 0.15.

Our argument has lost its force; three times out of twenty gets to be more probable than we would want. So what is needed for a multiple comparison of means is a different test. The t test is good, but *if and only if* it is done once. The problem gets worse if we add groups. If we have four groups, there are six comparisons, and so on. The hypothesis $(\bar{X}_1 \neq \bar{X}_2)$ is the only one that we can test using a t test; for a hypothesis that takes the form $(\bar{X}_1 \neq \bar{X}_2 \neq \bar{X}_3)$ we need some other kind of statistical procedure. This procedure is called the *analysis of variance* [ANOVA].

HOW ANALYSIS OF VARIANCE WORKS

Perhaps the best way to learn about the analysis of variance is to look at an example. Suppose that we are developing a new test of sensitivity to nonverbal communication. We think that individuals involved in the arts would be good people to pretest our ideas, since the arts are good training grounds in subjective meaning. We prepare a videotape of an actor presenting a message with ten specific nonverbal messages in it, and then we recruit people in the arts to view it. We end up with a group of actors, a group of singers, a group of painters and a group of poets. Here are the numbers of successful identifications of the nonverbal messages by each of the groups:

Table 10.1			
Actors	*Singers*	*Painters*	*Poets*
7	6	4	3
3	10	2	4
4	8	2	5
3	5	1	4
6		2	
		1	

Who did the best? First we would calculate the means $(\bar{X}_j)$ of the four different groups (Notice that n_i is the number of people in each group). Obviously, we need to add up the scores (ΣX_i), but we also need to do some other calculations. Here are our first steps:

	Actors	Singers	Painters	Poets
			Table 10.2	
	Actors	Singers	Painters	Poets
n_i (count)	5	4	6	4
ΣX_i (sum)	23	29	12	16
$\overline{X}_j$ (average)	4.6	7.25	2.0	4.0

We can see immediately that the singers were the best at identifying nonverbal messages. Painters were pitiful, at 2.0, and the poets and actors were about the same, at 4.0 and 4.6 respectively. But can we prove this statistically? We can't do it with t tests, so we must look for something else.

You will recall that the *variance* in any group of numbers expresses how widely the numbers are dispersed, or scattered. In the collection of scores above, the overall mean was 4.21 and the variance was 5.73 (the standard error was 2.39). But if we look at the means of the four groups—actors, singers, poets and painters—we see that the groups vary widely. If we would take that variance away (subtract the variance among the means from the overall variance), the remaining variance would be smaller. If (and it's a big if) the overall variance is caused by the differences in the classifications, then it would be sensible to do this and ask how much difference it made. The analysis of variance is a method by which we do this. It is a method to assess the *variance among the group means* and compare it to the rest of the variances among this group of scores. If we calculated the total variance, then the variance among the four group means, and then subtracted the group means from the total variance, then we would have the *residual* (leftover) variance. If this variance is *significantly* smaller than the variance caused by the groupings, then we could say that the groups differ from one another.

The *F* Test

In statistics, comparing one variance to another is done by means of the F test, another distribution like t and z. This statistic was invented by Sir Ronald Fisher, for whom it is named. The F test is actually derived from a number of distributions rather than just one, and each one is characterized by not one but two different numbers for degrees of freedom. Its formal definition is presented in statement (7).

$$F = \frac{\sigma^2_{between}}{\sigma^2_{within}}$$

(7)

Let's continue with our example. Let's take what we have so far and perform two new calculations. First we calculate the square of each number (ΣX_i^2) and then get the total of each group squared and divided by the number of cases in the group $\frac{(\Sigma X_i)^2}{n_i}$.

These intermediate calculations are a short-cut method to assessing the variances within the collection of scores. In this method we calculate the "sums of squares" and the "mean square" which is a close approximation of the variances. Here is our new table:

Table 10.3

	Actors	Singers	Painters	Poets	Totals
	7	6	4	3	
	3	10	2	4	
	4	8	2	5	
	3	5	1	4	
	6		2		
			1		
n_i	5	4	6	4	19
ΣX_i	23	29	12	16	80
$\overline{X}_i$	4.6	7.25	2.0	4.0	
ΣX^2_i	119	225	30	66	440
$(\Sigma X_i)^2/n_i$	105.8	210.25	24	64	404

Correction Term

Our first step is to calculate what is called the *correction term*. This is defined as the total sum of the scores squared $[(\Sigma\Sigma X_{ij})^2]$ or 80^2 and divided by the overall total of people (or cases) in the table (Σn_{ij} or 19). Another way of putting this definition is in formula form:

$$c = \frac{\left(\sum\sum X_{ij}\right)^2}{\sum n_{ij}}$$

This works out to be 336.8. Now we are ready to calculate the sums of squares and the means squares. First we take the total of each score squared (440) and subtract the correction term. This gives us the *total sums of squares*, which is usually written SS_T. More formally we might express this as:

$$SS_{TOTAL} = \sum\sum X_{ij}^2 - \frac{\left(\sum\sum X_{ij}\right)^2}{\sum n_{ij}}$$

Now we need to calculate the sum of squares between the groups.

$$SS_{BETWEEN} = \sum\left(\frac{\sum X_{ij}^2}{n_i}\right) - \frac{\left(\sum\sum X_{ij}\right)^2}{\sum n_{ij}}$$

When we put the actual numbers in the equations, they look like this:

$$SS_{TOTAL} = 440 - \frac{(80)^2}{19}$$

and

$$SS_{BETWEEN} = \frac{23^2}{5} + \frac{29^2}{4} + \frac{12^2}{6} + \frac{16^2}{4} - 336.8$$

Remember that 80^2 divided by 19 is 336.8. The sum of squares for between groups is 67.25 and the sum of squares for total is 103.2. We need one more calculation, however—the sum of squares for "within." This is a simple calculation, since it is the sum of squares for total minus the sum of squares for between groups: 103.6 – 67.7, or 35.9. The simplified calculations follow:

$SS_{BETWEEN} = 404.05 - 336.8 = 67.25$
$SS_{TOTAL} = 440 - 336.8 = 103.2$
$SS_{WITHIN} = SS_{TOTAL} - SS_{BETWEEN} = 103.2 - 67.25 = 35.95$

The Summary Table

The next step is to place these various sums of squares in a summary table. This kind of summary is tabulated primarily to illustrate how the mean squares are calculated. But there is one last element in the table that we have not yet calculated: the degrees of freedom. This important aspect of the analysis of variance is slightly different than the degrees of freedom you encountered doing the t test. Since the variance between the group means is based on the number of group means, the degrees of freedom is $n_j - 1$, or in this case, 4–1, or 3. The overall variance is the overall total minus one, or $n_y - 1$, or 18. Then the degrees of freedom for the "error" or residual term (within groups) is the degrees of freedom for total minus the degrees of freedom for between groups: 18 – 3, or 15. Degrees of freedom are abbreviated in the summary table as df. This is how the summary table looks:

Table 10.4
Summary of Analysis of Variance

Source of Variation	df	SS	MS	F
Between Groups	3	67.25	22.42	9.34
Within Groups	15	35.95	2.4	
Total	18	103.2		

The mean squares are derived by dividing the sums of squares by their respective degrees of freedom. The F statistic is derived by dividing the mean square (between groups) by the mean square (within groups). If you look back through these calculations, you will see that the calculations for the mean squares are exactly the same as the calculations for variance, except that we went at it a little differently. Now the problem is done, except for figuring out what it means! The F statistic is like the t statistic in that we now wish to know whether it is "significant" or not. Once again, we need a table.

When we turn to appendix D, table 1, we see that it is titled "Significance of F at the 0.05 level," and table 2 is titled "Significance of F at the 0.01 level." These tables are more complicated than the ones for the t tests, in that each F has two degrees of freedom. When you look at table 1, you will see a row of numbers going down the left-hand column. This indicates the first degree of freedom, and a row of numbers going across the top of the table, which indicates the second degree of freedom. The label in the table's upper left-hand corner indicates df_1 and df_2. Remember that in our example, the F that we calculated had 3 and 15 degrees of freedom. So we look at the row that indicates "3" and read over to the column labelled "15." The value indicated is 8.70. Our calculations gave us a value of 9.34, so we know that our significance is greater than 0.05. If we look at table 2 (significance of F at the 0.01 level), we see that the tabled value is 5.42. This tells us that our hypothetical problem produced an event that is rarer than once in twenty, and rarer than once in a hundred.

The Critical Difference

Our conclusion, then, is that there is a significant difference among the four groups, and that it would make sense to further examine the means to see where the significance lies. There are a number of ways to examine the differences among the means—to see if poets are different from painters, singers from actors, and so forth. There are many different methods to calculate differences among means following the analysis of variance, but here we will examine one of the simplest.[1] This is the method of establishing a critical difference between means, based on a t test using the mean square within as the best estimate of the pooled variances. The critical difference is how large the differences between the means will have to be before we consider it significant. We find this range by using the following formula:

$$CD = t\sqrt{\frac{2ms_{WITHIN}}{n\ (per\ group)}}$$

(8)

In expression (8), CD stands for the critical difference, the t stands for the value that a t test would have if the difference we are seeking is to be significant, the MS_{WITHIN} comes from the summary of analysis of variance table, and the n is the number of respondents per group. In our example, the frequencies are different, so we need to get the harmonic mean of the frequencies. Here is how the *harmonic mean* of the frequencies is calculated:

$$\bar{n} = \frac{\sum n_j}{\dfrac{1}{n_1} + \dfrac{1}{n_2} + \dfrac{1}{n_3} + \dfrac{1}{n_4}}$$

In our example the total number of groups ($\sum n_j$) is 4, and the number of people within each group are 5, 4, 6, and 4. This makes our calculation look like:

$$\bar{n} = \frac{4}{\dfrac{1}{5} + \dfrac{1}{4} + \dfrac{1}{6} + \dfrac{1}{4}}$$

One divided by five is 0.2, one divided by 4 is 0.25, one divided by 6 is 0.167, and one divided by 4 is 0.25; then, 0.2 + 0.25 + 0.167 + 0.25 is 0.867. Finally, 4 divided by 0.867 is 4.61. So we can use 4.61 as the average for the number of responses per group in expression (8). To continue with this calculation, we need to establish a value for t, so we look at appendix C. Our value for degrees of freedom is 15, since it is based on the degrees of freedom in the mean square within. A t at the 0.05 level with 15 degrees of freedom is 2.131, so we use that value in the calculation.

$$CD = 2.131 \sqrt{\frac{2 \times 2.4}{4.6}}$$

We calculate that 2 times 2.4 is 4.8; 4.8 divided by 4.6 is 1.043; and the square root of 1.043 is 1.02. Therefore, 1.02 times 2.131 is 2.17. In other words, the critical difference is 2.17. Let's see how we use that.

First we arrange the means from highest to the lowest. We see that the singers had a mean of 7.25 and the painters had a mean of 2.0. Putting them in order results in the following:

Singers	7.25
Actors	4.6
Poets	4.0
Painters	2.0

If the critical difference is 2.17, then the difference between the painters and the poets is not quite large enough (2.0), but the difference between the painters and the actors is (2.6). The difference between the actors and the poets is small and therefore insignificant. But the difference between the poets and the singers is large enough to qualify. In other words, we can look at the range of differences as we arrange the means from lowest to highest, and, using the critical difference that we calculated, see where the significant differences are.

Effect Size

Another important aspect of the analysis of variance is the *effect size*. Effects can be significant but not very large. In general the effect size is defined as the amount of variance explained by the models involved in the study, that is, the degree to which the theory (or hypotheses) reduces randomness, or chance, in the population drawn for study. Effect size is usually designated by ω^2, or "omega squared." It is calculated using the following formula (Hays, 1973, p. 485):

$$est \; \omega^2 = \frac{SS_{BETWEEN} - (J-1)MS_{WITHIN}}{SS_{TOTAL} + MS_{WITHIN}}$$

(9)

In this formula, the sums of squares are taken from the summary of analysis of variance table. As we mentioned earlier, researchers typically do not include these tables in the interest of saving typesetting costs and space, so the reporting of effect size is even more important. Effect size is typically a proportion, which can be understood as the proportion of overall variance explained by the model. Often researchers report effect size as "E," which is a similar concept but is calculated slightly differently.

ASSUMPTIONS MADE BY THE ANALYSIS OF VARIANCE

The analysis of variance looks to be an excellent way to look for differences among means, and it is widely used by researchers in the social sciences. But there are some important statistical assumptions that need to be made if it is used. The first is that the subpopulations (in the example above, the groups of poets, painters, singers, and actors) are drawn from normally distributed populations. The second is that the distributions are not skewed, or J-shaped. In other words, the groups themselves should not depart significantly from normal. Obviously it is important that the cases be randomly drawn (Hays, 1973, p. 467).

However, one researcher, Dee Norton, showed through an elaborate computer analysis that even if the assumptions are badly violated, the analysis of variance will serve well as a statistical test, providing that the significance levels of the tests are doubled (Lindquist, 1956).

In the next section, we will examine the analysis of variance for multiple effects, or for interaction. In these tests, there is an additional assumption that the frequencies or numbers in each of the cells are equal, or, at least, proportional.

ANALYSIS OF VARIANCE FOR MULTIPLE EFFECTS

One of the most interesting problems in research occurs when different influences are brought together to cause multiple effects in combination. To see how this works, let us look at another example.

Suppose you have been hired by the ABC advertising agency to decide what kinds of television commercials to run in an upcoming campaign. They have two kinds of commercials in mind: one with sexual innuendo in the message, and another more innocuous presentation. But they are concerned about gender differences in their findings. Here are the results of their pilot data:

	Women	Men
	12	15
	16	13
Ordinary	14	9
Commercial	11	9
	12	8
	14	11
	79	65
	10	19
	9	16
	14	18
Suggestive	13	23
Commercial	17	14
	15	15
	78	105

It looks as if the suggestive commercial is more effective overall, but we can see that there is a big difference in the way men and women react to it. There is a *different* difference in the table, so we would say that there is an *interaction*, that is, an effect that doesn't act the same at different levels. This is what interaction really means: "A difference that differs differently." You will see how this works as we analyze the data.

We can test this interaction by doing the following calculations. First we need to get the sum of all the scores squared:

$$\sum X^2_{ij} = 12^2 + 16^2 + 14^2 \text{ etc} \ldots = 4749$$

Then we need to get the total of all the scores in the table:

$$\sum X_i = 70 + 65 + 88 + 105 = 327$$

Then we calculate the correction term:

$$(\sum\sum X_{ji})^2 / N_{ij} = (327)^2 / 24 = 4455.375$$

Now we can calculate the total sum of squares:

$$SS_{TOTAL} = \sum X^2 - ((\sum X_j)^2 / N)$$

This works out to be:

$$4749 - 4455.375 = 293.625$$

Now we need to do something different from the analysis of variance in the first example. We do this by calculating the sums of squares for the subgroups. First we look at the differences caused by gender:

79 + 78 = 157 (Women)
65 + 105 = 170 (Men)

Now we square each of these totals and divide them by the number of cases in the group (12);

$$\frac{157^2}{12} + \frac{170^2}{12} = \frac{53,549}{12} = 4462.416$$

The sum of squares for gender is below:

$$SS_{GENDER} = 4462.416 - 4455.375 = 7.04$$

Then we can do the same for the content of the commercial.

79 + 65 = 144 (ordinary)
78 + 105 = 183 (suggestive)

Remember, we square each of these subtotals and divide them by the number of respondents (cases):

$$\frac{144^2}{12} + \frac{183^2}{12} = \frac{54225}{12} = 4518.75$$

Now we can calculate the sum of squares for the content of the commercial:

$$SS_{CONTENT} = 4518.75 - 4455.375 = 63.375$$

So far we have done the calculations exactly as if we were testing each of these elements by themselves in a simple analysis of variance. Now we are ready for something different: the sum of squares for "cells." This is the sum of squares for each group, treated as if the groups were the variable we were testing. Here is how we calculate this sum of squares:

$$\frac{6241}{6} + \frac{4225}{6} + \frac{6084}{6} + \frac{11025}{6} = \frac{27575}{6} = 4595.833$$

The sum of squares for cells, therefore, is

$$SS_{CELLS} = 4595.833 - 4455.375 = 140.458$$

Now we are ready to calculate the interaction within content and gender. The sum of squares for interaction is

$$SS_{CONTENT \times GENDER} = SS_{CELLS} - SS_{GENDER} - SS_{CONTENT}$$

or

$$140.458 - 7.04 - 63.375 = 70.04$$

We only need one more thing to complete the analysis—the error, or "within." Here is how we get it:

$$SS_{WITHIN} = SS_{TOTAL} - SS_{GENDER} - SS_{CONTENT} - SS_{CONTENT \times GENDER}$$

This works out to be:

$$293.6 - 7 - 63.4 - 70 = 153$$

Now for the degrees of freedom. The total number of cases in the table was 24, and each comparison is the number of elements in the comparison minus one. Since the gender and content comparisons were only two conditions, their degrees of freedom are 2 -1, or 1. The interaction is their degrees of freedom times one another, or 1 times 1 which is 1. The degrees of freedom for each are listed below:

$$df = \quad SS_{TOTAL} = 24 - 1 = 23$$
$$SS_{GENDER} = 2 - 1 = 1$$
$$SS_{CONTENT} = 2 - 1 = 1$$
$$SS_{GENDER \times CONTENT} = (2 - 1) \times (2 - 1) = 1$$
$$SS_{WITHIN} = 23 - 1 - 1 - 1 = 20$$

Now we are ready to do the summary table. We place the sums of squares in the table, calculate the mean squares by dividing each one by the degrees of freedom, and we calculate the F by dividing the appropriate mean square by the mean square for within. In this example, we have an F for gender, one for content, and one for interaction.

Summary Table of the Analysis of Variance				
Source	*SS*	*df*	*MS*	*F*
Commercial	63.375	1	63.375	8.27
Gender	7.04	1	7.04	<1
Comm. X Gender	70.04	1	70.04	9.13
Within	153.296	20	7.66	
Total	293.625	23		

We can look in our tables to see what the F values indicate. At the 1 and 20 intersections of the table, we see the value here is 4.3. This means that at the .05 level, an F of 4.3 would be significant. The F for the commercial type above is 8.27, so it is significant. The value for gender is not significant. But the interaction effect is significant, with an F value of 9.13. What exactly does this mean? If we look at figure 10.1, we can see the mean scores graphed. This graph shows us that the women in the analysis didn't exhibit any differences for the two types of commercial, but that the differences in the study are due to the men only. If you average the men and women together, you would find that there would be differences between the two commercials, but this kind of averaging *hides* the real difference, which is that the difference exists only with men. This is what we meant when we said earlier in this section that interaction really means: "A difference that differs differently." In other words, the significant F for the commercial is essentially meaningless. The rule for two-factor analyses of variance, therefore, is that we look first for the interaction effect; and if it is significant, we can safely ignore mean effects. If the interaction is not significant, then the main effects can be important.

Figure 10.1
Mean Scores Graphed for Ordinary and Suggestive Commercials

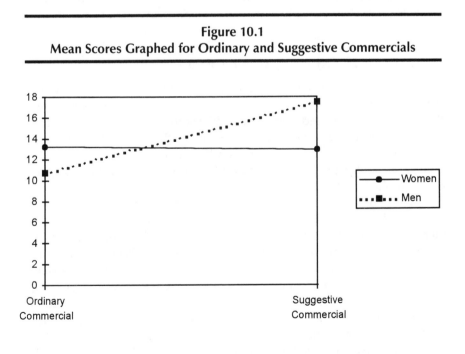

At one time it was customary to include the summary tables for the analysis of variance in research reports, but now researchers simply report their F values and the degrees of freedom. For example, Berger and Jordan (1992) report: "A 2 X 4 ANOVA [Analysis of Variance] of the familiarity index using sex as the between-subject factor and goal as the within-subject factor revealed only a significant effect for goal, F (3.66) $= 11.55, p < .001$" (p. 138). This means that when Berger and Jordan tested to see if familiar topics had different effects on the plans individuals make for interpersonal communication, they did not find a significant effect for gender, but only for the kinds of goals that were important in the interaction. Further the F had 3 and 66 degrees of freedom, and it turned out to be 11.55, which has a probability value of less than once in a thousand.

ANALYSIS OF VARIANCE ON THE COMPUTER

If the calculations in this chapter seemed to be time-consuming, you may wish to use the computer to do the work for you, just as you did in the previous chapter. The first step in performing the analysis of variance on a computer is to enter the data. First let's look at doing it on the PC.

Excel and the Analysis of Variance

First you activate Microsoft Excel. We'll be using the data from the "Analysis of Variance for Multiple Effects" that appeared earlier in this chapter, so you will need to type more labels than we did with the t test example. First enter "women" and "men" at the top of the columns. Then as you go down the columns, identify whether the commercial was "plain" or "suggestive" in the left hand column. Type in the labels as shown in figure 10.2.

The labels are arbitrary to Excel, but will show up again when Excel finishes the analysis. From the Tool menu click on Data Analysis, then choose "Anova: Two-Factor With Replication" from the list shown. Then type in the data range. In this data set, you want Excel to read from the A1 cell to the C13 cell. Enter "A1:C13" in the Input Range space. Then Excel wants to know how many cases there are in your subgroups, so enter "6" in the Rows Per Sample space. Than all you have to do is click OK and Excel does the rest. The output is reproduced in figure 10.3. You will notice that, as with the t test, Excel calculates the α level for us, and gives an exact value of 0.009 for the style of commercial, 0.349 for gender, and 0.0067 for the interaction between the two effects.

Figure 10.2   Input in Microsoft Excel for ANOVA

	Women	Men
Plain	12	15
Plain	16	13
Plain	14	9
Plain	11	9
Plain	12	8
Plain	14	11
Suggestive	10	19
Suggestive	9	16
Suggestive	14	18
Suggestive	13	23
Suggestive	17	14
Suggestive	15	15

When we did the problem by hand, we only could place the α level between certain values. This is one distinct advantage of the computer.

Analysis of Variance and SAS

Now let's look at how the mainframe would do the same problem using SAS. Excel is limited in that it will only take two different factors and will not do some of the other kinds of more sophisticated analyses. But it is a good way to solve problems that are fairly straightforward.

We need to identify each score as to its category: what kind of commercial it was, and whether it was the score of a male or a female. So you can see in the job listing that the first line after the CARDS; statement is 9 PLAIN FEMALE. Each additional score is listed this way. But now SAS needs to know what each of these things are on the data lines, so we need to go back to the INPUT step and specify what they are. First you identify the number as a SCORE and then you identify each subsequent element. So the input statement looks like this:

INPUT SCORE COMRCL $ GENDER $;

Remember that SAS won't take a name larger than eight characters and that alphanumeric terms are followed by a dollar sign. When you are finished entering the numbers, you are ready to ask for the analysis of variance. In this example we used the General Linear Model procedure, but we could also have used the ANOVA procedure.

Figure 10.3 Output in Microsoft Excel for ANOVA

Anova: Two-Factor With Replication						
SUMMARY	Women	Men	Total			
Plain						
Count	6	6	12			
Sum	79	65	144			
Average	13.16667	10.83333	12			
Variance	3.366667	7.366667	6.363636			
Suggestive						
Count	6	6	12			
Sum	78	105	183			
Average	13	17.5	15.25			
Variance	9.2	10.7	14.56818			
Total						
Count	12	12				
Sum	157	170				
Average	13.08333	14.16667				
Variance	5.719697	20.33333				
ANOVA						
Source of Variation	SS	df	MS	F	P-value	F crit
Sample	63.375	1	63.375	8.275299	0.009327	4.35125
Columns	7.041667	1	7.041667	0.919478	0.349062	4.35125
Interaction	70.04167	1	70.04167	9.145811	0.0067	4.35125
Within	153.1667	20	7.658333			
Total	293.625	23				

Here are the statements we need:

PROC GLM; CLASSES COMRCL GENDER;

MODEL SCORE= COMRCL | GENDER;

MEANS COMRCL | GENDER;

TITLE CHAPTER

The complete listing is presented in figure 10.4. The resulting output is presented in figure 10.5.

You will notice that the SAS output listed 9.15 as the F value for the interaction. Excel was more precise, stating that it was 9.145811, and the worked example above gave an answer of 9.13. These differences are due to the various rounding as we work through the problems.

Figure 10.4

```
//A EXEC SAS
DATA INP;
INPUT SCORE COMRCL $ GENDER $;
CARDS;
9 PLAIN FEMALE
16 PLAIN FEMALE
14 PLAIN FEMALE
11 PLAIN FEMALE
12 PLAIN FEMALE
8 PLAIN FEMALE
15 PLAIN MALE
13 PLAIN MALE
9 PLAIN MALE
9 PLAIN MALE
8 PLAIN MALE
11 PLAIN MALE
10 SEXY FEMALE
12 SEXY FEMALE
18 SEXY FEMALE
16 SEXY FEMALE
17 SEXY FEMALE
15 SEXY FEMALE
19 SEXY MALE
16 SEXY MALE
18 SEXY MALE
23 SEXY MALE
14 SEXY MALE
15 SEXY MALE
PROC GLM; CLASSES COMRCL GENDER;
MODEL SCORE= COMRCL | GENDER;
MEANS COMRCL | GENDER;
TITLE CHAPTER10 EXAMPLE;
```

Figure 10.5 General Linear Models Procedure

Dependent Variable: SCORE

Source	DF	Sum of Squares	Mean Square	F Value	Pr > F
Model	3	166.33333333	55.44444444	6.06	0.0042
Error	20	183.00000000	9.15000000		
Corrected Total	23	349.33333333			

R-Square	C.V.	Root MSE	SCORE Mean
0.476145	22.13339	3.02489569	13.66666667

Source	DF	Type I SS	Mean Square	F Value	Pr > F
COMRCL	1	140.16666667	140.16666667	15.32	0.0009
GENDER	1	6.00000000	6.00000000	0.66	0.4276
COMRCL*GENDER	1	20.16666667	20.16666667	2.20	0.1532

Source	DF	Type III SS	Mean Square	F Value	Pr > F
COMRCL	1	140.16666667	140.16666667	15.32	0.0009
GENDER	1	6.00000000	6.00000000	0.66	0.4276
COMRCL*GENDER	1	20.16666667	20.16666667	2.20	0.1532

EVALUATING RESEARCH WITH
THE ANALYSIS OF VARIANCE

Since analysis of variance is so commonly used, it is important for us to understand how it is used. The principal rationale for its employment is the fallacy involved in multiple t tests, and usually we would not see the analysis of variance used when there are only two conditions to be tested. However, when interaction is implicated, testing factors with only two factors is acceptable. After the decision to use analysis of variance has been made, it is important to examine the assumptions that legitimize its use: that the distributions that make up the subgroups are normal, that the instances have been randomly drawn from a larger population, that the distributions are approximately the same size, and that the numbers of cases in the subgroups are proportional. Violation of these assumptions results in an inflated test of significance and can seriously compromise the outcome of an investigation.

NOTE

[1] Some of these comparisons include the Duncan Multiple Range test, the Newman-Keuls Multiple Range test, the Tukey test, and Scheffe's test. The choice of method in most instances depends on the nature of the data analyzed, the consequences of making Type I and Type II errors, and the predilections of the researcher. For simple ways of calculating each of these, see Bruning & Kintz (1977).

Chapter Eleven

Regression and Correlation

COVARIANCE

One of the most important tasks in research is to show how one variable is related to another, usually in a causal way. A relationship of this type is especially important in communication, where we usually think of messages as producing effects, such as changes in behavior or attitudes. We are used to causes and effects in the natural world, especially in mechanical ways. Bacteria cause disease, and asbestos causes emphysema. Our doctor on the *Today* show (at the beginning of the book) assumed that smoking caused lung cancer.

Unfortunately, human beings often accept spurious accounts of causation in our reasoning. For example, people "know" that talking to their computers helps them to work better! Fortune tellers masquerading as spiritual advisers make a good deal of money telling gullible people about what "causes" good fortune. Sometimes what we think is a cause is not really a defensible cause.

How do we conclude that a cause exists? The rules are simple. First the two variables (cause and effect) must *covary*, that is, when one goes up, the other should go up, and when one goes down, the other should also go down. If you remember variance from our previous chapters, then you can handle *covariance*, a related concept. Remember the following equations?

$$\sum_{i=1}^{n} X_i - \bar{X} = x_i$$

$$\sum_{i=1}^{n} Y_i - \bar{Y} = y_i$$

If the collection of scores has both an X and a Y for each instance, then there can be *covariance*, which is defined as the degree to which the scores *vary together*. If when one gets bigger, the other also gets bigger, there is a lot of covariance. When one gets bigger and the other gets smaller, there isn't a lot of covariance. Mathematically, the covariance is defined as:

$$\frac{\sum_{i=1}^{n} x_i y_i}{n-1} \tag{10}$$

If we believe that the variables are connected in a causal way, we would expect the variables to covary. Second, the effect should occur later in time than the cause (Asher, 1983). In addition, there should be some relationship between the cause and the effect—an earthquake in Peru may well cause disturbances in coffee prices, but certainly isn't going to have much effect on people's evaluation of O. J. Simpson.

BASIC PRINCIPLES OF REGRESSION

In addition to simply asserting that one event causes another, most researchers would like to get an idea of how much and to what extent these events are related. To describe such a relationship is to model it (Poole & McPhee, 1994). The best way to do this in research is to use *regression*.

Before we go on, we might clarify the term a bit. The word regression is used in many ways. One is a psychological term for returning to a more infantile response. When a person who has been out of high school for thirty years still acts like the football player he always wished he had been, psychologists call this *regression*. In addition, there is another form of regression, which occurs when any test or procedure is repeated. When this happens, any given score tends to return to the mean of the collection of scores. This is called regression toward the mean. This type of regression, which we will discuss further in this chapter, is the relationship of one variable to another, highly quantifiable using the procedure called the least squares. Let's look at an example.

Suppose that a researcher believes that married couples are happy only when they communicate with one another; that is, couples that talk together a lot will be happier than those that don't. The researcher measures the amount of time each week spent in communicative activity, and also asks each couple how happy they are. The researcher could divide the couples into two groups: a "high" group which talks a lot, and a "low" group, which doesn't talk much. The researcher could test the means of the groups for significance, using a t test. Or the researcher could divide the couples into high, medium, and low groups, and perform an analysis of variance. But the researcher thinks regression might be a better way. She proceeds as follows.

First the scores are arranged in an array, and given a variable name. The hours spent each week in communicative activity are called X and the satisfaction with the relationship is designated as Y. Any name would do, but these variables are common conventions in statistics. Also X and Y are easier to write down in formulas. Table 11.1 shows how the numbers look in tabular form.

Table 11.1 Communication Activity and Relationship Satisfaction Scores

Case (couple number)	Hours per week spent in Comm. Activity	Reported "Satisfaction" with Relationship			
	X	Y	XY	X^2	Y^2
1	2	3	6	4	9
2	5	6	30	25	36
3	3	4	12	9	16
4	7	6	42	49	36
5	2	4	8	4	16
6	6	8	48	36	64
7	4	6	24	16	36
8	9	9	81	81	81
9	8	9	72	64	81
10	4	5	20	16	25
Σ (sum)	50	60	343	304	400

The next step is to use the method of *least squares*. There are many ways of proceeding, but the simplest is to use a technique called *simultaneous linear equations*. Here's how it works. We want to get the answers to the unknowns in the following equation:

$$Y_i = a + b X_i$$

In each case (1 through 10) we know what Y_i and X_i are (in case number 9, Y is 9 and X is 8; in case number 6, Y is 8 and X is 6, and so on). But we don't know what a and b are. The method of least squares tells us that we can find these values if we solve the following simultaneous equations:

I. $\Sigma Y = na + b\Sigma X$

II. $\Sigma XY = a\Sigma X + \Sigma X^2$

Solving for a and b involves substituting the values from the calculations above. $\Sigma Y = 60$; $n = 10$; $\Sigma X = 50$. $\Sigma XY = 343$ and $\Sigma X^2 = 304$. If we substitute these values into the equations above, we get

I. $60 = 10a + 50b$

II. $343 = 50a + 304b$

Don't get confused because we changed the positions of the a's and b's in the second set of equations. If you remember your algebra, you will remember that it is more conventional to write values with the variables following the numerals. Now we are ready to solve, using the arithmetic method. This method involves an operation that we can perform on any equation: if we add, multiply, or subtract on both sides, the value of the equation remains constant. A standard method of solving equations in two unknowns involves adding or subtracting the equations from one another. So if you multiply one equation by a particular value, you can arrange it so that the value of one of the terms can be equal in both equations, so that if you subtract, the value for that term becomes zero. This is easier to do than to describe. So let's do it: First multiply the first equation by 5, and call the new equation Ia.

I. 60 $= 10a + 50b$

II. 343 $= 50a + 304b$

(5 x I.) Ia. 300 $= 50a + 250b$

Subtracting Ia from II gives: $43 = 0 + 54b$

Therefore b equals 43 divided by 54, or 0.7962.

Now that we know what b is, we can solve for a. Since equation I tells us that $60 = 10a + (50 \times 0.7962)$, then $60 = 10a + 39.81$. This means that $20.19 = 10a$, or a equals 2.019. Therefore, our predictive equation looks like this (where Y_T represents the theoretical Y score):

$$Y_T = 2.019 + 0.7962X_i$$

There are many other ways of arriving at this equation, but this may be the simplest. Another method is to calculate b first, using the formula

$$b_x = \frac{\sum X_i Y_i}{\sum Y_i^2} \tag{11}$$

and then calculate a by the following formula

$$a = \overline{Y} - b\overline{X}$$

Whether the method used[1] is simultaneous equations or the method above is less important than the uses that we can find for the equation $Y_i = a + b\,X_i$. Just looking at it lets us know that if X is zero, then Y will be equal to a. In this example above, a is slightly more than 2. So this means that no matter what, couples are going to be at least satisfied with their relationship to the degree of 2 on this scale, even if they never talk. Then we know that if we increase communication activity between the couple, we can get a specific amount of good out of it. In this data set, we see that one increment in the X score produces about 0.8 of an increment in the Y score. This relationship might have great theoretical significance, especially in terms of the relationship that we think talking has to satisfaction in a relationship. So for each level of X we can predict a specific amount of Y that the theory would tell us should be there.

In this example, we would expect that for each point of satisfaction, couples talk more to each other by an increment of 0.8 on the researcher's scale. While this is not always useful in every situation, we can see that the quantitative approach may indeed have some theoretical significance for some relationships.

Another very useful aspect of this equation is that it has a visual element to it that can tell us a good deal. We can make a graph in two dimensions that expresses the relationship between these two variables. If we draw a vertical line that expresses the satisfaction with the relationship, and a horizontal line that denotes the hours spent communicating, we can graph the particular positions of each respondent in our example (see figure 11.1).

The circles with the numbers are the positions of each couple on this graph. You can see that as the hours per week spent in communicating go to the right, the satisfaction goes higher. This general trend is more precisely charted when we graph the *regression line* determined by the formula $Y_T = 2.019 + 0.7962 X_i$. All this means is that for each value of X we can calculate the ideal or theoretical value of Y by multiplying the value of X times 0.7962, and then adding 2.019. For example, if X is 5, then Y is 2.019 plus 5 x 0.7962, or 2.019 plus 3.981, or 6. When all the "theoretical values" of Y are entered on the graphs, they produce a general pattern of a line, such as the one in figure 11.2.

You notice immediately that the line starts at about Y=2 and proceeds upward. The rate at which the line proceeds upward is called the *slope* of the line, and it is an extremely important concept in theory-building. Since the degree of slope is determined by the b value in

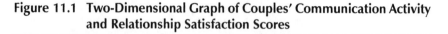

Figure 11.1   Two-Dimensional Graph of Couples' Communication Activity and Relationship Satisfaction Scores

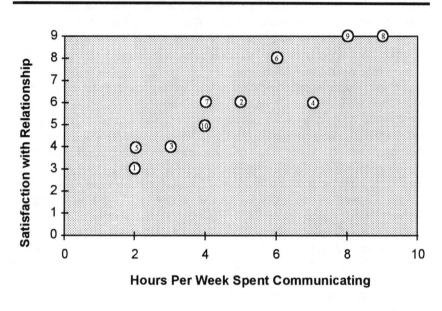

the equation, the slope is often referred to as the beta (β) of the curve. If you are interested in the stock market, you have already encountered this term.

The main thing that we need to know about this theoretical line that we have produced is "how good a picture of the relationship is it?" We approach this question from the point of view of the "explanation" of the variance. What do we mean by "explaining" variance? We will now begin exploring this question by calculating the variance of the Y scores. If we look at the table of the scores presented below, we can see that the mean of the Y scores is $(\overline{Y}) = 6.0$. The variance of the Y scores is calculated by the following formula:[2]

$$\sigma_Y^2 = \frac{\sum (Y_i - \overline{Y})^2}{N}$$

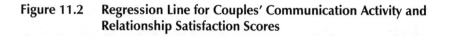

Figure 11.2   Regression Line for Couples' Communication Activity and Relationship Satisfaction Scores

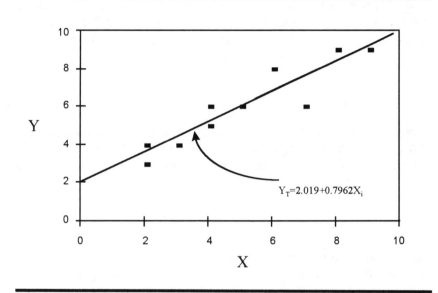

$Y_T = 2.019 + 0.7962X_i$

Table 11.2   Calculations for Communication Activity and Relationship Satisfaction

Couple #	Y	$Y_i-\bar{Y}$	$(Y_i-\bar{Y})^2$	Y_T	$(Y-Y_T)$	$(Y-Y_T)^2$
1	3	-3	9	3.61	-0.61	0.3721
2	6	0	0	6.00	0.0	0.0
3	4	-2	4	4.41	-0.91	0.1681
4	6	0	0	7.59	-1.59	2.5281
5	4	-2	4	3.61	0.39	0.1521
6	8	2	4	6.80	1.20	1.440
7	6	0	0	5.20	0.80	0.640
8	9	3	9	9.19	-0.19	0.0361
9	9	3	9	8.39	0.61	0.3721
10	5	-1	1	5.20	0.20	0.0040
$\sum=$	60	0	40	60	0	5.7488

From table 11.2, you can see that the sum of all the squared deviations $[\Sigma(Y_i - \overline{Y})^2]$ is 40, and when it is divided by 10, you get 4. Therefore the variance of the Y scores is 4. But let's look at another kind of variance. If we subtract the theoretical Y score from each Y score, we get quite a different value. If we square that deviation, we get a different kind of variance which is called the variance around the regression line:

$$\sigma^2_{reg} = \frac{\sum(Y_i - Y_T)^2}{N}$$

Plug in the numbers from table 11.2 into the formula above, and the *variance around the regression line* is 0.5749. Another way to calculate this kind of variance is to use the formula:

$$\sigma^2_{reg} = \frac{\sum Y_i^2 - a\sum Y_i - b\sum X_i Y_i}{N}$$

The reason we think this formula is important is that the X variable (in this case, the communication variable) is used in this equation to calculate the variance. The mean and the variance of the satisfaction scores give us a degree of knowledge about any given score, in that we know that a certain percentage of them will fall into areas of the normal curve on either side of the mean.[3] However, if we also know what the X score is, we can predict better. How much better is expressed by the relationship between the variance around the regression line and the general variance.

Significance of the Regression Line

You will remember from chapter 10 that the F statistic was the result of comparing one variance with another. In that chapter we also compared the variance among the means caused by our experimental groups with the residual variance. Also in chapter 10 you saw the formula

$$F = \frac{\sigma^2_{between}}{\sigma^2_{within}}$$

Here we will calculate F again, but we will use this formula instead:

$$F = \frac{\sigma^2_Y}{\sigma^2_{Y_{reg}}}$$

In our example, the variance of Y is 4 and the variance around the regression line is 0.5748. To further simplify, 4 divided by 0.5749 is 6.96. Looking in the F table (for 1 and 9 degrees of freedom), we see that $F_{.05}$ is 5.12, so 6.96 is sufficiently large for us to think the ratio is significant.

Correlation and the Regression Line

These two variances tell us a great deal more, however. First of all, we can see that the regression line variance is a good deal smaller than the overall variance. How much smaller is sometimes described as the *coefficient of determination*, or *variance explained*. The statistical term for it is R^2. We calculate it as we did F but with the numerator and denominator flip-flopped: we divide the variance around the regression line (0.5748) by the overall variance (4) and subtract it from 1. This amounts to 1 - 0.1437, or 0.856. The square root of this number is called the *correlation coefficient*. We symbolize it as R, since it is the square root of R^2. Therefore, $R = \sqrt{R^2} = 0.925$. Many researchers skip the regression procedure and calculate the correlation coefficient directly by using the following formula:

$$R_{XY} = \frac{n\sum XY - (\sum X)(\sum Y)}{\sqrt{n\sum X^2 - (\sum X)^2}\sqrt{n\sum Y^2 - (\sum Y)^2}} \quad (13)$$

This is a serious mistake for many reasons. First, much information is lost. The slope and the beginning point of the regression have important theoretical information for the researcher. Second, the correlation coefficient by itself is misleading. It is based on the idea of the amount of variance explained, but it is inflated, since it is the square root of the variance explained. As you look at the square roots of various proportions, you will see how this is so. A correlation coefficient of 0.5 seems relatively robust, but when you square it to get the amount of variance explained by the relationship, you only get 0.25—one fourth. A communication study that only explains one-fourth of the variability in its outcome is of less value than one that explains more.

ALTERNATIVE FORMS OF REGRESSION

The straight line relationship expressed in figure 11.2 is aesthetically pleasing, but is rare in nature. Most relationships between causes and effects are less regular, and don't look like straight lines. Information, for example, is a *logarithmic* function, that is, its alterations are usually expressed in terms of the logarithm (to the base 2) of the information content. So a very useful kind of regression for communication researchers is *polynomial* regression, that allows for different kinds of relationships between causes and effects. Let's look at an example.

Polynomial Regression

Suppose we have a researcher who wants to help the doctor on the *Today* show that we mentioned at the beginning of the book. This researcher has instituted a program of computer-generated presentations that are designed to create more positive attitudes about the health care system. Then the researcher wishes to explore the relationship between these attitudes and subsequent compliance with their doctor's recommendations. These two variables are presented below.

Table 11.3

	Attitude toward Health Care (X)	X^2	Compliance with Program (Y)	XY	Y^2
1	5	25	9	45	81
2	7	49	9	63	81
3	6	36	9	54	81
4	8	64	10	80	100
5	9	81	11	99	121
6	5	25	8	40	64
7	4	16	6	24	36
8	0	100	10	100	100
9	1	121	13	143	169
10	4	16	7	28	49
11	3	9	6	118	36
12	2	4	8	116	64
13	12	144	15	180	225
14	13	169	16	208	256
15	1	1	7	7	49
16	1	1	8	8	64
17	15	225	22	330	484
18	15	225	20	300	400
19	14	196	17	238	289
20	13	169	16	208	256
$\Sigma=$	158	1676	227	2189	3005

If we use the procedure described earlier in this chapter, we will want to get the unknowns for the simultaneous linear equations:

$$\text{I. } \Sigma Y = na + b\Sigma X$$
$$\text{II. } \Sigma XY = a\Sigma X + b\Sigma X^2$$

Solving for a and b (as we did before) involves substituting the values from the calculations above. These values include: $\Sigma Y = 227$; $n = 20$; $\Sigma X = 158$; $\Sigma XY = 2189$; and $\Sigma X^2 = 1676$. If we substitute these values into the equations above, we get

$$\text{I. } 227 = 20a + 158b$$
$$\text{II. } 2189 = 158a + 1676b$$

Now we are ready to solve, using the method we used before. Remember that we can add or multiply on both sides of the equation, and the value of the equation remains constant, and that one method of solving equations with two unknowns involves subtracting the equations from one another. In the previous example we multiplied the first equation by 5. In this example we need to find the number that represents the proportion 158/20. This proportion is equal to 7.9. Once again, our new equation is designated as Ia.

$$\text{I. } 227 = 20a + 158b$$
$$\text{II. } 2189 = 158a + 1676b$$
$$(7.9 \times \text{I}) \quad \text{Ia. } 1793.3 = 158a + 1248.2b$$

Subtracting Ia from II gives:

$$395.7 = 0 + 427.8b$$

Therefore b equals 395.7 divided by 427.8, or 0.925.

Now that we know what b is, we can solve for a. Since equation I tells us that $227 = 20a + (158 \times 0.925)$, then $227 = 20a + 146.2$. This means that $80.85 = 20a$, or a equals 4.0425. Therefore, our predictive equation looks like this:

$$Y_T = 4.0425 + 0.925X_i$$

This relationship is graphed in figure 11.3.

We can calculate the variance around this regression line with the formula:

$$\sigma^2_{reg} = \frac{\Sigma Y_i^2 - a\Sigma Y_i - b\Sigma X_i Y_i}{N}$$

Figure 11.3   Regression Line for Attitude toward Health Care and Compliance with Program Scores

---

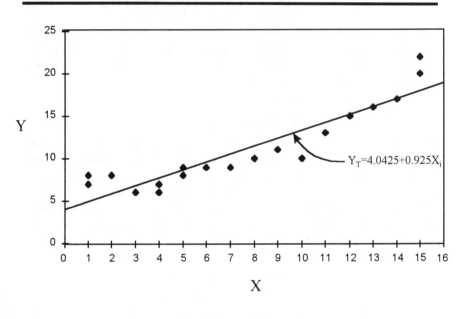

$Y_T = 4.0425 + 0.925X_i$

X

If we substitute the values from the problem into this formula we get

$$\sigma^2_{reg} = \frac{3005 - 4.0425(227) - 0.925(2189)}{20}$$

which works out to be 3.1263. The variance of Y is given by the formula

$$\sigma^2_Y = \frac{\sum Y^2_i - \bar{Y}\sum Y_i}{n}$$

(See chapter 4.) This works out to be 21.42. Remember the following equation:

$$F = \frac{\sigma^2_Y}{\sigma^2_{Y_{reg}}}$$

The variance of Y is 21.42 and the variance around the regression line is 3.12 (we are rounding); 21.42 divided by 3.12 equals 6.86. Looking in the F table (for 1 and 19 degrees of freedom), we see that $F_{.05}$ is 4.38, so 6.86 is sufficiently large for us to think the ratio is significant. Calculating R^2 is done the opposite way, dividing 3.12 by 21.42 gives us 0.1457. Subtracting that from 1 yields 0.8543. The square root of 0.8543 is 0.924. This is a hefty correlation.

But look again at figure 11.3. Many of the scores are some distance from the regression line and there is a real possibility of the scores lying in some other geometric order than a straight line. It is possible that the real relationship is curvilinear. The equation form that produces a curved line is called a *quadratic* equation, and takes the form:

$$Y_i = a + b X_i + c X^2_i$$

In order to solve this equation with three unknowns, rather than two, we need to have three expressions:

I. $\sum Y \quad = n a + b \sum X + c \sum X^2$
II. $\sum XY = a \sum X + b \sum X^2 + c \sum X^3$
III. $\sum X^2 Y = a \sum X^2 + b \sum X^3 + c \sum X^4$

In addition, we need some new values derived from the X and Y relationships. They are:

$\sum Y^2 \quad = 3005$
$\sum X^2 Y = 25953$
$\sum X^3 \quad = 20162$
$\sum X^4 \quad = 258380$

When we place these values into the three equations, we get

I.   227 $\quad = 20a + 158b + 1676c$
II. 2189 $\quad = 158a + 1676b + 20162c$
III. 25953 $= 1676a + 20162b + 258380c$

Solving these equations with three unknowns is slightly more complicated than solving them in only one. Simplification is the key. Here's how we do it.

First, we solve for c. The first step is to eliminate the a value arithmetically. The first equation contains "20 a" and the second "158 a"; 158 divided by 20 is 7.9. So we multiply all the terms in equation I by 7.9. Then we subtract this new equation from equation II. This produces a new equation which we will call equation A.

$$\begin{array}{rl}
\text{II.} \quad 2189 &= 158a + 1676b + 20162c \\
-(7.9 \times \text{I.}) \quad 1793.3 &= 158a + 1248.2b + 13240.4c \\
\hline
\text{Equation A.} \quad 395.7 &= 427.8b + 6921.6c
\end{array}$$

Then let's do the same thing with equations II and III. To eliminate a from the second and third equations, we need a different constant. Equation II contains the value "$158a$" and equation III the value "$1676a$." 1676 divided by 158 is 10.6. Therefore we need to multiply equation II by 10.6. Subtracting the two equations produces equation B:

$$\begin{array}{rl}
\text{III.} \quad 25953 &= 1676a + 20162b + 258380c \\
-(10.6 \times \text{II.}) \quad 23203.4 &= 1676a + 17765.6b + 213717.2c \\
\hline
\text{Equation B.} \quad 2749.6 &= 2396.4b + 44662.8c
\end{array}$$

Now we have two equalities that are more manageable, equation A and equation B. We can solve them for c as we did in the simpler example. By multiplying equation A by 5.602, we eliminate the b term:

$$\begin{array}{rl}
2749.6 &= 2396.4b + 44662.8c \\
-(5.602 \times \text{A.}) \quad 2216.71 &= 2396.4b + 38774.8c \\
\hline
\end{array}$$

Now we can solve:

$$532.9 = 5888c$$

and we see that c is equal to 0.0905.

Next we can take our value for c and put it in equations I and II, to solve for b. Here is how that works:

$$\begin{array}{rl}
\text{I.} \quad 227 &= 20a + 158b + (1676 \times 0.0905) \\
\text{II.} \quad 2189 &= 158a + 1676b + (20162 \times 0.0905)
\end{array}$$

or

$$\begin{array}{rl}
\text{I.} \quad 227 &= 20a + 158b + 151.68 \\
\text{II.} \quad 2189 &= 158a + 1676b + 1824.66
\end{array}$$

Simplifying these equations (putting all the unknowns on one side) produces:

$$\begin{array}{rl}
\text{Ia.} \quad 75.3 &= 20a + 158b \\
\text{IIa.} \quad 364.3 &= 158a + 1676b \\
-(7.9 \times \text{Ia}) \quad 594.9 &= 158a + 1248.2b \\
\hline
230.6 &= 427.8b \\
-0.539 &= b
\end{array}$$

Note that b has a negative value. Now solving for a is easy.

$$\text{Ia.} \quad 75.3 = 20a + 158 \, (\text{-}0.538)$$

or

$$\text{Ia.} \quad 75.3 = 20a - 85.0$$

Adding 85.0 and 75.3 produces 160.3, and dividing by 20 produces a value of 8.02 for a. Our final equation now is

$$Y_T = 8.02 - 0.538 X + 0.0905X^2$$

Figure 11.4 shows the kind of line that this equation produces.

Figure 11.4 Quadratic Equation Graphed for Attitude Toward Health Care and Compliance with Program Scores

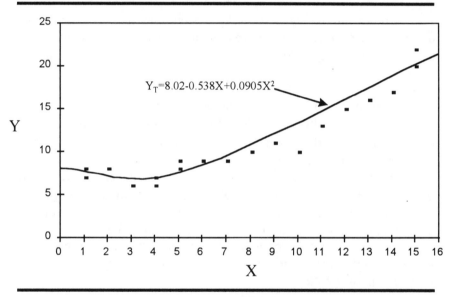

The next step is to calculate the variance around this line. The variance around a quadratic regression line is given by the formula:

$$\sigma^2 \ of \ Y_T = \frac{\sum Y^2 - a\sum Y - b\sum XY - c\sum X^2 Y}{n}$$

This value works out to be 0.7831. The variance (σ^2) of Y = 21.42, 21.42 divided by 0.7831 = 27.35. This is the F statistic that determines the significance of the new regression line. You will note that it is much larger than the straight line. The coefficient of determination (R^2) is

$$1 - \frac{0.7831}{21.42} \quad or \quad 1 - 0.0365 \quad or \quad 0.9635$$

Therefore, R = 0.9815. It is clear that the curved line is a much better fit than the straight one.

Multiple Regression

Another interesting form of regression analysis occurs when we believe that a given effect has more than one cause. The predictive equation for multiple regression is:

$$Y_t = a + b_1 X1_t + b_2 X2_t$$

Notice that there are now two predictors, X1 and X2, rather than one; and there are two different values for b, b_1 and b_2. In our previous example, we studied a dependent variable that measured compliance with a medical regimen, and was "predicted" by an "attitude" variable. But suppose we add another prediction—the seriousness of the health problem. More people might comply with medical instructions when the problem is serious, but not so much if it isn't. So we could examine both "seriousness" and "attitude" as independent variables.

In order to solve an equation for three unknowns, we proceed just as we did in the case of the polynomial regression example. We need to solve the three equations:

$$\sum Y = na + b_2 \sum X_2$$

$$\sum X_1 Y = a \sum X_1 + b_2 \sum X_1^2 + b_2 X_1 X_2$$

$$\sum X_2 Y = a \sum X_2 + b_2 \sum X_1 X_2 + b_1 \sum X_2^2$$

The result of solving these equations is not one, but two regression coefficients, b_1 and b_2. A visual representation of these two coefficients requires a three-dimensional graph, not a two dimensional one, like the one in figure 11.1. But the same principles hold for the overall correlation coefficient. We call the result the *multiple correlation coefficient*. We can calculate this coefficient a number of ways, but we will not go into detail in this book.[4]

Regression and Historical Data

An extremely interesting use of regression is in the analysis of historical data. Sometimes the researcher will have statistics about the history of a given industry or group. Regression can tell us the specific characteristics of these data, often much better than other analytic techniques. Let us look at an example from the telecommunication industry.

Each year, the amount of money spent on television by advertisers has increased. These billings are available from a number of sources. In the years between 1968 and 1978, these billings grew by almost 5 million dollars every year. To use regression to chart this growth, first simplify the figures—and then, if possible, use an odd number of years for your analysis. Using the years 1968 to 1978, and simplifying, we can see that the midpoint year is 1973. If we call that year "zero," then the other years can be charted as short distances from this zero.

		Table 11.4		
Year	*X*	*TV Billings (Y)*	*X²*	*XY*
1968	-5	2.9	25	-14.5
1969	-4	3.2	16	-12.8
1970	-3	3.2	9	-9.6
1971	-2	3.6	4	-6.4
1972	-1	3.6	1	-3.6
1973	0	4.0	0	.0
1974	1	4.4	1	4.4
1975	2	4.7	4	9.4
1976	3	6.0	9	18.0
1977	4	6.8	16	27.2
1978	5	8.1	25	40.5
Totals	0	50.1	110	52.6

Remember that the equations to calculate a two-element regression are:

$$\text{I.} \quad \Sigma Y = n\,a + b\,\Sigma X$$
$$\text{II.} \quad \Sigma XY = a\Sigma X + b\Sigma X^2$$

But, since $\Sigma X = 0$ (we made it that way on purpose!), then $\Sigma Y = n\,a$, or $a = \Sigma Y / n$. Similarly, $\Sigma XY = b\Sigma X^2$ or $\Sigma XY / \Sigma X^2 = b$. In the problem above, $a = 50.1/11$ or 4.55; $b = 52.6/110$, or 0.478. The theoretical description (in mathematical terms) of the growth for these eleven years is $Y_T = 4.55 + 0.478\ X$. As you look at the growth, however, you might well conclude that a straight line is not an appropriate way to describe it, and try a polynomial description instead. Or you might well apply a correction for the inflation multiplier in each of these years and test to see if television billings grew faster than inflation. Any number of analyses are interesting and worthwhile.

REGRESSION AND THE COMPUTER

The calculations in this chapter can be onerous (especially if your problem has lots of data), so you may wish to use the computer to do the work for you, just as you did in the previous chapter. The first step in performing regression analysis on a computer is to enter the data. First let's look at doing the calculations on the PC.

Excel and Regression

First you must get into Windows, and then activate Excel. You do not need to put in labels, because Excel will call the variables X and Y just as we have been doing in this chapter. See figure 11.5 to see how the data from this chapter will look.

When you're finished entering in the data, click on the Tools menu and then select Data Analysis. This will bring up a menu that includes many options. Select Regression. You will then see a screen that asks you to put in the ranges for your data. So for the first one, enter B1:B20. For the second one, enter A1:A20.[5] Then select any options you want, and select the OK button. You should get an answer that looks like figure 11.6.

If all goes well (and no mistakes were made), you should get the same answer for the problem that we did earlier in the chapter. Excel calls the a value the *intercept* and the b value the *X variable*. This is because the regression line intercepts the zero axis at that value. The printout gives a value of 4.042777 for the intercept and 0.924965 for the X variable. These are close enough for most of us! You will notice that Excel calculates the α level for us, and gives a value of F of 105.3407. Part of this difference stems from the use of N-1 (and the subsequent values for the variances). But part of it stems from the use of mean squares as the base for calculation, as opposed to the direct method presented earlier in the chapter. All this means is that Excel is far less conservative in its procedures than the more direct method. In

Figure 11.5   Input in Microsoft Excel for Regression Analysis

5	9
7	9
6	9
8	10
9	11
5	8
4	6
10	10
11	13
4	7
3	6
2	8
12	15
13	16
1	7
1	8
15	22
15	20
14	17
13	16

other words, Excel will get us a "significant" answer more easily. When we did the problem by hand, we only could place the α level between certain values. This is one distinct advantage of the computer. Remember from chapters 9 and 10, that each one of these computer programs has an algorithm (a built-in section that makes calculations) that computes the exact probability of any value of the test result. We probably don't really need them, but sometimes it's nice to have them.

If you selected the check boxes for the Residual Plots, Line Fit Plots, and/or Normal Probability Plots on the screen where you entered the ranges for your data, you will notice the plot(s) with the Excel output. For many kinds of research reports, these plots will be useful in your final presentation. One of the plots is presented in figure 11.7.

Figure 11.6   Output in Microsoft Excel for Regression Analysis

SUMMARY OUTPUT

Regression Statistics	
Multiple R	0.924155198
R Square	0.854062829
Adjusted R Square	0.845955209
Standard Error	1.864006653
Observations	20

ANOVA

	df	SS	MS	F	Significance F
Regression	1	366.0086255	366.0086255	105.3407495	5.9756E-09
Residual	18	62.54137447	3.474520804		
Total	19	428.55			

	Coefficients	Standard Error	t Stat	P-value	Lower 95%	Upper 95%	Lower 95.0%	Upper 95.0%
Intercept	4.042776999	0.824990747	4.900390719	0.000115232	2.309534415	5.776019583	2.309534415	5.776019583
X Variable 1	0.924964937	0.090121221	10.26356417	5.9756E-09	0.73562713	1.114302743	0.73562713	1.114302743

RESIDUAL OUTPUT

Observation	Predicted Y	Residuals
1	8.667601683	0.332398317
2	10.51753156	-1.517531557
3	9.59256662	-0.59256662
4	11.44249649	-1.44249494
5	12.36746143	-1.367461431
6	8.667601683	-0.667601683
7	7.742636746	-1.742636746
8	13.29242637	-3.292426367
9	14.2173913	-1.217391304
10	7.742636746	-0.742636746
11	6.817671809	-0.817671809
12	5.892706872	2.107293128
13	15.14235624	-0.142356241
14	16.06732118	-0.067321178
15	4.967741935	2.032258065
16	4.967741935	3.032258065
17	17.91725105	4.082748948
18	17.91725105	2.082748948
19	16.99228612	0.007713885
20	16.06732118	-0.067321178

Figure 11.7   X Variable 1 Line Fit Plot in Microsoft Excel

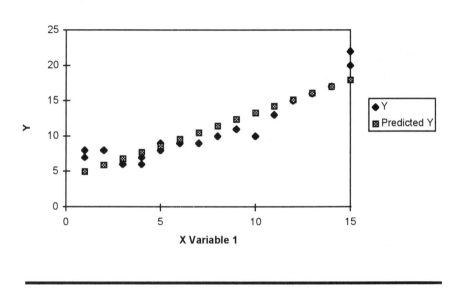

You will look in vain for methods of doing polynomial regression on Excel, or multiple regression. The program just doesn't have it. So to do these types of problems, we need more power, which we get on the mainframe. So let's look at how the mainframe would do the same problem using SAS.

Solving Regression Problems with SAS

The first step, as with Excel, is to enter the data. Figure 11.8 illustrates the same problem data from above entered into a SAS job file.

If you look at the input statement, you will see that we named the first variable "ATTITUDE" and the second one "HEALTH." Note that SAS will only accept names that are eight characters long. First we ask SAS to do a simple regression problem with the model statement:

PROC GLM; MODEL HEALTH =ATTITUDE;

Then to work the polynomial problem, we used the model statement:

PROC GLM; MODEL HEALTH =ATTITUDE ATTITUDE*ATTITUDE;

Figure 11.8   SAS Job for Regression Analysis

```
//REGRE JOB 2615-50002,CLASS,TIME=1
/*PASSWORD PVC96
//A EXEC SAS
DATA HEALTH;
INPUT ATTITUDE HEALTH;
CARDS;
5 9
7 9
6 9
8 10
9 11
5 8
4 6
10 10
11 13
4 7
3 6
2 8
12 15
13 16
1 7
1 8
15 22
15 20
14 17
13 16
PROC GLM;MODEL HEALTH=ATTITUDE;
PROC GLM; MODEL HEALTH =ATTITUDE ATTITUDE*ATTITUDE;
PROC PLOT; PLOT HEALTH*ATTITUDE;
PROC PRINT;
TITLE BOOK11;
```

The term ATTITUDE*ATTITUDE[6] instructs SAS to multiply ATTI-TUDE by itself, which is the same as X_i^2.

The SAS output is presented in figure 11.9.

In the first page you will notice that we got the same answers for the simple regression that we did with Excel and with the demonstration problem. There are some slight differences when we examine the

Figure 11.9 Output of SAS Job for Regression Analysis

The SAS System

General Linear Models Procedure

Dependent Variable: HEALTH

Source	DF	Sum of Squares	Mean Square	F Value	Pr > F
Model	2	412.94708045	206.47354023	224.96	0.0001
Error	17	15.60291955	0.91781880		
Corrected Total	19	428.55000000			

R-Square	C.V.	Root MSE	HEALTH Mean
0.963591	8.440781	0.95802860	11.35000000

Source	DF	Type I SS	Mean Square	F Value	Pr > F
ATTITUDE	1	366.00862553	366.00862553	398.78	0.0001
ATTITUDE*ATTITUDE	1	46.93845493	46.93845493	51.14	0.0001

Source	DF	Type III SS	Mean Square	F Value	Pr > F
ATTITUDE	1	5.67195597	5.67195597	6.18	0.0236
ATTITUDE*ATTITUDE	1	46.93845493	46.93845493	51.14	0.0001

Parameter	Estimate	T for H0: Parameter=0	Pr > |T|	Std Error of Estimate
INTERCEPT	7.954730389	11.49	0.0001	0.69211627
ATTITUDE	-0.512928780	-2.49	0.0236	0.20633320
ATTITUDE*ATTITUDE	0.088871205	7.15	0.0001	0.01242725

polynomial regression output. Our resulting equation in the worked example was $Y_T = 8.01 - 0.538 X + 0.0905X^2$. SAS, on the other hand, gives us an equation with the values $Y_T = 7.954 - 0.512 X + 0.088X^2$. These differences are due to rounding errors. SAS works these problems with exact figures, out to nine decimal places! It is doubtful whether this accuracy is necessary in the social sciences.

We could have done a multiple regression problem quite easily, but would have to add the second predictor in the data set. We would have needed to modify the input statement to reflect the new predictors. Suppose we thought that the health behavior would also be affected by the age and the gender of the respondents. In this case, we would enter age and gender next to the health and attitude variables, and have a new input statement, such as:

INPUT ATTITUDE AGE GENDER HEALTH;

Then in our model statement, we would have asked SAS to do it this way:

PROC GLM; MODEL HEALTH = ATTITUDE AGE GENDER;

This model statement produces regression coefficients for each of the independent variables as well as a multiple coefficient for the entire model. There are many different kinds of multiple regression models, such as PROC STEPWISE that adds variables to the predictive equation one by one, to see how much influence each has in combination with the other.

Lastly, we asked SAS to plot the problem, using the statement:

PROC PLOT; PLOT HEALTH*ATTITUDE;

You will notice that the plot that SAS draws is not nearly as finished as the one produced on Excel (see figure 11.10). Newer SAS procedure (SASGRAPH and others) can produce better visuals, but standard mainframe programs were designed to use printers without the capacity that most of our printers now have.

Figure 11.10   Line Plot Output of SAS Job for Regression Analysis

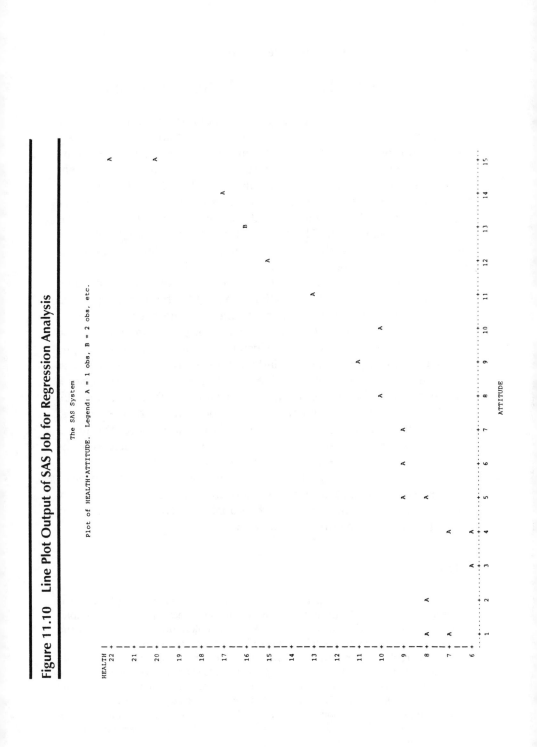

EVALUATING RESEARCH USING REGRESSION

You may have noticed in this chapter that little emphasis has been placed on correlation and much more on regression. This reflects a growing opinion among researchers that correlational methods obscure relationships among data, rather than reveal them. Simple linear regression contains a wealth of information lacking in correlation. The first term in the regression equation tells us what the zero value of the dependent variable is; that is, what we could expect it to be if our "cause" was nonexistent. The second terms tells us *how much* of an increase in the independent variable is needed before "significant" increases in the dependent variable are observed.

Since the use of correlation is very common, your first step would be to estimate how strong the relationship might actually be, expressed in terms of the amount of variance explained. Remember that correlation (R) is the square root of the coefficient of determination (R^2), so converting correlation into the coefficient of determination is simple. One only has to square the correlation. If a research report states that the correlation between two variables is 0.6, then squaring 0.6 gives a value of 0.36, the actual proportion of variance explained by the relationship. You can see why correlation is popular with researchers. Generally it magnifies the apparent size of the relationship. You might scan a few research reports and see if you think the conclusions of the author is justified by the actual size of the relationship!

But most variables in communication research are not simple—and the use of polynomial regression and multiple regression are absolutely essential to deal with most relationships. Oversimplification is one of the worst problems in social science.

NOTES

[1] Another method used to calculate the values of a and b is matrix algebra. This is the method used by Pedhazur (1982). Simultaneous linear equations are simpler and more accessible to most students. When we look at multiple regression and polynomial regression, it will be clear why this is a good method.

[2] You may remember that the best estimate of the variance of a population is obtained by using N-1 instead of N. However, for this example, we are not estimating—we are simply looking at a finite set of scores to discover some of the characteristics of them. This difference, however, gives us trouble when we use computers to calculate some of these problems. Mostly computers use N-1 because most of the time the research is trying to make some sense out of larger populations.

[3] See chapter 8 for a refresher on the normal curve.

[4] Several options are available. Pedhazur (1982, pp. 59–63) proceeds by calculating the squared deviations of each of the collections of scores. Edwards (1976, pp. 152–155) uses a similar technique. Pedhazur advocates the use of matrix algebra in solving these problems.

[5] Excel considers the Y variable to be in the second column.

[6] The symbol "*" in many computer languages indicates multiplication. SAS is written in a language called "PL1," while SPSS is written in an older language called FORTRAN. Neither of these languages are widely used today.

Chapter Twelve

Analyzing Frequencies
Chi-Square

We have now examined some very important statistical procedures, the z score, the t test, the analysis of variance, and regression. These examples of statistical reasoning depend on a number of *assumptions*, primarily those of the normal curve. One assumption is that samples or instances have been drawn from a group of numbers or observations that are normally distributed, and the means and variances are relatively consistent. Strictly speaking, when the assumptions are violated, the inferences that follow are also violated. A statistical test that does not make these assumptions, then, is therefore highly desirable in certain circumstances.

Another kind of problem arises in the application of z scores, t tests, analysis of variance, and regression—the nature of the numbers that are used to form the database. All of these procedures assume at least ordinal measurement on the variables in question; that is, that some quantitatively defensible scheme is employed to score them. For example, the usual attitude scales fit the definition because they range from strong to weak. Androgyny scores resulting from a personality test also fit this model. But in many kinds of research this level of measurement is not possible.

Suppose you are involved in an effort to promote literacy in your community—and have designed a brochure that advocates a "literacy center" that would provide instruction in basic reading and writing for adults in your community. Your goal is to obtain signatures on a petition to your city council to dedicate an unused city building as a literacy center. You mail your petition to everyone in your town, and ask for signatures. Then in two weeks, you and your coworkers set up a booth at a local mall, and when people come by, you ask them to sign the petition. You suspect that more women will sign this petition than men, because historically women have been more sensitive to educational issues, and you are designing the next advertising campaign for the literacy center. Accordingly, you examine the signatures you obtain to see if more women signed than men. You instruct your coworkers to mark an M or an F on your signature sheets. When the mall closes that night, you find that you have 289 women's signatures and 211 men's signatures.

Remember the basic premise of statistical argument? You feel that your sample produced a greater degree of women's signatures—78 more. But a skeptic could say, "Sure, but that's just chance. Tomorrow would be different." You need a probability test. However, you don't have means to compare with a t test—all you have is signatures in two categories, either men or women. This set of numbers is an example of *frequency* data, in that it consists of frequency counts in one category or another. There is a statistical test for frequencies, and it is called chi-square (χ^2).

The chi-square statistic has another advantage for much research: it is an assumption-free test, that is, it doesn't depend on sampling from a normal population. It has its own set of probabilities and its own logic. χ^2 is related to z scores, in that $\chi^2 = z^2$ when z is normally distributed with a mean of zero and a standard deviation of 1. In short, χ^2 is a probability distribution similar to the other distributions we have seen, and can be used to analyze frequency data.

BASIC CALCULATIONS

Let's return to the literacy project and the signatures at the mall. You would like to show that the frequency of women's signatures is *significantly* greater than the men's signatures. Here's how you do it: First, decide what the frequencies would be if there were no differences between the genders. An obvious one is 50 percent in each category. If there is no difference, then 50 percent is the *expected frequency*. You had a total of 289 women's signatures and 211 men's signatures, for a total of 500. Fifty percent of 500 is 250, so your expected frequency is 250. However, this is not what you got. What you got is called the *observed frequency*.

Now you are ready to calculate χ^2. You use the following formula:

$$\chi^2 = \sum_{i=1}^{n} \frac{(O_i - E_i)^2}{E_i}$$

In this formula, O is the observed frequency, E is the expected frequency, and n is the number of observations. In our signature example, we see the following frequencies:

Group	O	E	O-E	(O-E)²	(O-E)²/E
Women	289	250	39	1521	6.08
Men	211	250	-39	1521	6.08

We get χ^2 by adding 6.08 and 6.08, which is 12.16. Degrees of freedom for chi-square is always K-1 (where K=the number of comparisons), so in this example it is 1. We next look in the table (in appendix E) for chi-square values with one degree of freedom, and find that 10.827 is the value given for a probability of less than one in one hundred. We therefore conclude that the signatures are different to the degree that it would have occurred by chance only once in a hundred times.

CONTINGENCY TABLES

Sometimes chi-squares are useful in testing *contingencies*. In the signature example above, you might well have concluded that the results might have been affected if fewer men come to the mall than do women. If you had that data, you might be right. Let's look at contingency analysis, however, by using a real example, not a hypothetical one.

When people get married, what do they call their in-laws? Do they use first names, do they use Mom or Dad, or what? Jorgenson (1994) studied the "addressing" behavior of married couples, and asked what they did. Respondents' answers fell into four categories: Mom or Dad, first names (Phil or Agnes), title (Mrs. Johnson), or no names at all (avoidance). Jorgenson found that his data contained more women than men, so he used a chi-square *contingency* analysis to see if there were differences throughout the table due to gender. Table 12.1 shows his data.

Table 12.1

	Husbands	Wives	Total
"Mom and Dad"	6	8	14
First Names	5	4	9
Title	3	2	5
No names	2	4	6
Total	16	18	34

To do an analysis using chi-square, the first step is to calculate an expected frequency for each of these cells. The overall number of responses is 34, 16 husbands and 18 wives. There were 14 Mom and Dad responses, 9 first names, 5 title responses, and 6 no names. The proportion of Mom and Dad responses were 14 divided by 34, or 0.412, the proportion of first names was 9 divided by 34, or 0.265, the proportion of title responses was 5 divided by 34, or 0.147, and the proportion of no name responses was 6 divided by 34, or 0.176. But these proportions must be adjusted to reflect the proportion of husbands and wives in the sample. There were 16 husbands, so their proportion was 16 divided by 34, or 0.471. There were 18 wives, so their proportion was 18 divided by 34, or 0.529. Now, to get the expected frequency for each cell, we take the proportion in the column, multiply it by the proportion in the row, and then multiply the result by the overall frequency. For example, in the cell indicating the number of husbands using Mom and Dad, the row proportion is 0.412 and the column proportion is 0.471. Multiplying these two proportions gives a new proportion, or 0.194. When this is multiplied by 34, the expected frequency is 6.6. In table 12.2 each of the cells shows the results of this calculation:

Table 12.2

	Husbands	Wives	Total
"Mom and Dad"	6	8	14
	(0.194)	(.217)	(0.412)
	6.6	7.38	
First Names	5	4	9
	(0.124)	(0.139)	(.264)
	4.21	4.73	
Title	3	2	5
	(0.069)	(0.077)	(.147)
	2.35	2.62	
No names	2	4	6
	(0.082)	(0.093)	(0.176)
	2.79	3.16	
Total	16	18	34
	(0.471)	(0.529)	

The next step is to calculate chi-square based on these frequencies. We can arrange them as table 12.3 shows.

Table 12.3

Cell	O	E	O-E	$(O-E)^2$	$(O-E)^2/E$
1	6	6.56	-0.44	0.193	0.003
2	8	7.38	0.62	0.384	0.052
3	5	4.21	0.79	0.624	0.148
4	4	4.73	-0.73	0.533	0.113
5	3	2.35	0.65	0.423	0.179
6	2	2.62	-0.62	0.384	0.147
7	2	2.79	-0.79	0.62	0.222
8	4	3.16	0.84	0.71	0.223
				$\chi^2 =$	1.078

We can look up the value 1.078 (with degrees of freedom of K-1, or 7) in our chi-square table and see that it falls far short of significance. We would then conclude that the contingency analysis does not yield a significant chi-square, and we should look no longer to see if men and women address their in-laws differently. If you look back to the chapter on analysis of variance (chapter 10), and review the material on *interactions,* you will notice many similarities between interactive analysis of variance and contingency chi-squares.

CHI-SQUARE AND HISTORICAL DATA

Often a statistical analysis can help us understand history. If you have read Walter Lord's book about the sinking of the Titanic, you may have been struck by the disparity in the proportion of first-class passengers who drowned as opposed to the third-class passengers (Lord, 1986). Looking at these frequencies might do two things for us: it will help us to work another problem with chi-squares, and it might show us how this kind of analysis can be applied to historical data. From Lord's book, we can get the numbers of people in first class, second class, and third class who were either saved or drowned (crew is omitted from this table). Then we can put them in a table like table 12.4.

Table 12.4

	1st Class	2nd Class	3rd Class	Total
Saved	203	118	178	499
Drowned	122	167	528	817
Total	325	285	706	1316

This is a large disparity, and we would wonder if the distribution might have happened by chance. Once again, the first step is to calculate the row and column proportions. We do that by taking the total number of passengers saved (499) and dividing it by the total number of passengers (1316), and then doing the same for the number of those drowned (817). Overall, we see that the proportion saved is 0.379 and the proportion drowned is 0.621. Then we do the same for each of the columns. The total number of first class passengers (325) is divided by the total number of passengers (1316), as is the total number of second-class passengers (285) and the number of third-class passengers (706). All of these proportions are given in table 12.5.

Table 12.5

	1st Class	2nd Class	3rd Class	Total
Saved	203	118	178	499
				(0.379)
Drowned	122	167	528	817
				(0.621)
Total	325	285	706	1316
	(0.247)	(0.217)	(0.536)	

Then we can calculate the expected frequency in each of the cells. Since first class passengers made up 0.247 of the total, and the number of people saved made up 0.379 of the total, the number of first class passengers saved (if the cell meets the expectations of the total table) would be 24.7 percent of 37.9 percent, or 0.094. If the expectations were uniform throughout the table, we would have expected 9.4 percent of the group to be in the cell designated by first class, saved.

Table 12.6

	1st Class	2nd Class	3rd Class	Total
Saved	203	118	178	499
	(0.094)	(0.082)	(0.203)	(0.379)
Drowned	122	167	528	817
	(0.153)	(0.135)	(0.333)	(0.621)
Total	325	285	706	1316
	(0.247)	(0.217)	(0.536)	

Then we do the same for each of the other cells to get the cell frequencies expected. These values are presented in table 12.7.

Table 12.7

	1st Class	2nd Class	3rd Class	Total
Saved	203	118	178	499
	(0.093)	(0.082)	(0.203)	(0.379)
	(122.388)	(107.912)	(267.748)	
Drowned	122	167	528	817
	(0.153)	(0.135)	(0.333)	(0.621)
	(201.348)	(177.660)	(438.228)	
Total	325	285	706	1316
	(0.247)	(0.217)	(0.536)	

Now we are ready to calculate chi-square. We have the observed frequencies and the expected frequencies. Table 12.8 (on next page) shows how we calculate the value of chi-square.

Looking up 134.36 in the chi-square table produces a highly significant result (with 5 degrees of freedom). Can we now agree with Lord that the class system produced the result? If we think about the class system and the organization of the ship, we would have to note that the first class passengers were all on the upper decks, and the third class passengers down in the third or fourth decks, far from the lifeboats. Chi-square shows us that there was a differential rate of rescue; our interpretive skills must tell us whether we think it was due to undue favoritism by the *Titanic's* crew or whether just the physical positioning of the passengers was the cause. This is an excellent illustration of what statistics can do and, more importantly, cannot do.

				Table 12.8	
Cell	O	E	O-E	$(O-E)^2$	$(O-E)^2/E$
1	203	122.4	80.6	6496.36	53.075
2	122	201.3	-79.3	6288.49	31.239
3	118	107.9	10.1	102.01	.945
4	167	177.7	-10.7	114.49	.644
5	178	267.7	-89.7	8046.09	30.056
6	528	438.2	89.8	8064.04	18.403
				CHI-SQUARE	=134.362

EVALUATING RESEARCH USING CHI-SQUARE

You will notice that chi-square is simple, easy, and not hard to interpret. Its very simplicity is the reason that there are few computer programs to calculate chi-square. Apparently those who write these statistical programs see little need for a procedure that is so easy to calculate. However, large interactive chi-square analyses can be done using SAS procedures CATMOD and BMDP. Sometimes these problems are worked using a technique called *log-linear analysis*, which uses essentially the same algorithms as do simple chi-squares.[1]

The most important aspect of chi-square analysis is that it is performed on *frequency* data, that is, on categorizations, rather than measurements. This means that it is more appropriate for many research studies that do not have interval and ratio scales for data.

One common error that occurs in chi-quare research is caused by having too few cases in the table. When the frequencies are lower than 10, look for a statement that an appropriate correction has been made. In a table with small frequencies, a more appropriate method is to use an exact probability test rather than chi-square.

NOTE

[1] Chi-square can be calculated in Excel by using the "Function" option. You can also calculate chi-square on the Internet, at http://www.cyber.vt.edu/mbo/privcom-mres/lectures/chisq/chiscript.html.

Chapter Thirteen

Working with Experiments

In the previous three chapters we studied analysis of variance, correlation, regression, and chi-square, all methods of testing how closely variables are associated with one another. At the beginning of chapter 11, we noted that often the source of our interest in correlation and regression comes from our desire to know whether a *causal* relationship exists between the variables. If we believe that the variables are connected in a causal way, we would expect the variables to *covary*, and correlation and regression measure the degree to which they do this. But measuring the amount of covariance is only the beginning of making a case for causation. In chapter 11 we noted that causation also implies that an "effect" should occur later in time than the "cause" (Asher, 1976). In addition, there should be some logical relationship between the cause and the effect—an individual's shoe size certainly has little to do with the kinds of movies he or she is likely to attend.

But even if a time sequence and a logical connection are present, we will still not accept a causal hypothesis until it has been demonstrated in a more formal way. We usually call this demonstration an *experiment*.

Let's look at an example. The role and relative importance of nonverbal communication is a central topic in modern communication research. Many believe that nonverbal messages constitute the largest part of the "meaning" in interpersonal communication (Mehrabian, 1972). On the other hand, other researchers tell us that the role of nonverbal communication is probably overstated and that verbal messages may be more important (Lapakko, 1997). How can these competing claims be resolved? An experiment in which specific nonverbal signals were compared to verbal signals would be one way, with a specific test of which one was more "effective." One first step would be to look at the effects of nonverbal signals in conversations. Unfortunately, when we observe naturalistic conversations, we note that facial expressions indicating emotions almost always accompany verbal messages indicating the corresponding emotion. How can we tell which is more important—the facial expression or the verbal messages that they accompany?

Researcher Michael Motley (1993) undertook to see what the relative roles of verbal and nonverbal signals in conversations might be. Motley wished to investigate *anger, disgust, confusion, happiness, sadness*, and *surprise* as they appear in facial expression. But a large problem in interpersonal research arises because in naturalistic conversations, individuals don't always exhibit the responses that we might wish them to. An individual might feel that his or her face was expressing happiness, but others might not think that the facial expression that was displayed actually conveyed that message. In addition, an observer might examine thousands of conversations before the appropriate facial expression appeared. Motley therefore undertook to create particular expressions by introducing varying situations in conversation.

He began by designing an experiment where naive respondents came to a room ostensibly to adjust a polygraph instrument. The polygraph task was bogus. In the room already were other students who acted as "confederates." All of the conversations in the room were videotaped. Here is how he created surprise:

> Spontaneous small talk began at the outset of the fake polygraph adjustment period. As early as was intuitively appropriate, the confederates directed the conversation toward school courses, and instructors. At one point the video subject was asked by one of the confederates who his or her favorite professor was. Regardless of the response, Confederate A disclosed that this professor was her favorite also and that she had recently heard that the professor was leaving the institution at the end of the present term. This announcement was designed to elicit surprise (p. 17).

After carefully identifying the taped segments and verifying that the nonverbal messages did indeed reflect the messages intended, Motley superimposed audio messages of varying emotional content with the videotapes and compared the overall effects of the audio and video together. He found that words (audio) tended to be far more important than the facial expressions (video) in the evaluation task. He concluded that facial expression is more appropriately viewed as an interjection in the conversation and that the vital content of the conversation is conveyed with words.

In this important experiment, we can note several factors at work. The experimenter created the situation that was of interest, rather than waiting to observe it when it occurred naturally. Second, he subjected his stimuli to independent, objective evaluation to see if it indeed reflected the characteristic in question. Third, he compared the factors in an orderly, controlled fashion. Motley's use of this communication *experiment* demonstrates a causal relationship that naturalistic observation never could. Experiments are a vital aspect of research, and have many important characteristics that distinguish them from other methods.

CHARACTERISTICS OF EXPERIMENTS

An *experiment* is a vital aspect of science, since it is the demonstration of a relationship in an artificially planned event. There are many elements involved in successful experiments, ranging from practicality to theoretical cogency. Of all of the possible factors, the three delineated by Cochran and Cox (1957) are the simplest and to the point. They point out that there are three factors that are vital in planning an experiment: first, a clear idea and a statement of objectives, second a clear and defensible plan for differentiation among experimental treatments, and third, a plan (usually statistical) for the analysis of the results. We will look at each of these in turn.

Objectives

The first and probably most important aspect of an experiment is a clear idea of what it is to accomplish. In the example about nonverbal communication cited above, first an underlying theory was articulated: a statement of the relative importance of nonverbal versus verbal communication in interpersonal situations. A specific objective was to compare facial expression of an emotion with a linguistic statement of that emotion and test whether or not the facial expressions were indicators or interjections. No other findings were expected.

Another important objective is to articulate how generalizable any finding should be. Many times research does not aim at wide generalization. If an experimenter wishes to know how an anti-smoking message is perceived by inner-city teenage girls, then wider generalization may not be necessary. In this case, the generalization would be confined to the "target" population, inner-city teenage girls. On the other hand, if the investigator wants to test a principle that might apply to everyone, then a different design would be indicated.

The conditions (if any) where the effect is important is another consideration in designing an experiment. Studies of television viewing often take place in a "laboratory," or some kind of room artificially designed to provide seating and a television screen. But most of us actually view television with friends or families, and at times that are considered "leisure." A determination of how important the context of viewing actually is may be critical to the interpretation of the experiment. The research concerning television and violence is especially vulnerable to conditional interpretation. Violence in children usually occurs in a social setting, and studies of children's interaction with television in artificial settings may be limited in usefulness. We will examine the setting of the experiment in more detail later.

The next important element in experimental research is the definition and operationalization of the experimental treatments.

Experimental Treatments

The definition of the experimental treatments stems from the objectives of the study. Are these treatments different in kind, or are they gradations of a single variable? Cochran and Cox mention an experimental design in which whiskey and water, rum and water, and gin and water are compared, to see which produces more intoxication (p. 11). If you designed an experiment of this type, it would not be possible to see what effects water itself might have. Rum might have a greater effect when mixed with water than it does when taken straight.

Another important aspect of design is a specification of what the comparisons might mean. In research focusing on small group decision-making, experimenters often pose a problem to groups and evaluate the solutions that varying groups might produce in response to the problem. Is it more important to know whether or not the groups produce the "right" answer, as opposed to producing answers of various qualities? This can be a vital early decision in planning the experiment. In other words, if there is only one right answer, we have a design that Cochran and Cox characterize as research designed to "spot the winner." But with problem solving it might be possible to distinguish among ranks of outcomes. A solution may not be "the" right one, but still may have good characteristics. In many investigations, varying degrees of "rightness" can be of interest.

Another important consideration asks if the experiment can be replicated in the "real" world. An experiment in which individuals are subject to extreme sensory deprivation (being placed in a tank of warm water, blindfolded and with cotton in one's ears) may never occur. On the other hand, experiments that make a respondent fearful or nervous have a much better chance of being replicated in more realistic settings.

Perhaps one of the most important considerations asks if control is possible. Later in the chapter we will examine some of the many aspects of the use of control groups, but the possibility of having control at all is an important one. Certain variables are not controllable. For example, if we are concerned about the effects of advanced placement in communication courses based on SAT scores, we might deduce that a real test of the effect would only come if we could deny enrollment in the course to some groups of students. Real control would only come, then, if those who wished to take the course (and who had a given level of SAT scores) were denied admission. Few institutions of higher learning would permit such a study. One of the most horrifying examples of an attempt to get a control group (however possible) arose when a group of researchers chose to deny treatment for syphilis to a group of men in Alabama. However well intentioned, we can see that such "control" is simply not possible given ordinary standards of decency.

In communication study, we often test characteristics of messages. Whether the treatments reflect "real language" or artificially created language is important. Jackson and Jacobs (1983) recommend the use of naturally occurring messages rather than artificially contrived ones in experimental study. Bradac (1983) points out that this is an unreasonable demand, and Hunter, Hamilton, and Allen (1989) point out that in "real life" many messages are contrived, not "natural." They note that advertisers and political speechwriters are examples of message designers of great importance in our culture that do not use "naturally occurring" language. In addition, they say that most communication researchers simply do not have the resources in time and energy to do as Jackson and Jacobs suggest and use multiple messages. However, the issue raised by Jackson and Jacobs is certainly important. Simple variation of message intensity might be a realistic goal.

Plan for Analysis

The third element mentioned by Cochran and Cox is a plan for analysis. The experiment will have little value if its results cannot be analyzed. The first step in such a plan is to decide what assessment techniques will be appropriate and to decide on a dependent variable that makes sense. Simple counting (such as incidence of participation in a small group study) often will suffice. At other times, a specific codebook might be prepared describing types and qualities of different communicative acts. Here is where previous research is invaluable; a good review of previous research will show the experimenter the kinds of differences and the nature of reactions that they can expect.

Choice of Statistical Test

Usually this is taken to mean a specific idea about what statistical test is appropriate for these data. In some cases, the most suitable statistical technique will be the analysis of variance, and in other cases, a simpler test—such as a chi square—would be appropriate. In a comparison that only pits one condition against another, the clear choice would be a *t* test. Multiple comparisons would call for analysis of variance, and if the independent variables are clearly quantifiable, then regression would be indicated. Too often researchers choose inappropriate statistics for the kind of results they wish. But the most important aspect of a plan for analysis would be an assessment of power.

Power. In experimental designs power is always important. Power is usually written as γ (gamma) and is defined as $1 - \beta$ (β, you will recall, is the probability of making a Type II error). Many researchers calculate power after the experiment, but it is much more desirable to do so before the actual experiment is undertaken. The traditional approach is to calculate a statistic called ϕ (Beyer, 1966), but Feldt and Mahmoud (1958) have devised a method of calculating another value that they call ϕ' (phi prime) which is simpler and easier to calculate. Both use power function charts. ϕ' is a function of the size of the difference that will be considered important, the size of the standard error, (or the "mean square within" in the analysis of variance) and the number of cases in each part of the analysis.

Importance of the Differences. Statistical decisions are always important but it is even more important to note that the use to which the finding will be put is even more important. One truly important aspect of regression analyses is that the regression equation tells us how much of a difference in the independent variable we need before we can expect differences in the dependent variable. In addition, the "effect size" measurements in the analysis of variance are crucial. But decisions about how important these differences will be can only be assessed by qualitative methods. Statistical analysis alone will not tell us how important it might be for individuals to be aware of the potential impact of alcohol and driving.

In the next section, we will examine some of the ways that we control comparisons and see what difference they can make.

DESIGN OF EXPERIMENTS

Suppose we believe that students learn communication skills better in an "open" environment, that is, in a classroom where students' participation is stimulated and encouraged. We may have come to this belief by observing many different classes and measuring the amount of student participation (perhaps by recording classroom sessions). After recording our data, we then measure the final achievement by students and by using regression, discover that high participation seems to be associated with accomplishment. But we still really don't know if the participation was the factor. For example, in the high participation classes, we might find teachers that are high in teacher "immediacy" (see chapter 14) and wonder if this was the factor that produced the greater accomplishment. Or we might see that greater participation took place in classes that met before lunch, rather than after lunch. Perhaps lunch made everyone sleepy!

The only way to decide if the participation is the key element is to have some kind of control imposed by the researcher. One method might be to devise classroom rules and assignments that encouraged student participation. For example, if students were responsible for presenting oral evaluations of their classmates' performances, we might define that activity as an "encourager." When we were ready to devise a curriculum that satisfied our definition of "high participation," then we have created an *experimental* group, which is defined as a group that contains the elements of our variable as we have defined it. Now we can go on to the next step.

Control Groups

Inherent in the idea of experiments is the notion of *control*. Control means that we are able to compare the *experimental* group to a group that is "normal" or which doesn't have the experimental elements in it. Researchers call these ordinary groups "control" groups, because they feel that they are *controlling* the presence or absence of the factor that is being studied. In medical research, we often see that researchers test treatments by using control groups. First they give a group of individuals an experimental medicine to see how it works, and then they compare this group with other groups that don't get the medicine. *The control group should be as nearly alike (have the same characteristics) to the experimental group as possible.*

Let's look again at our example about participation in the classroom, and assume that we have at least one control group of communication classes that is as similar to our experimental group as possible. It should be clear that we are not talking about single classes any more, but groups of classes which all meet at the same time, with similar students, and with teachers who are also as similar as possible. While this isn't always possible, it is necessary to make an attempt in order to achieve a reasonable deduction of cause and effect.

But what about the possibility that some of the students in one of the groups were better to start off with? This would certainly affect the assessments and the validity of our *t* test. One way to adjust for that is to measure achievement prior to the experiment. We call this measurement a "pretest." Since we have a pretest, then it is logical to call the final measurement a "posttest," and the difference between the two is an "improvement" or "change" score. Our design looks like this:

GROUP	Participation	Control
PRETEST	Yes	yes
POSTEST	Yes	Yes

But suppose the pretest caused some changes through alerting the students and teachers that something was being studied. Knowledge that you are in an experiment has been termed the "Hawthorne effect" and definitely is an important factor in design. We could control for this effect by creating yet another control group, without a pretest. The design now takes these dimensions:

GROUP	Participation	Control-1	Control-2
PRETEST	Yes	No	Yes
POSTEST	Yes	Yes	Yes

And to add the ultimate in control—to control for the effects of the initial assessment on the participation group—we get a design like this:

GROUP	Participation-1	Participation-2	Control-1	Control-2
PRETEST	No	Yes	Yes	Yes
POSTEST	Yes	Yes	Yes	Yes

This design controls for both pretest effects and control group effects. If we substitute the term "Experimental" for "Participation" in the table, we will have a general description of such a design. This design is sometimes called the "Solomon Four-Group" design. Variations on this design can be utilized depending on how important the effects of the pretest might be for a given experimental effect.

Statistical Control

One way of controlling an experiment is to use random selection as a method of assigning individuals to experimental or control groups. The basic idea behind this is that if you select participants in the experiment randomly and if you get enough of them, then all of the other problems associated with control will disappear. If you recall the characteristics of the normal curve (from chapter 8) you will remember that if people are selected at random, then some will be on one side of the curve and some will be on the other. For an experiment, you hope that any factors that might impair your results will balance out. If you will review the methods of taking a random sample in chapter 8, you will remember that one of the most common devices is to use a table of random numbers to help you select the experimental subjects.

The theory behind statistical control is a strong one, and it usually works. Most researchers, however, prefer to utilize more formal methods of control.

Interactive Designs

Chapter 10 introduced the interactive analysis of variance, and if you review this chapter and consider the example about the commercials that have provocative content, then you will have the basic idea behind an interactive design. Remember that a producer wished to test whether a commercial with suggestive content would be better than a commercial with ordinary content, and the example illustrated how the difference *interacted* according to the gender of the receiver. This was a basic "two-by-two" interactive design, which is very common in research. This is how the design in chapter 10 looked:

	Men	Women
ORDINARY COMMERCIAL		
SUGGESTIVE COMMERCIAL		

You remember that the worked example produced a significant interaction, in that men liked the suggestive commercial but women did not. There are several other kind of interactive designs that we might consider. For example, suppose you wondered if chronological age might be a factor in this evaluation. If you split your respondents into three age groups, your design might now look like this:

	MEN			WOMEN		
	18–25	26–45	47–70	18–25	26–45	47–70
ORDINARY COMMERCIAL						
SUGGESTIVE COMMERCIAL						

This is a "three by two by two" design, and can be analyzed exactly like the "two by two." The calculations are a little more involved and there are several interaction effects: a three-way interaction among all three factors, and three two-way interactions among each factor. As with the two-by two design, main effects are deemed important only if the larger interactions are not present.

Repeated Measures Designs. One problem with adding factors is that it makes it necessary to add respondents. If you needed fifteen respondents per cell then you would have had sixty total in your two-by-two design (15 times 4). But if you go to a two-by-two-by-three design, then your needs triple. Now you need 180 respondents! This can be an inordinate task, especially if your research assessment takes a lot of time.

One way of approaching this problem is to use the repeated measures, or within-subjects design. In this design you give the same experimental treatment to a single respondent. In the example above, you might give both the suggestive commercial and the ordinary one to the same people. Now you can test age and gender, but have cut the size of your sample by half. There are many variations on the kinds of within-subjects designs that are available, but all are predicated on the basic notion that the variance due to one individual is considerably different that the variance between individuals (Lindquist, 1956). Special statistical treatment is necessary (Bruning & Kintz, 1977), but is easily accomplished with typical mainframe computer programs.

Special Problems in Experimental Design. Fixed effects model (Type I SS) applies to the group that is studied ONLY. The experimental "treatments" are FIXED, and not random (Hays, 1973, p. 458). Most of the time the analyses of variance are calculated using the fixed effects model. All the calculations in chapter 10 make this assumption. Hays (p. 524) uses the example of different experimenters as an example of random effects. In addition, we could have "mixed" effects where the fixed effects and random effects are mixed. These effects are calculated differently from the fixed effects models. If a researcher is using SAS, then type II and type III effects are automatically calculated, and can be used.

In communication research, Jackson and Jacobs (1983) have pointed out that the typical communication experiment is an example of random effects. They note that the use of designs involving messages (for example, different contents in persuasive messages). They cite instances where researchers vary aspects of messages, such as "intensity" by varying a single word or phrase ("this belief is mistaken" vs. "this belief is idiotic"). They point out that to be sufficiently generalizable, more than one message should be employed. Bradac (1983) points out that this is an unreasonable demand, and that most communication researchers simply do not have the resources in time and energy to do as Jackson and Jacobs suggest.

The basic issue involves whether message content should be included as a factor in research involving language. The implications of the Jackson and Jacobs arguments is that when language is a variable, it should include multiple topics, rather than a single topic. In other words, in a study that examined language intensity, not only should varying levels of intensity be studied, but several different topics should also be included in the design. Strict interpretation of the analysis of variance admits no other interpretation. However, Burgoon, Hall, and Pfau (1991) performed an analysis using multiple messages in the style advocated by Jackson and Jacobs. They found little differences due to the multiple message effect and conclude that Jackson and Jacobs' claims are unwarranted. This conclusion is based on one comparison only, however, and does not refute the basic theoretical problem posed by Jackson and Jacobs. In designing experiments one should plan on testing for random effects. Most of the time the differences will be minimal, but minimal or not, it makes little sense to ignore an important theoretical assumption which could possibly play an important part in interpretation of results.

OTHER EXPERIMENTAL DESIGNS

The previous designs have been centered on situations occurring in a "laboratory." We may think of a laboratory as a special area in a building that has test tubes, electronic apparatus, and Bunsen burners strategically located. Actually, in the social sciences, a laboratory can be any specialized setting, such as a classroom or lounge. Some television studies have taken place in a day-care center, with toys and other play-things scattered about. The key idea behind a laboratory is that the setting is *controlled,* that is, the noises, interruptions, and other distractions of everyday life are absent. Of course, the laboratory should be as conducive as possible to the purpose of the experiment, but the most important aspect involved is the control of conditions. Often in "communication research laboratories" there will be audio and video recording equipment, together with one-way glass for observation.

Non-Statistical Comparisons

One of the leading scholars in behavioristic psychology, Judson S. Brown, felt intuitively that certain types of replication were inherently more convincing than statistical tests. In his theory of the multiplicative nature of drive (motivation), Brown performed several replications of the crucial experiment on a number of animals. They all conformed to a curved-line model hypothesized by Brown (1960). This kind of reasoning is fairly common in the physical sciences, especially astronomy. An exact replication may be even more convincing than a statistical aggregation.

Field Studies

Another interesting way of designing experiments occurs in more naturalistic settings, often called "field" experiments. An advertising campaign might well select two markets that are similar in size and demographic characteristics and sponsor a series of commercials in one city and not the other. Buffalo, New York and Wilkes-Barre-Scranton in Pennsylvania might be two such matches. This kind of experiment is never perfect, in that people travel and communicate with one another. Nonetheless, this "test-market" technique is quite common and produces useful data.

Surveys as Field Experiments. Feinburg and Tanur (1990) have proposed an approach to survey research that combines survey methods and experimental methods. Suppose you feel that the way a question is being asked is going to influence the response you get. If you review the nature of questionnaires in chapter 7, you will recall many instances in which the nature of the question had an influence on the responses. In addition, we might also think that the workers in the survey (the people that actually make the calls and take down the answers) might have an influence in the way the results were tabled.

So suppose that it's the year 2000 and Jack Kemp and Al Gore are running for President. You have two items for your political poll. Item one goes like this:

> **Given the unprecedented success of the Clinton-Gore team in stimulating the economy while protecting the environment, for whom do you plan to vote for president?**

Or

> **Given the disgraceful scandals in the White House in fundraising and other immoral acts in the last four years, for whom do you plan to vote for president?**

Then you could assess your poll workers and see who planned to vote Republican, who planned to vote Democratic, and have a design for your poll that looked like this:

	Pro-Republican Question	Pro-Democratic Question
Republican Poll Worker		
Democratic Poll Worker		

The truth is that most commercial (and academic) survey researchers like to pretend that their questions and their workers are totally unbiased. There is a simple reason for this—they are in the business to make money, and casting doubts on their accuracy is a good way to go out of business. However, common sense tells us that no researcher is totally unbiased, and no question is totally objective. It would seem to make good sense to control for this bias in the design of a survey, rather than pretend a perfection that is clearly not attainable.

Field Research in Interpersonal Communications. Charles

Berger (1995) and his associates have hit on an interesting way of conducting research in natural settings that still retains much of the flavor of experimental research. These researchers were interested in the complexity of plans inherent in interpersonal communication, and tested some of their hypotheses by going to a local mall and asking strangers directions. They chose locations that were easy or hard to get to. Unknown to the respondent, one of the researchers (usually behind the respondent) timed response latency. The researchers felt that difficult destinations would produce greater response latency, and in this expectation, they were proved correct.

Difficulties with this kind of study are legion. No idea of exact demographics or pre-test knowledge or ability is available, and the location of the sample can be crucial. Nonetheless, this is a promising avenue of research, and one that deserves more attention.

EVALUATING EXPERIMENTAL RESEARCH

The only real justification of all the time and trouble for an experimental study is to impose the control necessary to arrive at a defensible position concerning cause and effect. There are many aspects of an experiment that an evaluator needs to be concerned with. Whether the situation in the experiment is sufficiently like that in the "real" world is the first major concern. Experimenters create the situation in a "laboratory" rather than waiting to observe it when it occurred naturally. They should always subject their stimuli to independent, objective evaluation to see if they indeed reflect the characteristic in question. Usually researchers call this a "manipulation check." Evaluators should then ask if the experimenters compared the factors in an orderly, controlled fashion.

Another important consideration asks if the experiment can be *replicated* in the "real" world. We mentioned above that an experiment in which individuals are subject to extreme sensory deprivation (being placed in a tank of warm water, blindfolded and with cotton in one's ears) may never occur. On the other hand, experiments that make a respondent fearful or nervous have a much better chance of being replicated in the real world. We will look later at the ethical aspects of experiments in communication in chapter 15.

Chapter Fourteen

Areas of Research in Communication

To this point in the book, we have examined the nature of theory and data and have compared various statistical procedures. You should now be familiar with z scores, t tests, the analysis of variance, regression and correlation, and the chi-square test. In each of the chapters discussing those topics, we have used specific examples to show the application of various tests. In this chapter, we will examine some of the various areas in which communication research occurs: interpersonal, small groups, organizational, intercultural, and communication education. You may already be familiar with these areas of research from previous communication courses.

The five areas covered are by no means an exhaustive list of important areas for communication study. Some other vital areas are persuasion, cognition, nonverbal signals, language, and political communication. This chapter contains just a sample of the field of research. If we attempted a discussion of all the important communication areas, the book would be many times larger. The five groups included are probably central to most communication study and serve as a good foundation to more advanced study. Keep in mind that no specific area of research demands any particular procedure.

INTERPERSONAL COMMUNICATION

The first and most obvious aspect of interpersonal communication is that it is direct, or face-to-face. But just being in the same room and being able to see one another doesn't produce interpersonal communication. It is important to emphasize that the communication should be intentional, personal, and direct. The important aspect of interpersonal communication is that it is dyadic—between two persons only.

Coding Couples' Interactions

Some researchers have developed detailed, at times elaborate, coding schemes when trying to categorize the verbal behavior of interactants. A good example is the coding system used by Burggraf and Sillars (1987) to classify couples' discussions that had been previously videotaped. Here is the way they classified various interactions in these videotapes.

I. *Avoidance Acts*. Acts which minimize explicit discussion of conflict.

    1. *Simple denial*. Unelaborated statements which deny that a conflict is present.

    2. *Extended denial*. Denial statements which elaborate on the basis of the denial.

    3. *Ambivalence*. Shifting or contradictory statements which elaborate on the basis of the denial.

    4. *Topic shifting*. Statements that terminate discussion of a conflict issue before the discussion has reached a natural culmination.

    5. *Topic avoidance*. Statements that terminate discussion of a conflict before an opinion has been expressed.

    6. *Nonresponsiveness*. Failure to acknowledge or deny the presence of a conflict following a statement or inquiry about the conflict by the partner.

    7. *Semantic focus*. Statements about the meaning of words or the appropriateness of labels that supplant discussion of conflict.

    8. *Process focus*. Procedural statements that supplant discussion of conflict.

    9. *Pessimism*. Pessimistic statements about conflict which minimize the discussion of conflict issues.

    10. *Abstractness*. Abstract principles, generalizations, and hypothetical statements that supplant discussion of concrete individuals and events related to conflict.

    11. *Joking*. Nonhostile joking that supplants the serious discussion of conflict.

II. *Confrontative Acts*. Verbally competitive and individualistic acts.

    12. *Faulting*. Statements that directly criticize the personal characteristics of the partner.

    13. *Rejection*. Statements in response to the partner's previous statement that indicate personal antagonism toward the partner as well as disagreement.

    14. *Prescription*. Demands, arguments, threats and other prescriptive statements which attempt to resolve conflict by getting the partner to change.

15. *Hostile questions.* Directive or leading questions which fault the partner.

16. *Hostile jokes.* Joking or teasing that faults the partner.

17. *Presumptive attribution.* Statements that attribute thoughts, feelings, intentions, or motivations to the partner that the partner does not acknowledge.

18. *Avoiding responsibility.* Statements that minimize or deny personal responsibility for conflict.

III. *Analytic Acts.* Nonevaluative giving and seeking of information about conflicts.

19. *Description.* Nonevaluative statements about observable events related to conflict.

20. *Disclosure.* Nonevaluative statements about events related to conflict which the partner cannot observe, such as thought, feelings, intentions, motivations and past history.

21. *Qualification.* Statements that explicitly qualify the nature and extent of conflict which the partner cannot observe, such as thoughts, feelings, intentions, motivations and past history.

22. *Soliciting disclosure.* Soliciting information from the partner about events related to conflict which one cannot observe.

23. *Negative inquiry.* Soliciting complaints about oneself.

24. *Problem-solving.* Statements that initiate mutual considerations of solutions to conflicts.

IV. *Conciliatory Acts.* Statements that accept responsibility for conflicts, emphasize shared goals or compatibilities and express positive evaluations of the partner despite occasional conflicts.

25. *Support.* Statements that express understanding, acceptance, or positive regard for the partner (despite acknow-ledgment of a conflict).

26. *Emphasizing commonalities.* Statements which comment on shared interests, goals, or compatibilities with the partner (despite acknowledgment of a conflict).

27. *Accepting responsibility.* Statements that attribute responsibility for conflicts to self or both parties. (Burggraf & Sillars, 1987, p. 283)

It is a clear strength of this study that their coding scheme is spelled out in such detail. You can see that this kind of research study involved a great deal of effort in the coding phase. The researchers watched videotapes of interactions and noted how often a particular communicative act took place. They took careful notes of how often and in what circumstances these differing events occurred. They could then compare the individual interactions.

Using Questionnaires to Classify Relationships

Probably the most dominant method in studying relationships is using questionnaires to elicit revealing responses. To explore this method more fully, we will examine the work of Mary Anne Fitzpatrick, who was the first to identify some of the most important aspects of relational life. You may remember her definitions of couple types and basic coding schemes presented in chapter 7.

According to Fitzpatrick, there are three basic dimensions of relational life that determine the nature of any particular couple. The first dimension is *autonomy/interdependence*. People need to be together, but at other times need to be apart. Fitzpatrick examined the amount of sharing and companionship in the marriage as well as how the couple organizes time and space. An *interdependent* couple has a high level of companionship, spends time together, and organizes their time to enhance interaction.

The second part of Fitzpatrick's dimensions is *ideology*. Each of us has beliefs, standards, and values about our relationships. Values concerning relationships can range from those stressing the importance of stability and predictability to those emphasizing the importance of change and uncertainty. We may not always think of ideas about relationships as ideology, but Fitzpatrick has characterized them this way, and it has been a very successful approach.

The third dimension is *communication*. Each of us tends to have different ideas about communication and tends to approach or avoid communicative activity in different ways. Just as individuals differ, couples also differ as to the degree they are willing to talk and be open in their relationship. This also is related to the way that couples vary as to their willingness to engage in conflict and their level of assertiveness with one another.

These dimensions are assessed by self report. For example, if someone agreed with the statement, "My spouse/mate has taken vacations without me (even if only for a day or two)," this would indicate separateness, as does "We go to bed at different times." Agreement with the statement, "We eat our meals (the ones at home) at the same time every day" indicates a traditional relationship. The statement, "We express anger at one another," indicates communication.

Fitzpatrick then looked at the ways these dimensions appeared in different couples and concluded that there were at least three basic types: *traditionals, independents,* and *separates.* To get an idea of how these types are constituted, let us look at some of Fitzpatrick's data.

Table 14.1 summarizes the results from five different samples totaling 1672 individuals responding to her questions. Here is how Fitzpatrick describes the different groups:

> Traditionals hold conventional ideological values in relationships, favor a high degree of interdependence between marital partners, and report that they are expressive with their mates. Independents hold fairly nonconventional values about relational and family life, favor interdependence in a relationship yet push for autonomy, and report that they are extremely expressive with their mates. Separates vacillate between having conventional and nonconventional ideologies of family life, are not companionate with their mates, and report a lack of expressivity in their relationships (Fitzpatrick, 1983, p. 56).

Table 14.1
Means on Questionnaire Items Across Five Samples (N=1672)

	Traditional	Independent	Separate
Ideological Views			
Ideology of traditionalism	4.97	3.93	4.88
Ideology of uncertainty	3.52	4.35	4.19
Autonomy/Independence			
Sharing	5.01	4.73	4.07
Autonomy	3.20	4.39	4.40
Undifferentiated space	4.44	4.41	3.88
Temporal regularity	4.71	3.23	4.41
Communication			
Conflict avoidance	3.94	3.60	4.54
Assertiveness	2.80	3.54	3.27

Fitzpatrick, M. A. (1983). Predicting couples' communication from couples' self-reports.

But the typology is not that simple. There are also "Mixed" couple types, in which the husband and wife describe their relationship differently. The major Mixed type uncovered in previous research is the *Separate/Traditional*, in which the husband defines the marriage as separate while his wife defines the same relationship as traditional. Fitzpatrick found this couple type so prevalent that she often found it necessary to examine them independently of the others.

Fitzpatrick refuses to generalize to the population at large from her data samples, as they were not all random samples of couples. However, she did examine some demographic indicators from the one major random sample generated to see if the couple types describe marriages at different points in the family life cycle rather than couple types permanently. The evidence was inconclusive (Fitzpatrick & Indvik, 1982).

Compliance-Gaining

One of the most common occurrences in interpersonal communication is that situation in which one participant wishes the other to do something, go somewhere, or think about something. Compliance is asked for, as most researchers put it. In organizational settings, persons in charge simply tell subordinates what to do, but in most of our relationships the same kind of authority is not present. For example, a friend of yours might say, "Could you do something for me? Next time I come to see you, would you keep your dog in another room? He slobbers all over me and I hate it." This is a clear example of compliance-gaining.

Miller, et al. (1977), in their examination of compliance-gaining techniques, asked individuals to imagine themselves in hypothetical situations in which compliance from another person would be desired. The experimenters presented these persons with Marwell and Schmitt's options (see table 4.4) and asked them to choose which technique they would use. The hypothetical relationships were varied: Some were interpersonal in nature and others were noninterpersonal, some were short-term relationships and others were long-term. For example, the noninterpersonal, long-term-consequence situation was described like this:

> You have been living six months in a house that you purchased. You learn that your next-door neighbors (the Smiths, persons with whom you have had only limited contact since moving in) plan to cut down a large shade tree that stands near your property in order to construct their new two-car garage. However, in the long run, loss of the shade tree will adversely affect the beauty of your home, your comfort, and, perhaps, the value of your home. How likely would you be to employ each of the following strategies in order to get the Smiths to leave the tree standing? (Miller et al., 1977)

Then each person was asked to mark each of the 16 choices in terms of the probability of choice. These researcher's results are expressed in table 14.2. You will see that in the interpersonal situation, the short-term strategy choices were altruism, altercasting, and liking.

But in the noninterpersonal situation, these same choices were threat, promise, liking, and expertise. Miller and his colleagues conclude that source traits, message choices, situational effects, and their

Table 14.2
Strategies Likely and Unlikely to be Used in Each of the Four Situations

INTERPERSONAL

	SHORT TERM	LONG TERM
Likely strategies	Altruism (M*=5.95 Altercasting+(M=5.81) Liking (M=5.29)	Threat (M=5.88) Altercasting+(M=5.82) Altruism (M=5.59) Liking (M=5.45) Promise (M=5.28)
Unlikely strategies	Moral appeal (M=2.42) Aversive Stimulation (M=2.42) Esteem–(M=2.45) Threat (M=2.51) Pre-giving (M=2.85)	Esteem–(M=2.17) Self-feeling–(M=2.25) Aversive Stimulation (M=2.51) Debt (M=2.74 Esteem+(M=2.94)

NONINTERPERSONAL

	SHORT TERM	LONG TERM
Likely strategies	Threat (M=5.83 Promise (M=5.79) Liking (M=5.62) Expertise+(M=5.36)	Expertise+(M=6.15) Expertise–(M=5.86) Altruism (M=5.52) Promise (M=5.23) Liking (M=5.21) Debt (M=5.17) Altercasting+(M=5.08)
Unlikely	Moral appeal (M=2.98)	Aversive Stimulation (M=2.28)

Source: Miller, G. R., Boster, F., Roloff, M. & Siebold, D. (1977). Compliance-gaining message strategies: A typology and some findings concerning effects of situational differences.

interactions are better predictors of the correct strategy choice than traditional reliance on source-oriented or message-oriented factors (1977, p. 51).

SMALL GROUP COMMUNICATION

Groups play an enormous part in our daily lives. In our jobs, in our families, and in our social life, we are closely identified with specific groups of others. Most decisions that we make—personal and organizational—occur in small groups. Large organizations, where most of us work, are probably best thought of as groups of groups. The fact that groups are everywhere means that we need to understand them and how communication works in group life. This underscores how important research in small groups can be. Frey (1994) has stated that the small group is *the* most important social organization.

Conformity in Small Groups

Let's look at an example of an artificially created group that formed the basis for one of the most important group experiments. Asch (1956) was interested in conformity and wanted to know what would happen when one person was a member of a group in which all the others expressed a clearly wrong opinion. The dramatic nature of the study has made it one of the most important ones in demonstrating this phenomenon systematically. In Asch's experiment, individuals arrived at a workroom and were told that they would be part of a study examining perception. Other individuals were already in the workroom. First the group was shown two cards, similar to the ones illustrated in figure 14.1.

Figure 14.1

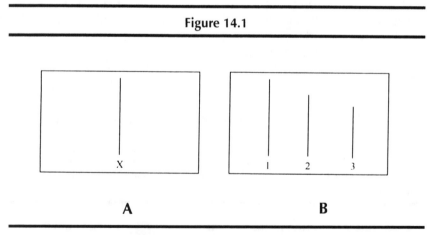

Then they were asked to identify which line on card B most closely resembled the line on card A. It is obvious that 1 is the correct answer. But the naive person (the late-arriving one) heard other members of the group respond 3, 3, 3, and so forth, all around the group. Unknown to this person, all the other participants were paid confederates of Asch and the psychology department. They pretended they saw 3 as the correct answer. Imagine how you would feel—you came to participate in an experiment and everyone present expressed answers that were totally wrong. What would you do?

Over thirty percent of Asch's subjects went along with what they saw as the majority. [Some circumstances mitigated this effect—when the naive person had a "partner" who gave correct answers, the conformity effect disappeared. This also was the case when the "partner" began giving correct answers late in the experiment, after a number of conforming responses.] Asch also studied varying sizes of groups and found that a majority of three was enough to produce this conforming response.

Asch asked those who went along with the false majority why they did it and classified the answers into three types: distortion of perception, distortion of judgment, and distortion of response. In the first group, people said they actually saw the lines as being in the wrong category. The second group said they saw the lines correctly but felt that they were probably wrong, since everyone else was unanimous. The last group said that they knew they were providing the wrong answer but just didn't want to make a fuss.

Asch's demonstration of conformity took place using a very obvious stimulus—the lines involved were unmistakably different, and the membership in the groups was not all that important to the participants. Deutsch and Gerard (1955) replicated Asch's data with more ambiguous stimuli and saw that the conformity effect was very much enhanced. They also concluded that when there was some pressure for normative effects (that is, when the group identity was more important) the effect was enhanced. The success of Asch's technique has inspired many group researchers to emulate this procedure of creating an artificial situation unknown to one or more of the group members and to observe the results.

Attitude Similarity in Small Groups

One good demonstration of attitude similarity within mock juries occurs in a study conducted by Brandstatter and his colleagues (1978). They researched the general effects of bias on the nature of decisions rendered in six-person mock juries. They believed that initial bias would affect the outcome of a jury's deliberation as well as the kind of verdicts rendered. In this study, 708 persons were given a questionnaire to measure possible bias toward the prosecution or the defense in a rape trial. It contained statements like "Next to murder, rape is the most serious crime imaginable" and "Rapists should receive severe prison sentences." Participants rated their response to the statements on a Likert scale. On the basis of the responses to the questionnaire the experimenters divided the jurors into three groups: Pro-Prosecution, (34%); Moderate, (33%); and Pro-Defense, (33%). All of these persons watched a videotaped trial, and then indicated their preference for the guilt or innocence of the defendant. After watching the trial, 63 percent indicated that they thought the defendant guilty, while 37 percent thought the defendant innocent. The initial attitude had only a slight effect on the judgments of innocent or guilty. Then these persons were divided into 128 six-person juries and were allowed to deliberate. In spite of the overwhelming number of guilty predispositions, only 49 of these groups (41.1%) were able to reach a verdict of guilty in the allotted time. Of all the mock juries, 41 groups (35.9%) voted not guilty, and 28 of the groups were unable to reach a decision. Based on a chi-square test, Davis and his coauthors claim that initial bias had significantly affected the number of guilty verdicts. Their data are illustrated in table 14-3. But these data do not actually represent a statistically significant difference when a contingency table chi-square was used to compare the effects of deliberation (Bostrom, 1983).

Table 14.3   Majority Size, Initial Bias, and Results of Jury Deliberations

Majority Size	Prosecution			Moderate			Pro-defense		
	G	H	NG	G	H	NG	G	H	NG
5–1	7	0	2	7	2	1	0	0	0
4–2	6	5	1	5	3	3	4	5	5
3–3	0	2	6	1	4	4	1	5	1
2–4	0	2	2	0	0	3	0	0	5

More careful analysis shows that the Asch effect certainly doesn't seem to operate in a jury situation. Apparently the bias toward or against prosecution is an important one, but not as important as proponents of the Asch effect would predict. In table 14.4 the different majorities are presented. You can see that each of the biases—pro-prosecution, moderate, and pro-defense—show different bias effects.

These judgments and the nature of the group composition have not been studied as much as we would like. The effect of the not-guilty minority seems out of proportion to its size. These and other questions are beginning to be studied by communication researchers.

Table 14.4	Verdicts and Initial Opinions about the Prosecution		
	Guilty Verdict	Hung Jury	Not Guilty Verdict
Pro-prosecution	20	9	11
Moderate	16	9	12
Pro-defense	11	10	18

ORGANIZATIONAL COMMUNICATION

Communicative activity takes place in many specific settings; the organizational setting is one in which most adults spend one-third of their lives. By organization we usually mean a fairly large group of persons, usually brought together for the purpose of performing some activity or enterprise. Organizational communication got its start as "business communication," in that most of the organizations studied were businesses where the principal goal was to make a profit or to create a product. However, non-profit groups such as hospitals or government agencies are also now included in organizational communication research since they share many of the characteristics of the profit-making groups.

Systems Theory in Practice

One outstanding characteristic of organizations is that almost every element in it is interconnected. If a change is made in one part of a system, another part of the system is also affected. This is the basis of systems theory. In studying organizations, systems theory is useful in that it reminds us that nothing has a simple effect in organizational life. An example may be helpful. In one large organization, the director of organizational communication (which included the organization's mail room) decided that mail delivery could be speeded up and a good deal of money could be saved by the implementation of a delivery system he called a "speed sort." Prior to this decision, each subunit in the organization had a mail address and the central post office for the organization sorted all incoming and interoffice mail into these categories and then delivered mail daily to these subunits. Under the new system the mail office would only sort into larger unit categories, which were amalgamations of the former subunits. In other words, instead of delivering mail to engineering plans, engineering development, and engineering drawing, the mail room only delivered to engineering as a whole. The result was that mail was out of the post office faster and the post office was able to reduce the personnel in its office by a third. The communications director won an award and was given a plaque commemorating his achievement.

The way the new system actually worked, however, was that the mail came to the engineering central office and still needed to be sorted into three separate piles. While the post office had done this in the past, now staff workers in the engineering office (and every other office in the organization) had to do the work originally done by the postal workers. While that mail had originally been taken around to the departments by the postal delivery, now a staff person had to be responsible for getting the mail to subunits. When someone was busy with a project, the mail delivery was likely to suffer. Mail piled up in these subunits, because no one was clearly responsible for the sorting and delivery of the mail. Engineers found that mail which had taken only a day or two to get around the organization was now stacked up and sometimes took three or four days. Failure to look at the organization as a complete system—in which one part of the group seriously affects another part of the group—resulted in a system that was worse than the original system.

Deleterious side effects can only be avoided by persistent efforts at interorganizational communication. When these effects occur, communication is often the best remedy. Systems theory has a wide utility and is a good foundation for research in organizational communication.

Organizational Inertia

As in other qualitative studies of communication, personal accounts are of central importance in studying organizational communication. An interesting example of these personal accounts relating to organizational inertia is reported by Altheide and Johnson (1980). They interviewed officers of the U. S. S. Walden, a warship assigned to the bombardment of the Vietnamese coast during the war in Vietnam. One of these officers reported that the aerial spotters would often exaggerate the amount of damage done by a particular salvo. When asked why, the officer reported:

> It was written in the regulations that damage assessment will be given at the completion of each mission. So even if there wasn't any damage, they'd give you some, because they had to justify—eventually the ship had to justify sending 300 shells onto a beach only to come back with no damage. I mean, no damage? The area Com-

mander is going to want to know why I am spending $18,000 a shell, or whatever it is, and why are you firing 300 of these shells against no target? (p. 212)

Altheide and Johnson further report on the procedure for enforcing this kind of fraudulent report. In another interview, a gunnery officer related:

> One time, I don't remember whether we had just arrived on the gun line in a particular area or whether we'd been firing there for a couple of days, but anyway, this time we ran into a green spotter. This was his first time out, although we didn't find this out until a couple of months later. It was our first mission of the day, I think, and he came over the phone and said due to the dense foliage he couldn't give us any battle damage assessment. The Old Man asked to ask him again, to tell him that we had to have damage, but the spotter repeated the same thing again, that he couldn't give us any. Well, the Captain got on the circuit and gave a call to the spotter's Commanding Officer and said, very to the point, I thought, no damage assessment for our rounds, and we pick up our marbles and go home. He didn't say it exactly that way, of course, but that was the message. Following this, we could hear the spotter's Commanding Officer get on the same circuit and he told him to fly a little lower and see if he couldn't find a few bunkers. The spotter could hear all of this, of course, and by this time, he knew what it was all about. He found some, too. (1980, p. 212)

After a few experiences like this, it is quite reasonable to see how those who are rewarded for this counterattitudinal reporting may easily come to believe that what they are saying is true. Clearly accounts of this nature find us insight that quantitative assessment would not. After completing their studies, these researchers concluded that large organizations engage in "propagandistic" activities within themselves, as well as for external consumption. "Reality" is "constructed" to fit organizational purposes. Ordinary survey research may not always be the best method to uncover such bureaucratic propaganda.

INTERCULTURAL COMMUNICATION

Studying the ways in which culture works in communication is not easy, because we are immersed in our own culture and it is difficult for us to sense the ways in which our culture affects us. Assumptions and rules that we follow seem "natural" or "given," just like the air. Quite often the only way we notice one of our own cultural rules is when we encounter a different rule in another culture, either while travelling, studying, or by some other means. For example, many Americans, while travelling abroad, are startled by the relatively casual manner in which many European merchants make change. In the United States, if you owe $9.98 and present a $10 bill, cashiers will be meticulous about returning the two cents due. In Ireland, insisting on the two cents will mark someone as an unpleasant tourist. In Singapore, no one bothers with pennies—everything is rounded off to the nearest five cents. Given these differences between cultures, it is easy to see why intercultural communication is a noteworthy part of communication research.

As another illustration of how habitual behavior is commonly accepted as "right" behavior, try this minor experiment. The next time you are served pie for dessert, it will undoubtedly be placed on the table with the point of the pie facing you. Almost everyone takes the first bite of the pie from the point. Try turning the pie around so that the point is facing away from you, and begin eating the pie crust first. You will find, first of all, that you will be uncomfortable; even more interesting will be the reactions of your dinner companions. Some will even find it disgusting. This is a simple act, but it shows that the way the pie is "supposed to be eaten" is a strong cultural norm and its violation produces a number of interesting effects.

Now imagine how you would react if you were having a business dinner in another country and the pie was served to you "backwards,"—that is, contrary to your expectations. Intercultural research looks for just such behavioral cues and teaches us that cultural patterns affect us both consciously and subconsciously.

One interesting example of an intercultural research study was conducted by Haidt, Koller, and Dias (1993), who used a set of stories about cultural events that stimulated social judgments for individuals in three different communities: Philadelphia, Recife (Brazil) and Porto Allegre (Brazil). Porto Allegre is a city of 1.4 million persons in the far south of Brazil. Most of its citizens are of European descent, and the area is generally very well-to-do. Recife is a city of almost 4 million persons in the northeast of Brazil. Its people are of mixed African and European descent and are very poor.

To illustrate the differences in the cultures, these researchers devised stories that had significant moral content and asked respondents in each of these communities a series of questions concerning: (a) Evaluation, (b) Justification, (c) Harm, (d) Bother, (e) Interference, and (f) Universality. For Evaluation the experimenters asked "What do you think of this story? Is it wrong, only a little wrong, or is it perfectly OK?" For Justification they asked "Can you tell me why?" To assess Harm, they asked "Was anyone harmed by this behavior?" Bother was assessed by asking "Imagine that you actually saw someone performing this act. Would it bother you or would you not care?" Interference was assessed by asking "Should this person [these people] be stopped or punished in any way?" The last assessment was Universality and was assessed by asking "Suppose you learn about two different foreign countries. In country A people [do that act] very often and in country B they never [do that act]. Are both of these customs OK or is one or both of them bad, or wrong?" When respondents think something is good or bad regardless of culture, then the principle is "universalized."

The stories used were designed to illustrate behavior usually not approved of in society but that didn't create harm to anyone other than the participants. The five stories were:

Story One: The Flag

A woman is cleaning out her closet, and she finds her old American [Brazilian] flag. She doesn't want it any more, so she cuts it up into pieces and uses the rags to clean her bathroom.

Story Two: Promise

A woman was dying, and on her deathbed she asked her son to promise that he would visit her grave every week. The son loved his mother very much, so he made the promise. But after the mother died, the son didn't keep his promise, because he was very busy.

Story Three: The Dog

A family's dog was killed by a car in front of their house. They had heard that dog meat was delicious, so they cut up the dog's body and cooked it for dinner.

Story Four: Kissing

A brother and sister like to kiss each other on the mouth. When nobody is around, they find a secret hiding place and kiss each other on the mouth, passionately.

Story Five: Chicken

A man goes to the supermarket once a week and buys a dead chicken. But before cooking the chicken, he has sexual intercourse with it. Then he cooks it and eats it.

Most of the responses were similar, but the researchers were more interested in the percentages of adults who felt that the people in these stories should be "stopped, or punished." Table 14.5 presents these percentages.

Table 14.5
Percentages of Adults Who Answered "Should be Stopped or Punished"

Story	Recife		Porto Allegre		Philadelphia	
	Low SES	High SES	Low SES	High SES	Low SES	High SES
Flag	63	23	53	17	50	17
Promise	57	7	23	7	20	3
Dog	57	40	50	33	80	10
Kissing	68	53	70	50	87	57
Chicken	79	50	87	63	80	27

Source: This table is adapted from Haidt, J., Koller, S. H. & Dias, M. G. (1993). Affect, culture, and morality, or is it wrong to eat your dog? *Journal of Personality and Social Psychology*, 65 (4), 613–628.

You can see that SES (Socio-Economic Status) made a much larger difference in the findings than did the nature of the city or the type of story that was presented. In Philadelphia, for example, 50 percent of the low SES adult respondents felt that an individual who cleaned the bathroom with the flag should be punished and only 17 percent of the individuals in the high SES group thought so. In Recife, 57 percent of the low SES respondents thought the man who didn't visit his mother's grave should be punished and only 7 percent of those who were in the high SES category thought so. It is interesting to note that one's socio-economic status had a larger influence than one's culture in this study.

Table 14.6 illustrates how many of the respondents *universalized* their reactions to the stories, that is, placed their responses into a framework of moral assessments. The same differences observed in table 14.5 to seem to hold. A fair conclusion of this research is that geography is indeed important, but socio-economic differences are probably more important in intercultural communication. The flavor of this investigations also gives us an idea how quantitative study can be used to answer specific questions.

Table 14.6
Percentages of Adults who "Universalized" Their Judgments

Story	Recife		Porto Allegre		Philadelphia	
	Low SES	High SES	Low SES	High SES	Low SES	High SES
Flag	50	24	67	13	50	3
Promise	87	28	53	23	40	20
Dog	60	13	60	17	57	7
Kissing	67	20	53	33	80	17
Chicken	87	43	87	57	87	23

COMMUNICATION EDUCATION

Enhancing communication skills has long been at the center of the educational process. To this end, many educational institutions require basic courses in which students practice communicative activities. The belief that practice in reading, writing, speaking, and listening produces "improvement" in these skills is widespread. Improving classroom practices is a never-ending task, and practical demonstration of the results of such improvement is not as easy. For most, convincing demonstration of improvement would depend on credible assessment procedures, which in turn would depend on the existence of testing procedures that are reliable, valid, and practical. As a consequence, a great deal of research in communication education focuses on the assessment process. Although mechanical aspects of assessment are important, decisions about the nature of the basic processes involved and their relative importance are fundamental, and require a good deal of study.

Goals of Communication Education

Clearly communication education aims at improving the abilities of students; therefore, communication skills are at the center of the process. The definition of communication competence is an object of research emphasis. Spitzberg and Cupach (1984) have defined competence as consisting of motivation, knowledge, and skills. Communicators need to be motivated to communicate and not be inhibited by social fears. They also need to possess knowledge about how communication works, as well as general knowledge about human beings and relationships. When these two aspects of competence are added to communication skills, a wider prospect for educational research emerges.

Motivation. Communication apprehension (approach and avoidance tendencies) is a widely used measure of motivation. The users of apprehension measures assume that since most everyone is motivated to communicate, and since apprehension interferes with this motivation, then the measurement of the apprehension is the central part of the assessment. Training in communicative skills (Kelly & Keaten, 1992) generally has been shown to reduce apprehension, but what caused it in the first place? What causes one person to talk while another remains silent? The assumption that "improving" communicative interactions consists of encouraging the reticent to speak more is a pervasive one; we should similarly be as interested in helping the loquacious speak less. But to do either, we need to understand these approach-avoidance tendencies a great deal better than we do at present.

James McCroskey (1970, 1977, 1978) developed a measure that he called the "Personal Report of Communication Apprehension" (PRCA). Previous measures had relied on "public speaking anxiety," but to McCroskey apprehension was more than that. He wrote, "[t]here are good reasons to believe that it [public speaking] is not the most important context in which anxiety can interfere with communication, and may not even be the most important context" (1970. p. 270). In order to extend the study of how anxiety is related to communication, he constructed a test that consists of assessments of more broadly based communicative activities.

Communication Skills. Skills in speaking, preparation, and delivery seem to be connected to a variety of other factors. For example, Rubin and Graham (1988) examined communicative behavior and success in college. They followed a group of students for over two years and concluded that students that talked more freely (were less apprehensive) did far better in college than those who did not. They discussed their results in terms of a model of communication competence. The connection between academic success and performance in college may well be tied to a relationship between cognitive ability and talking (Allen & Bourhis, 1996). These investigators found that talkers were slightly more intelligent than nontalkers.

Assessment of public speaking skills is conducted using a coding sheet, much as is done in interpersonal research. The section on interpersonal communication research mentioned the various methods of "coding" communication behavior. Here is a typical coding scheme, together with a numerical value, for evaluating classroom speeches:

A fair (2) speech exhibits problems in one or more of these aspects:
The speech is delivered extemporaneously.
The speech conforms to the type assigned.
The speech conforms to time limits.
The speech is prepared at the assigned time.

An average (3) speech meets the following standards:
exhibits coherent organization with clear purpose and easily
identifiable main ideas;
exhibits reasonably good delivery skills; and
is acceptable grammatically and in pronunciation and
articulation;

A good (4) speech meets the standards for a "3" speech and:
demonstrates skill in selecting appropriate strategies and supporting materials;
and demonstrates skill in extemporaneous delivery and
spontaneous
interaction with the audience.

An excellent (5) speech meets all the standards for a "3" speech and a "4"
speech and at least three of the following:
deals with an unusually challenging topic;
demonstrates exceptional skill in selecting strategies and supporting materials;
achieves a variety and flexibility of mood and manner suited
to subject matter, the audience, and the speaker him/herself;
and/or demonstrates skillful mastery of internal transitions
and of emphasis in the preparation of the speaker's ideas.

When using a coding sheet like the above, researchers need to train raters to evaluate consistently. Usually two or three raters are used, and reliability is calculated using Cronbach's *alpha*.

Knowledge. Usually research in communication competence defines "knowledge" as a body of information that helps us plan communication attempts and also enables us to evaluate communication success. The segment on "speech criticism" typically included in basic public speaking courses allows instructors to evaluate the knowledge students have acquired about the process of public communication. Research in this area would entail the measurement of knowledge attained in a course and its relationship, if any, to other factors, such as delivery or audience analysis.

Listening

We are concerned about deficiencies in listening ability because we feel that this deficiency may hamper academic performance or the quality of a relationship. Training in listening is different from training in speaking, in that listening is seldom directly observed. Clearly the first task in testing is to decide what we think good listening should be. Early assessment of listening depended on the lecture model. The operational definition of listening ability, therefore, was the ability to remember the content of a short piece of prose delivered orally.

Of course, memory for factual content is not the only way to define listening, and many researchers pointed out that a good listener could detect affective cues about the speaker's state of mind, rather than the content of the message. It was typical to call this "interpersonal" listening—looking for affective rather than factual content. Of course, the speaker's affective state is importantly influenced by the relationships with the interactant. An early test of this type was the Jones-Mohr Listening test (Watson and Barker, 1984). In this test, speakers used vocal intonations to indicate various affect states, and respondents were asked to identify the states. Little interest was shown in using the Jones-Mohr procedure, and the lack of a theoretical basis for its construction contributed to the lack of interest in this test.

Later tests followed the development of new cognitive models, specifically inspired by research in memory. These models are the basis of today's testing of listening. Research in memory demonstrates that memory has different components. Most of us think that we simply remember something or we do not. Actually memory varies widely. Sometimes we remember information presented to us for a brief time and then forget it. Cognitive researchers have called this short-term memory. Memory that persists is usually called long-term, and various researchers have posited a number of intermediate processes. Memory for words is different from memory for images and events.

Since listening seems to make use of memory in a fundamental way, a productive approach to measuring listening might be based on models of memory. The use of memory as a model led to the hypothesis that verbal decoding can be divided into several components: short-term listening, short-term with rehearsal, and lecture listening (Bostrom and Waldhart, 1980; 1988; Bostrom, 1990). This approach led to the development of the Kentucky Comprehensive Listening Test (KCLT). In one section of this test, responses were elicited immediately after information was presented. In a second section a response was elicited after a significant pause occurred—rehearsal listening. The KCLT also contained a traditional lecture test and a test of affect detection. Research showed that short-term listening seemed to have little relationship to cognitive abilities, such as intelligence tests.

Good short-term listeners apparently performed better in oral situations (Bostrom and Waldhart, 1980). This finding has been replicated in a number of different settings. In a study of managerial effectiveness, short-term listening skill was demonstrated to be the best discriminator between good and poor branch managers in banks (Alexander, Penley, and Jernigan, 1992). In another setting, short-term listening was the best single predictor of upward mobility in an organization (Sypher, Bostrom, and Seibert, 1989). Other communicative abilities were important, but this measure of listening was the strongest predictor. In an interview study, Bussey (1991) found that those with good short-term skills asked more questions of their interviewees than did those with poor short-term skills. Comparisons of other listening phenomena, such as accelerated speech (King and Behnke, 1989) provide strong evidence for the claim that short-term listening is qualitatively different from long term, and investigation of short-term listening in interpersonal settings indicates that it is importantly related to other interpersonal abilities.

Though the KCLT does have an interpretive component, many researchers felt that affective messages were more important than it seemed to indicate. The Watson-Barker Listening Test (WBLT) contained more interpretive material. Developed in 1983, the WBLT has a greater emphasis on interpersonal relationships than does the KCLT, and further includes "instruction-following" (Watson and Barker, 1983). This test does include short-term retention as a separate scale but does not have the emphasis on short-term with rehearsal that appears in the KCLT. A video version is available, and this test is particularly suited to listening training in applied situations.

Note

[1]   For an example, consider one of the major television stations in a city like St. Louis—at times the audience can reach over 100,000. The network news broadcasts have audiences in the millions, and special events like the "Superbowl" in professional football reach close to 100 million persons.

Chapter Fifteen

Research and Ethical Concerns

Ethics is the study of right and wrong—of good and bad. We may not have been aware of them, but questions of morality—ethical questions—have appeared throughout this book, and we have looked at the dilemmas created in exploring human interaction. Ethical issues are a fundamental part of communication research, even though we may not be accustomed to thinking of them in this way. How do ethical issues relate to research?

You may remember "Dolly," the sheep that was cloned in Scotland in 1996. Selective breeding of animals for useful characteristics, such as better wool, tastier meat, and greater strength and speed has been a central activity of farming since the dawn of time. But no matter how carefully farmers selected animals for breeding, the process always included a chance that genetic characteristics of the father and mother would combine in unacceptable ways. Cloning—the ability to generate genetic material that is *exactly* the same as the parent animal—reduces this chance. So animal breeders—especially the owners of champion race horses—liked the idea!

But if animals can be cloned, could human beings also be cloned? More importantly, *should* they? Would you like your child to be exactly like you? Would the possibility exist that we could breed children that were not nearsighted, have inherited resistance to disease, and look like Tom Cruise? You can see that research in cloning human beings involves more than just the mechanics of producing the appropriate DNA in an embryo. Important issues involved are the nature of parenting, the basic idea of what a human being is (or should be) and who is capable of making these choices. These are all *ethical* questions. The absence of any strong ethical system to make judgments about cloning led President Clinton to ban all federally supported research concerning cloning human beings. The difficulty that we have in coping with the cloning problem shows how important ethical issues are to research.

Communication research is a form of social science that has special ethical concerns. The fundamental nature of communication implies a basic ethical judgment that most of us take for granted. Without an ethical foundation, communication makes no sense. This ethical foundation stems from a judgment of the value of the *other person*. It implies a fundamentally cooperative attitude as a basic prerequisite for the communicative act. Business, government, and the arts all depend on this basic orientation. Being other-oriented is the foundation of ethics.

Any research involves ethical judgments, but the basic nature of communication means that ethics is especially important to us. In this chapter we will explore some of the ethical issues that arise when we do communication research, and look at the basic nature of these judgments. Then we will explore some of the basic steps all researchers must take to make sure they are proceeding ethically.

SOURCES OF ETHICAL IDEAS

Phillip Lieberman, a prominent linguist, examined both evolutionary and neurological elements in his book *Fundamentally Human: Evolution of Speech, Language, and Selfless Behavior* (1991). Lieberman contends that the evolution of speech and communication itself is tied into "selfless" motives. He believes, in other words, that the evolution of humanity, together with the structure of our nervous system, provides evidence that most of us are "other-oriented"; and in the communication instance, are "receiver-oriented."

When this principle is expressed so simply, we may immediately think of the exceptions—the liars, the crooks, and all those who take advantage of others. You may even have memories of a salesperson who advertises a new car "at cost," but when writing up the deal figures in his or her commission, the rental on the building, the interest on the loan, and some fancy extras as part of the "cost." But the only reason these people are able to do what they do is that the rest of us assume that they are honest. In other words, the presence of the universal ethical assumption (which most of us possess) is the reason the crooks are able to succeed.

ETHICS AND COMMUNICATION RESEARCH

Some procedures in research carry ethical implications that are obvious. In chapter 13 we discussed an important aspect of experimental research—the "control group" that would make causal reasoning more convincing. But the notion of certain kinds of control can be inherently objectionable. One of the most horrifying examples of the attempt to get a control group (however possible) arose when a group of researchers chose to deny treatment for syphilis to a group of men in Alabama. However well intentioned, we can see that this kind of "control" is simply not ethical.

Striving for objectivity is itself an ethical concern. Denying (or downplaying) personal interests to benefit others implies a strong ethical motive. Here is how one researcher put it:

> When we speak of objectivity in science, we do not mean that scientists are completely free from bias; rather we mean that good research utilizes experimental and data analysis procedures and standards that prevent biases from influencing the outcome of tests. Ideally, any personal beliefs the researchers have about the eventual outcome of the experiments should play no role in the outcome. Researchers with totally opposite preconceptions should arrive at the same results upon following the same procedures. (Mussachia, 1995. p. 34)

To look more specifically at ethical issues in research, let us look again at chapter 13. In that chapter, we examined a communication experiment where the relative importance of verbal and nonverbal signals were studied (Motley, 1993). The researcher found it necessary to engage in several activities that we might consider unethical. First he deceived his respondents by telling them that they were to participate in an exercise where a polygraph was to be adjusted. Actually the individuals were being studied to see how their facial expression affected the content of a conversation. Motley's confederates further deceived the respondents by giving them messages which weren't true, but which were designed to create reactions of surprise, anger, and the like. Whether this deception represents a serious ethical concern or not is an important problem. Most communication researchers believe that the information produced by Motley's experiment had great value; greater by far than any minor harm that might have been done by the deceptions that were used. But how can we justify such a position?

Each of us must justify our own ethical ideas against some larger framework of ethics; some sense of right and wrong. Let's look at some of the ethical characteristics to which most of us adhere.

FORMULATING ETHICAL POSITIONS

One of the difficulties we have in dealing with ethics is that most of us don't have a well-developed vocabulary of ethical statements that form a starting point for describing our own feelings. It might worthwhile to review a highly regarded ethical theorist for fundamental ethical statements. One of these is the modern ethical philosopher Harry Girvetz (1973). He has assembled what he thinks are the fundamental assumptions that must be made before any dialogue in ethics (valuation) is possible. These assumptions are:

(1) that we ought to act one way or the other;

(2) that we make these choices as free agents;

(3) we ought to act with concern for others even to the point of acting contrary to our own interest

(4) we ought to act with respect for law;

(5) that some things can be judged as good or bad based on a justificatory system of some kind;

(6) that descriptive and prescriptive judgments are distinguishable; and

(7) that moral suasion is possible.

Girvetz' assumptions could well be the assumptions subsumed by most communication research. Girvetz' method is to follow the logical implications of these assumptions, arriving at defensible bases for value systems. The value system of communication would differ from the value system of other disciplines in that part of the subsuming structure is different. Girvetz' method is challenging and more broadly applicable than we might first think.

Ethics and Empiricism

Empirical researchers tend to neglect ethics, possibly because of their uncritical commitment to the "scientific method." What usually accompanies a commitment to science is the assumption that scientific statements are amoral and the scientific enterprise is without an ethical dimension. Few ideas seem to be more deeply embedded in Western philosophy than the distinction between statements of valuation and statements of scientific principle. This assumption has probably been strengthened by the practice of studying individuals' valuations as objects. Ethical statements have been analyzed as statements of "attitude," "opinion," "schema," "constructs" and the like. This process of treating values as an object of study has had the effect of distancing the researcher from the process studied. In Milton Rokeach's system, for example, varying beliefs are placed into a layered system, in which the central, or "primitive," beliefs are those which are held with great tenacity and are considered to be universal by the believer (1960, pp. 40–42).

While Rokeach could have classified these central beliefs as "values," he chose not to. He explained them by invoking cultural, demographic, or specific personality characteristics.

In short, the uncritical acceptance of a "scientific" worldview by those of us who consider communication as a branch of social science may have prematurely foreclosed serious inquiry into ethical questions. Empiricists would appear to be value-free. But are they really?

Careful analysis of empirical research in communication reveals a well-developed ethical system. Even if we used what Girvetz referred to as "abortive" escapes from ethical skepticism—intuitionism, prescriptivism, and instrumentalism. Even if we use these escapes, we can still find ethics expressed in the work of social science. Let's look at an example from a well known line of communication research—verbal aggression.

Infante and Wigley (1986) have carefully analyzed the nature of verbal aggressiveness. Those scoring high on this scale seem to have a persistent personality trait that leads to attacking others' self-concepts and not their ideas. At no point in the research report do Infante and Wigley baldly state, "these are evil persons." But at the end of the report, the authors do tell us that verbal and physical aggressions should be "treated" (1986, p. 67). Most of us would agree that one should only attack ideas and not persons. This type of ethical assertion underlies a good deal of our research on face issues, on relationships, and on bargaining.

The underlying ethic in social science is sometimes well hidden. It has been typical to characterize specific value systems by the name we attach to them. One spectacular instance of this was the common use of the "F-scale" in the 1950s which purportedly measured "fascistic" personalities. More subtle instances of the same process can be found in our characterization of multi-valued ethical systems as "open" rather than "closed," "complex" rather than "simple," and other pejorative namings.

One major theme running through the analysis of communication theory was that methodology and content cannot be separated. It may be possible that is true for the bulk of social science as well. Carl Hempel (1965, p.86) offers an instructive analysis of the interaction of science and values. He notes that since all "findings" in science are probabalistic in nature, the level of acceptance or rejection of hypotheses are a vital part of the structure of scientific thought. He goes on to show that the levels of acceptance vary with the valuational outcomes implied in a particular research project. That is, we care more about outcomes that reflect strongly held ethical systems. The practice of science, Hempel demonstrates, can no more be separated from value systems than can scientists themselves.

For example, the editor of a journal might well accept and publish data that account for 20 percent of the variance in a given set of observations. A judge, however, when deciding whether to send someone to the penitentiary would demand a more stringent prediction. The terms "Type I" and "Type II" error are familiar ones, and the only way that researchers can analyze these two types of risk is through valuational statements.

Hardly any scientific question is exempt from the process. Astronomy and paleontology might seem to qualify as "pure" knowledge, but the theological disputation that has resulted from these two disciplines seems to indicate that even Halley's comet and the demise of the dinosaurs have valuational implications. We must admit to ourselves that distinguishing between ethics and science is one of the stories that empiricists tell themselves—one of the root myths of social science. It is a useful myth: most of us believe in it. But belief does not make it any less than a myth!

Ethics and Qualitative Research

One of the principal goals of qualitative study is to approach the problem without preconceived notions and allow the respondents to furnish data in depth and at length. However, this doesn't mean that the data gathering is totally without ethical dilemmas. When a qualitative researcher finds it useful to actually participate in the particular setting in order to gain insight about the communicative interactions that they study, they face the same problem of informed consent and honesty that quantitative researchers do.

In addition, qualitative researchers often study themes that have strong ethical overtones. A good example is found in Mary-Jeannette Smythe's in-depth study of themes in women's stories conducted at a fitness center, called "Bodyworks." Smythe (1995) participated as a member of the fitness club, and conducted both free and "guided" conversations. She kept copious field notes. Here are some of the responses that she recorded:

Respondent A:

I think my saddest day was two days after we brought Chas [her infant son] home from the hospital. I was getting ready to take some laundry downstairs and saw my reflection in the hall mirror. At first I thought I had picked up more clothes than I realized because I looked so damn huge. I just stood there and gaped at myself. When I realized all I was carrying was three shirts and some underwear, I bawled my eyes out. But right then I started thinking about how I was gonna figure out how to get back into shape and that meant coming to class on a regular basis. See, I was nursing, and I knew that I couldn't strictly diet or starve myself, so conditioning and fat-burning were the only hope for salvation. Right then I knew what I was going to have to do.

Respondent B:

Part of my motivation for sticking with an exercise regime is grounded in simple vanity. The name of the game is "beat the clock." Activity doesn't halt the aging process, but it can actually slow the onset of certain unmistakable and unattractive aspects, so I'm planning to keep moving as long as I'm able. And, when people tell me how great I look, that is an extra payoff, because the real issue is the way I feel when I slip into something the same size I was wearing umpteen years ago. That is one smug, but sweet moment, and I like the power rush it gives me.

Respondent C:

It is a sexist society and no matter how much you and I may hate that, it doesn't change one damned thing. So my choice is to acknowledge the gifts I got from the goody bag and polish these for the best performance. After all it's me I am nurturing in the long run, whether that means making myself look like the most qualified lawyer for a promotion in the firm, or the most enjoyable dinner partner for an evening on the town. I think that anyone who ignores their potential that way is in deep, deep denial.

Smythe's principal task was to let the respondents provide their own framework for their responses. After presenting her data, she concluded that "to be a woman is to be embodied, to be deeply and enduringly involved with one's corporality." The idea that "being a woman" is primarily a physical definition has strong ethical dimensions.

A Communication Research Ethic

There is a well-developed ethic in communication theory. Examining the bulk of communication research, in the same way that we have studied Infante and Wigley above, would produce a well developed set of ethical assumptions. Here are some examples of the types of assumptions that are necessary when communication takes place:

(A) Altruism is not only possible, but necessary

(B) Equivalency among persons is the rule

    (1) reciprocity and turntaking should result

    (2) collectivist communication goals are best

    (3) trust is essential

    (4) respect is fundamental

(C) Persuasion is superior to coercion

(D) Self-deception is counter-productive

These statements are a crude beginning toward what might be called a "communication" research ethic. The second step would be to utilize the techniques recommended by Toulmin and Girvetz to develop the system. Toulmin asks that we accept a few more assumptions that many of us might not wish to use: (a) incompatibility of opposing ethical statements, (b) the close relationship ethical statements have with our feelings, and (c) the elocutionary force they have in the structure of argument.

If we would adopt the statements above as our communication research ethic, we would be clearly far ahead of the usual ethical practice in research. In 1989, the National Institute of Health required that graduate students involved in federally supported research receive training in the ethics of research. These training programs generally boiled down to:

Do not invent (fudge) data

Do not steal data, or take credit for others' work

Do not hurt your research subjects (McGee, 1996)

There is yet another benefit to be realized from the introduction of values to communication study. The introduction of valuational statements can add a good deal to our analysis of the suitability of theoretical or methodological issues. We have already seen a poorly developed attempt to introduce ethical content into the practice of social science in our treatment of those persons who we have cavalierly called "subjects" for so many years.

Ethical arguments have a real impact on what we have taken to be an issue of "pure" theory, and the application of ethical principles might be as important a consideration as any other in the selection of a fundamental theoretical stance.

What possible moral issues are involved in subjectivist thought in social science? The answer can be found by a simple procedure—asking the social scientist whether the aim of research is to prove the researcher right, or to prove the researcher wrong. The differentiation in goals is at heart an ethical issue. Researchers who are involved in systems that cannot possibly turn up a negative result are truly unethical persons, even if they have convinced themselves of the rightness of their position. An excellent example of a system that had no corrective principle was the "cognitive dissonance" studies of the sixties. Everything that happened was "explained" by invoking the existence of "dissonance," even when the experiment came out in a way quite different from that predicted by the experimenters.

The largest question that we face in communication research is: Who should decide?

Institutional Review Boards

To help with this problem, the U.S. federal government has insisted that all institutions that accept federal funding have an internal review procedure to examine ethical and moral concerns with research. The precipitating incident in establishing these boards was the publication of a study by Stanley Milgram (1963) in which the researchers induced naive individuals to press levers that they thought represented painful shocks in other persons. Milgram persisted in the procedure until individuals refused to go any further. One of the aspects about this research that was alarming was the potential psychological damage to the subjects who truly believed they were administering shocks to another human being. Institutional review boards were designed to protect human subjects.

The way an Institutional Review Board (IRB) works is that researchers are required to submit research proposals in writing prior to the conducting of the experiment. The boards are usually composed of researchers from other disciplines, as well as individuals from the community, often priests or rabbis. One difficulty is the delay before researchers receive approval for their plans. Another problem lies in the social belief that human beings are more vulnerable than they might actually be. Anne Nicotera provides a personalized account of how it feels to work in a system where IRBs, as other bureaucratic entities, have gone beyond their original purpose. Here is how she describes her experiences with IRBs:

> I had a doctoral student whose dissertation research involved assessing people's responses to graffiti. Since the production of graffiti is illegal, he was not allowed to ask people if they had ever written on a wall. His interview protocols were so restricted that he had to abandon some important research questions. All this because the production of graffiti is illegal, and these interviewees might be put at risk of being identified!

My understanding of the IRB function is to make sure people are not getting hurt by careless or unethical researchers, but too often I think IRB committees take it upon themselves to promote their own value judgements as to what makes for good research. I believe the IRB should make anonymous voluntary survey research exempt, regardless of the content of the survey, asking only that the researcher sign an affidavit that the survey meets the requirements for exemption and attach a copy of the survey. In that same vein, I believe that the IRB's role should be restricted *only* to reviewing the plan for *data collection* and confidentiality/anonymity to assess potential risk to participants. Where risk exists, they should require that appropriate consent and debriefing/counseling be provided.

Shouldn't someone make sure social scientists' and other researchers' plans for data collection are not hazardous? I know that given free license, I wouldn't willingly hurt anyone, but I'd probably be thankful if some oversight of mine which could bring some research participant harm were brought to my attention by a responsible, cooperative committee. The key here is a *cooperative* committee, one comprised of persons who are supportive of the social science research effort, and who confine their activities to the assessment of data collection and confidentiality and their potential risks to subjects.

My main point . . . is that although IRBs definitely do not work well, and they severely impede the social scientific effort, the principle of human subjects protection should be maintained. To quote numerous grandmothers, let's not throw the baby out with the bath water.

Nicotera's views on the current state of the IRBs in large institutions, such as universities, are shared by many researchers.

SUMMARY AND CONCLUSIONS

While few of us are used to thinking about theoretical issues in an ethical way, sometimes ethics is more important than any of the other aspects of communication. Ethics is the study of right and wrong—of good and evil—and underlies the whole question of why study anything in the first place. Typically we see ethics studied as a critical theory, with its underlying search for meaning. Action theories have specific, unspoken ethical assumptions, that some very disturbing implications. Surprisingly, a strong basis in ethical behavior appears in empirical theories that has also been overlooked in the past.

Basic altruism is at the foundation of communicative theories, and each of us needs to work on our own basic ethical positions. A reasonable "communication ethic" could be based on the following propositions:

(A) Altruism is not only possible, but necessary
(B) Equivalency among persons is the rule
    (1) reciprocity and turntaking should result
    (2) collectivist communication goals are best
    (3) trust is essential
    (4) respect
(C) Persuasion is superior to coercion
(D) Self-deception is counter-productive

Not too long ago, science was known as "natural philosophy" and ethics as "moral philosophy." We need to consider this distinction very carefully and ask ourselves if "moral philosophy" doesn't underlie almost everything else. Perhaps we separate ethical issues because our commercial and public behavior lacks so much of it. If this is the case, we need to reconsider not only the way we think about communication, but about the rest of our intellectual life.

Appendix A
Random Numbers

Random Numbers

```
0 8 9 5 6 4 4 8 9 4 0 7 5 9 7 0 4 5 3 1 2 7 8 6 6
8 2 4 4 8 8 0 2 6 5 5 0 3 5 9 1 3 8 6 8 8 3 1 8 5
3 1 2 3 7 6 4 1 1 4 3 5 2 7 4 9 3 2 7 5 5 4 7 6 2
2 3 8 1 8 6 6 1 0 8 4 1 0 5 0 4 8 5 3 7 8 7 6 5 7
0 0 4 3 6 5 5 2 3 5 2 4 3 3 9 3 2 5 2 0 8 4 6 2 1
1 2 8 9 7 5 8 9 7 8 6 7 4 0 4 0 4 9 7 8 5 0 2 9 8
9 8 4 6 9 9 0 8 0 2 3 2 8 0 5 4 5 0 6 7 6 2 3 9 8
0 7 3 6 9 5 1 6 3 8 0 5 9 0 0 2 0 9 3 6 8 8 2 4 3
2 2 3 9 5 7 9 4 0 6 7 3 6 9 6 4 1 7 3 6 5 1 8 2 6
4 9 5 6 9 3 1 4 7 8 1 5 6 7 2 2 4 6 3 6 5 4 2 1 2
4 0 6 6 8 5 4 3 7 8 3 2 6 8 1 2 2 7 0 6 5 3 5 8 4
6 3 3 2 0 3 9 7 0 2 3 6 9 5 3 4 1 6 1 8 3 9 4 3 3
0 6 1 8 4 2 1 8 6 7 5 4 1 9 0 3 2 4 1 5 7 7 4 0 8
2 2 4 2 9 6 8 5 8 2 6 1 0 7 6 1 7 9 2 0 9 2 8 7 8
8 3 2 3 0 7 4 3 5 8 9 0 8 0 5 8 8 7 1 3 6 0 1 3 9
2 3 1 8 2 3 1 0 9 0 0 8 9 1 2 0 3 7 0 2 0 1 8 1 7
0 8 7 3 4 4 5 1 8 7 4 5 1 9 9 0 3 2 2 3 1 2 6 4 6
5 8 5 6 7 6 1 0 1 6 7 0 2 1 9 1 6 3 2 0 1 1 5 5 9
6 1 1 0 5 1 3 6 7 7 7 8 2 4 5 9 3 0 7 6 7 9 1 1 6
5 3 6 1 2 7 2 6 2 7 3 3 6 8 2 6 5 5 8 4 2 4 2 1 8
8 7 3 9 5 1 1 8 4 1 8 5 6 6 0 6 9 2 2 6 8 2 5 8 5
2 9 1 9 9 5 6 1 8 6 6 4 0 5 0 0 8 8 2 5 9 2 0 1 2
8 1 0 2 1 7 2 0 2 7 6 8 4 8 0 2 6 2 8 0 8 3 6 0 7
9 7 1 5 5 7 4 6 1 5 6 5 9 9 2 2 7 1 2 7 0 0 5 0 9
6 3 7 9 8 8 7 4 9 5 0 3 3 0 3 7 0 7 5 8 1 2 8 3 1
9 4 2 2 1 3 2 0 5 6 0 6 0 9 0 9 3 1 7 8 1 2 3 1 1
5 2 8 5 1 0 2 4 6 0 8 3 4 2 9 0 2 4 0 5 2 7 8 8 8
7 9 7 1 3 7 2 4 6 3 8 4 0 2 5 5 4 6 1 6 5 4 6 3 0
0 1 5 0 6 5 1 1 8 0 9 4 1 1 2 6 1 4 2 0 8 6 3 1 0
5 8 1 7 4 7 5 6 2 1 9 3 7 4 0 4 6 4 6 9 6 7 5 0 6
2 5 0 7 5 1 6 0 4 0 4 1 9 4 9 8 3 6 3 8 0 0 1 7 9
8 8 3 7 8 1 4 6 3 8 0 5 6 4 4 3 5 0 6 9 5 5 0 6 0
4 3 1 8 7 3 4 1 7 1 6 1 5 2 7 9 4 0 2 9 9 6 8 7 6
9 1 4 7 7 4 3 7 4 2 5 5 0 2 1 1 1 4 0 6 4 7 5 9 6
8 6 0 8 2 9 3 4 3 4 7 6 9 6 1 8 2 3 3 8 3 4 6 8 3
3 3 0 6 2 3 8 7 4 3 8 3 1 1 5 9 7 4 4 4 9 7 6 0 9
1 8 2 0 2 9 8 8 0 1 6 8 0 7 5 6 0 8 3 9 2 1 1 2 0
4 7 4 1 1 8 5 9 6 9 7 7 8 0 8 0 8 5 7 2 6 9 4 6 7
7 2 8 1 1 0 4 0 5 0 0 8 2 5 7 4 9 4 0 6 9 7 1 8 0
8 4 0 0 8 1 8 7 1 5 0 1 3 7 3 1 1 4 1 9 7 1 7 8 5
1 5 0 5 3 1 9 7 5 0 3 7 6 3 4 7 2 2 0 5 0 0 7 5 1
6 8 5 1 2 4 1 0 4 6 2 5 9 9 3 2 5 6 0 1 2 0 6 7 7
7 6 5 5 4 6 1 9 1 1 7 9 9 9 6 6 7 1 3 7 7 4 8 8 2
7 8 2 4 2 1 6 4 3 9 7 2 6 6 5 7 0 1 2 8 9 7 1 4 5
9 0 3 3 8 1 3 5 1 4 2 8 7 7 0 3 5 8 0 8 4 2 6 6 4
5 5 4 8 6 5 6 8 0 3 2 0 4 8 4 5 6 6 5 4 7 1 3 1 2
0 6 4 9 7 7 9 8 0 6 4 0 9 2 4 7 8 2 5 1 7 2 3 5 2
6 0 6 7 8 0 8 7 6 8 5 0 1 3 4 3 0 4 7 0 5 2 4 1 3
1 6 3 6 4 9 6 5 3 5 5 3 0 3 3 8 3 7 9 1 1 5 8 2 2
2 1 5 9 7 1 2 6 4 4 5 0 2 1 4 5 1 1 7 0 4 0 1 3 0
```

Random Numbers (*continued*)

```
5 0 3 9 1 8 3 8 9 5 5 6 7 3 0 6 7 9 7 1 4 9 2 3 3
3 5 8 1 8 1 6 3 4 7 0 6 7 7 8 9 6 2 0 8 5 0 4 3 7
7 0 6 4 0 6 9 0 5 9 3 3 7 7 1 1 4 4 3 8 0 6 2 1 8
1 0 4 9 2 7 8 1 6 4 4 9 3 2 9 6 7 3 2 4 2 6 4 9 6
7 7 7 0 3 2 5 7 9 3 0 5 6 6 5 8 7 6 2 8 5 2 5 3 8
3 1 4 2 0 1 2 3 5 8 0 4 9 9 9 5 6 4 8 6 4 3 5 0 8
8 7 9 8 4 6 4 1 7 0 8 6 0 0 6 1 7 0 9 0 2 9 8 4 2
5 0 6 9 7 6 4 6 4 9 6 6 0 5 3 2 7 9 2 4 4 4 0 6 5
0 9 7 6 2 3 7 3 6 5 7 7 4 8 5 9 4 9 6 6 0 9 5 6 3
1 1 2 9 9 4 6 0 0 6 3 7 1 3 1 9 1 2 6 6 0 8 7 5 2
9 5 5 5 1 9 7 5 9 0 3 2 1 5 6 1 1 1 2 8 3 5 9 5 5
5 6 2 2 6 5 2 0 4 0 5 8 1 8 6 1 2 3 9 0 3 4 3 0 3
3 0 8 5 5 8 7 5 1 7 1 0 7 0 2 7 4 9 9 5 4 9 3 4 6
1 9 4 1 2 5 8 1 2 4 4 9 7 5 9 7 5 8 8 6 2 2 2 4 0
1 6 0 1 7 5 6 9 4 1 7 3 2 2 6 5 1 4 5 9 8 9 9 2 4
9 4 3 4 6 5 3 2 3 0 8 5 6 6 1 1 0 6 6 6 9 6 0 1 1
3 8 5 2 2 5 3 1 3 4 8 8 2 8 7 5 4 6 4 6 4 0 3 3 4
6 5 9 8 7 5 1 5 0 1 3 1 3 5 7 1 1 7 6 6 6 6 8 4 5
9 9 7 6 9 8 8 7 0 6 1 5 7 9 7 1 5 9 7 9 2 6 7 1 1
3 2 8 0 3 7 7 6 8 3 1 2 6 3 0 8 1 4 8 6 1 2 6 6 8
8 9 9 2 9 7 7 4 2 3 3 5 9 2 3 5 8 6 7 3 0 6 4 9 9
5 2 2 0 3 2 8 7 3 4 1 2 6 8 9 6 8 9 4 1 7 6 8 2 9
9 3 7 1 9 8 3 6 0 2 8 6 3 5 3 0 1 6 1 3 3 8 3 4 8
0 6 7 9 9 0 3 7 7 2 6 0 7 7 1 1 8 1 2 9 9 7 8 0 6
6 5 3 1 0 4 2 4 5 1 4 9 5 3 9 0 2 2 4 5 9 9 9 0 0
4 1 8 9 1 7 4 3 6 4 4 6 6 6 0 7 6 3 2 5 8 2 0 6 8
4 5 4 7 1 1 4 5 0 4 7 9 4 0 6 1 2 1 9 4 9 9 0 2 3
2 5 4 3 3 6 3 1 4 0 9 3 7 9 1 1 8 8 1 8 0 3 1 9 5
4 3 6 4 0 1 7 8 2 0 4 9 5 9 7 9 0 3 3 7 2 9 9 4 0
2 3 8 5 4 4 3 3 0 6 1 0 7 3 5 3 1 3 2 0 6 0 9 1 7
1 6 4 8 7 9 9 9 1 3 1 0 8 6 7 5 6 9 0 3 1 6 8 2 0
4 8 1 6 3 4 5 0 2 7 5 7 0 8 3 2 4 8 5 3 2 9 6 8 1
4 2 1 9 4 6 2 3 0 1 1 6 1 0 7 2 .2 3 4 8 7 9 1 4 6
4 0 7 6 5 4 2 9 5 3 3 9 0 6 3 0 2 5 4 9 5 3 6 0 8
8 4 9 3 0 8 2 8 4 0 4 5 6 9 0 6 8 1 1 4 6 7 4 8 1
1 7 6 3 8 1 4 6 2 2 9 4 5 0 3 5 7 0 0 2 4 1 7 1 2
5 6 4 6 9 0 1 5 1 5 5 0 3 1 4 5 1 2 7 0 2 4 9 9 6
0 3 6 0 7 1 4 8 0 3 5 4 8 8 0 4 0 6 7 3 3 1 1 7 4
6 7 2 9 0 4 2 9 2 6 4 6 4 6 4 6 9 4 6 2 3 9 4 8 8
0 3 1 4 5 9 5 0 8 2 6 5 0 8 5 8 0 7 5 0 9 5 3 1 5
7 3 0 9 3 6 1 9 3 1 3 9 8 3 9 7 7 6 6 5 3 0 2 6 8
8 6 7 9 6 6 8 3 4 0 5 9 5 1 7 8 0 1 0 8 9 7 1 4 6
4 9 5 8 6 8 0 4 4 4 5 6 7 4 8 1 7 1 4 9 2 9 5 1 9
6 0 3 9 9 5 8 4 4 1 5 4 0 6 8 6 0 2 0 0 1 8 8 8 0
4 1 0 5 3 6 3 5 0 6 4 0 0 1 2 1 8 2 9 5 4 8 7 2 5
5 2 7 9 6 5 7 4 5 1 3 3 8 8 4 4 0 4 1 8 9 1 1 6 5
3 4 6 1 2 1 8 7 4 7 6 3 3 5 0 0 7 9 1 6 4 0 7 4 6
8 2 2 0 8 8 8 7 3 8 3 1 5 8 4 9 5 1 9 1 7 9 7 9 9
4 8 7 0 7 8 9 4 3 0 9 2 3 5 4 7 2 1 4 6 6 8 6 3 2
9 0 4 3 8 0 1 5 7 6 7 1 6 3 0 5 7 3 7 1 0 9 5 6 6
```

8	2	8	9	7	9	6	9	7	9	0	8	2	9	8	1	5	6	9	3	2	9	2	3	3
9	4	6	9	2	6	8	4	4	7	8	3	5	1	0	1	3	9	9	2	9	0	4	0	8
5	6	7	4	2	7	4	1	2	7	3	1	5	8	3	1	0	7	3	8	7	5	2	5	1
8	0	9	9	8	3	2	9	7	5	5	8	0	5	2	1	3	4	2	3	8	6	8	3	6
6	7	0	3	7	9	8	8	2	0	9	1	0	6	0	7	2	4	5	1	3	3	5	1	0
8	1	3	0	0	8	3	4	8	8	3	4	8	9	9	2	0	4	3	9	6	7	6	5	7
1	7	6	2	5	8	6	2	6	6	8	0	8	3	9	8	8	7	4	2	1	3	3	3	2
9	9	7	1	7	5	9	1	3	2	4	6	0	5	9	0	7	3	8	2	3	5	4	7	1
0	4	6	4	0	1	7	9	9	3	6	8	1	5	3	7	1	1	9	5	1	0	1	4	8
9	7	8	2	1	2	9	7	2	0	6	4	2	5	2	7	0	8	1	1	9	7	7	7	0
2	4	6	4	6	3	6	7	5	2	0	0	5	4	7	3	3	4	1	0	7	4	4	0	9
8	5	4	5	4	7	7	4	0	0	5	0	6	4	2	8	8	0	8	0	9	9	0	5	8
5	8	6	7	6	6	4	7	0	1	4	9	9	5	7	2	1	4	1	1	9	7	7	3	5
1	3	8	1	4	7	0	7	4	8	8	4	4	0	1	2	5	1	4	8	1	7	7	3	2
4	1	5	9	7	9	5	6	6	7	4	5	6	1	8	8	8	2	8	9	0	0	9	2	5
9	5	4	7	0	6	8	1	2	1	4	0	4	5	8	3	1	6	0	1	9	7	5	6	0
3	7	2	7	4	1	4	8	3	6	4	1	6	1	9	0	4	1	3	2	6	8	9	2	5
9	7	1	8	1	0	8	3	6	0	1	7	5	0	6	3	2	7	9	2	5	6	2	9	9
9	9	9	9	1	9	4	2	6	9	5	8	5	6	8	3	9	8	6	9	9	6	8	2	5
9	3	0	1	8	1	5	8	8	1	1	4	4	6	6	4	1	0	9	6	6	7	5	5	8
7	9	4	6	8	9	0	6	6	9	5	4	3	1	9	5	1	9	5	6	2	8	2	7	4
3	5	5	4	5	2	5	2	2	1	4	8	2	0	9	1	8	4	3	5	0	3	2	6	5
6	7	2	1	9	0	5	4	3	3	9	8	9	0	1	2	6	6	1	3	0	4	5	4	1
4	0	5	3	9	2	6	3	2	2	0	4	2	0	9	1	0	0	8	8	8	0	2	8	1
2	1	5	7	3	7	3	6	2	8	9	3	2	8	7	9	6	7	9	5	1	9	5	5	4
8	2	9	1	7	6	5	0	5	7	4	2	4	7	5	1	4	2	8	4	0	2	0	4	5
0	4	9	2	5	9	9	8	7	4	7	3	2	2	1	7	7	1	9	5	1	4	4	9	4
3	8	6	7	5	6	1	5	3	0	9	0	8	4	0	4	6	7	2	2	6	8	4	3	5
7	1	8	8	3	6	3	7	4	3	6	3	3	0	1	3	4	9	7	3	8	9	2	3	6
2	3	0	4	7	4	6	9	9	9	8	7	4	4	2	8	1	4	4	4	0	0	·6	0	8
8	6	4	4	0	7	1	2	9	6	3	1	3	4	9	1	6	2	9	3	7	6	1	1	0
0	5	5	4	6	7	7	9	6	9	0	2	5	5	3	5	8	5	1	2	9	6	9	3	9
5	7	4	3	2	8	8	4	4	2	0	8	9	6	3	0	5	1	1	2	7	3	7	8	0
8	3	2	7	1	2	7	0	2	9	1	1	7	1	5	4	8	1	9	1	2	5	0	5	3
3	1	2	1	0	7	7	3	0	4	7	1	3	8	9	3	8	7	2	7	5	1	4	8	9
0	7	9	7	0	6	4	5	3	0	5	8	2	7	3	7	3	0	6	2	4	3	3	9	1
9	0	3	4	4	3	1	8	2	1	0	4	5	9	7	2	9	0	5	5	4	7	1	5	9
1	5	7	9	2	9	5	2	8	9	1	8	6	4	2	3	4	0	6	1	4	1	7	9	9
7	3	8	2	7	8	4	7	5	9	3	4	2	9	9	4	8	3	1	1	6	5	1	5	6
2	4	0	4	4	0	4	5	0	7	6	4	9	2	0	5	3	9	2	8	1	1	8	0	2
2	9	9	9	6	6	8	0	6	9	4	0	8	4	2	4	0	4	6	0	2	1	2	2	4
5	8	2	2	2	1	7	7	2	5	9	4	2	1	7	2	1	7	7	9	3	3	5	9	8
7	3	7	4	3	6	3	0	9	9	1	6	3	9	2	3	0	2	6	8	9	8	9	0	7
8	8	9	7	6	2	9	9	0	1	2	0	0	1	0	2	4	7	8	9	6	6	9	7	8
1	4	0	9	6	1	0	9	8	7	0	5	8	0	6	5	8	0	5	0	1	9	3	0	1
1	6	4	2	4	7	6	7	7	3	5	9	3	2	2	9	2	7	8	6	3	7	7	8	1
1	2	9	8	1	2	5	7	7	9	6	8	4	4	0	6	3	3	1	1	6	7	2	5	8
5	7	7	5	3	5	5	5	6	7	9	4	3	1	5	7	2	7	6	9	7	6	1	0	3
2	4	7	9	1	7	2	8	3	4	4	1	1	1	3	0	6	9	1	4	8	8	7	5	6
0	2	5	9	4	0	8	2	5	6	0	4	7	1	6	3	6	5	5	6	1	1	6	7	6

Appendix B
Areas Under the Normal Curve

Areas Under the Normal Curve: Proportion of Area Under the Normal Curve Between the Mean and a z Distance from the Mean

$\frac{x}{o}$ or z	.00	.01	.02	.03	.04	.05	.06	.07	.08	.09
0	0000	0040	0080	0120	0160	0199	0239	0279	0319	0359
1	0398	0438	0478	0517	0557	0596	0636	0675	0714	0753
2	0793	0832	0871	0910	0948	0987	1026	1064	1103	1141
3	1179	1217	1255	1293	1331	1368	1406	1443	1480	1517
4	1554	1591	1628	1664	1700	1736	1772	1808	1844	1879
5	1915	1950	1985	2019	2054	2088	2123	2157	2190	2224
6	2257	2291	2324	2357	2389	2422	2454	2486	2517	2549
7	2580	2611	2642	2673	2704	2734	2764	2794	2823	2852
8	2881	2910	2939	2967	2995	3023	3051	3078	3106	3133
9	3159	3186	3212	3238	3264	3289	3315	3340	3365	3389
1 0	3413	3438	3461	3485	3508	3531	3554	3577	3599	3621
1 1	3643	3665	3686	3708	3729	3749	3770	3790	3810	3830
1 2	3849	3869	3888	3907	3925	3944	3962	3980	3997	4015
1 3	4032	4049	4066	4082	4099	4115	4131	4147	4162	4177
1 4	4192	4207	4222	4236	4251	4265	4279	4292	4306	4319
1 5	4332	4345	4357	4370	4382	4394	4406	4418	4429	4441
1 6	4452	4463	4474	4484	4495	4505	4515	4525	4535	4545
1 7	4554	4564	4573	4582	4591	4599	4608	4616	4625	4633
1 8	4641	4649	4656	4664	4671	4678	4686	4693	4699	4706
1 9	4713	4719	4726	4732	4738	4744	4750	4756	4761	4767
2 0	4772	4778	4783	4788	4793	4798	4803	4808	4812	4817
2 1	4821	4826	4830	4834	4838	4842	4846	4850	4854	4857
2 2	4861	4864	4868	4871	4875	4878	4881	4884	4887	4890
2 3	4893	4896	4898	4901	4904	4906	4909	4911	4913	4916
2 4	4918	4920	4922	4925	4927	4929	4931	4932	4934	4936
2 5	4938	4940	4941	4943	4945	4946	4948	4949	4951	4952
2 6	4953	4955	4956	4957	4959	4960	4961	4962	4963	4964
2 7	4965	4966	4967	4968	4969	4970	4971	4972	4973	4974
2 8	4974	4975	4976	4977	4977	4978	4979	4979	4980	4981
2 9	4981	4982	4982	4983	4984	4984	4985	4985	4986	4986
3 0	4987	4987	4987	4988	4988	4989	4989	4989	4990	4990
3 1	4990	4991	4991	4991	4992	4992	4992	4992	4993	4993
3 2	4993	4993	4994	4994	4994	4994	4994	4995	4995	4995
3 3	4995	4995	4995	4996	4996	4996	4996	4996	4996	4997
3 4	4997	4997	4997	4997	4997	4997	4997	4997	4997	4998
3 5	4998									
4 0	49997									
4 5	499997									
5 0	4999997									

Appendix C
Table of *t* Values

This table is abridged from Table III of Fisher and Yates, *Statistical Tables for Biological, Agricultural, and Medical Research*. Reprinted by permission of Addison Wesley Longman, Ltd.

Distribution of *t*

df	Level of significance for one-tailed test					
	10	05	025	01	005	0005
	Level of significance for two-tailed test					
	20	10	05	02	01	001
1	3 078	6 314	12 706	31 821	63 657	636 619
2	1 886	2 920	4 303	6 965	9 925	31 598
3	1 638	2 353	3 182	4 541	5 841	12 941
4	1 533	2 132	2 776	3 747	4 604	8 610
5	1 476	2 015	2 571	3 365	4 032	6 859
6	1 440	1 943	2 447	3 143	3 707	5 959
7	1 415	1 895	2 365	2 998	3 499	5 405
8	1 397	1 860	2 306	2 896	3 355	5 041
9	1 383	1 833	2 262	2 821	3 250	4 781
10	1 372	1 812	2 228	2 764	3 169	4 587
11	1 363	1 796	2 201	2 718	3 106	4 437
12	1 356	1 782	2 179	2 681	3 055	4 318
13	1 350	1 771	2 160	2 650	3 012	4 221
14	1 345	1 761	2 145	2 624	2 977	4 140
15	1 341	1 753	2 131	2 602	2 947	4 073
16	1 337	1 746	2 120	2 583	2 921	4 015
17	1 333	1 740	2 110	2 567	2 898	3 965
18	1 330	1 734	2 101	2 552	2 878	3 992
19	1 328	1 729	2 093	2 539	2 861	3 883
20	1 325	1 725	2 086	2 528	2 845	3 850
21	1 323	1 721	2 080	2 518	2 831	3 819
22	1 321	1 717	2 074	2 508	2 819	3 792
23	1 319	1 714	2 069	2 500	2 807	3 767
24	1 318	1 711	2 064	2 492	2 797	3 745
25	1 316	1 708	2 060	2 485	2 787	3 725
26	1 315	1 706	2 056	2 479	2 779	3 707
27	1 314	1 703	2 052	2 473	2 771	3 690
28	1 313	1 701	2 048	2 467	2 763	3 674
29	1 311	1 699	2 045	2 462	2 756	3 659
30	1 310	1 697	2 042	2 457	2 750	3 646
40	1 303	1 684	2 021	2 423	2 704	3 551
60	1 296	1 671	2 000	2 390	2 660	3 460
120	1 289	1 658	1 980	2 358	2 617	3 373
x	1 282	1 645	1 960	2 326	2 576	3 291

Appendix D
Distribution of F

Note: df_1 = rows of table (for degrees of freedom in denominator) — within
df_2 = rows of table (for degrees of freedom in numerator) — between

Table 1 Significance of F at 0.05 Level

df_2 \ df_1	1	2	3	4	5	6	7	8	9	10	12	15	20	24	30	40	60	120	∞
1	161.4	199.5	215.7	224.6	230.2	234.0	236.8	238.9	240.5	241.9	243.9	245.9	248.0	249.1	250.1	251.1	252.2	253.3	254.3
2	18.51	19.00	19.16	19.25	19.30	19.33	19.35	19.37	19.38	19.40	19.41	19.43	19.45	19.45	19.46	19.47	19.48	19.49	19.50
3	10.13	9.55	9.28	9.12	9.01	8.94	8.89	8.85	8.81	8.79	8.74	8.70	8.66	8.64	8.62	8.59	8.57	8.55	8.53
4	7.71	6.94	6.59	6.39	6.26	6.16	6.09	6.04	6.00	5.96	5.91	5.86	5.80	5.77	5.75	5.72	5.69	5.66	5.63
5	6.61	5.79	5.41	5.19	5.05	4.95	4.88	4.82	4.77	4.74	4.68	4.62	4.56	4.53	4.50	4.46	4.43	4.40	4.36
6	5.99	5.14	4.76	4.53	4.39	4.28	4.21	4.15	4.10	4.06	4.00	3.94	3.87	3.84	3.81	3.77	3.74	3.70	3.67
7	5.59	4.74	4.35	4.12	3.97	3.87	3.79	3.73	3.68	3.64	3.57	3.51	3.44	3.41	3.38	3.34	3.30	3.27	3.23
8	5.32	4.46	4.07	3.84	3.69	3.58	3.50	3.44	3.39	3.35	3.28	3.22	3.15	3.12	3.08	3.04	3.01	2.97	2.93
9	5.12	4.26	3.86	3.63	3.48	3.37	3.29	3.23	3.18	3.14	3.07	3.01	2.94	2.90	2.86	2.83	2.79	2.75	2.71
10	4.96	4.10	3.71	3.48	3.33	3.22	3.14	3.07	3.02	2.98	2.91	2.85	2.77	2.74	2.70	2.66	2.62	2.58	2.54
11	4.84	3.98	3.59	3.36	3.20	3.09	3.01	2.95	2.90	2.85	2.79	2.72	2.65	2.61	2.57	2.53	2.49	2.45	2.40
12	4.75	3.89	3.49	3.26	3.11	3.00	2.91	2.85	2.80	2.75	2.69	2.62	2.54	2.51	2.47	2.43	2.38	2.34	2.30
13	4.67	3.81	3.41	3.18	3.03	2.92	2.83	2.77	2.71	2.67	2.60	2.53	2.46	2.42	2.38	2.34	2.30	2.25	2.21
14	4.60	3.74	3.34	3.11	2.96	2.85	2.76	2.70	2.65	2.60	2.53	2.46	2.39	2.35	2.31	2.27	2.22	2.18	2.13
15	4.54	3.68	3.29	3.06	2.90	2.79	2.71	2.64	2.59	2.54	2.48	2.40	2.33	2.29	2.25	2.20	2.16	2.11	2.07
16	4.49	3.63	3.24	3.01	2.85	2.74	2.66	2.59	2.54	2.49	2.42	2.35	2.28	2.24	2.19	2.15	2.11	2.06	2.01
17	4.45	3.59	3.20	2.96	2.81	2.70	2.61	2.55	2.49	2.45	2.38	2.31	2.23	2.19	2.15	2.10	2.06	2.01	1.96
18	4.41	3.55	3.16	2.93	2.77	2.66	2.58	2.51	2.46	2.41	2.34	2.27	2.19	2.15	2.11	2.06	2.02	1.97	1.92
19	4.38	3.52	3.13	2.90	2.74	2.63	2.54	2.48	2.42	2.38	2.31	2.23	2.16	2.11	2.07	2.03	1.98	1.93	1.88

df																			
20	2 42	2 52	2 61	2 69	2 78	2 86	2 94	3 09	3 23	3 37	3 46	3 56	3 70	3 87	4 10	4 43	4 94	5 85	8 10
21	2 36	2 46	2 55	2 64	2 72	2 80	2 88	3 03	3 17	3 31	3 40	3 51	3 64	3 81	4 04	4 37	4 87	5 78	8 02
22	2 31	2 40	2 50	2 58	2 67	2 75	2 83	2 98	3 12	3 26	3 35	3 45	3 59	3 76	3 99	4 31	4 82	5 72	7 95
23	2 26	2 35	2 45	2 54	2 62	2 70	2 78	2 93	3 07	3 21	3 30	3 41	3 54	3 71	3 94	4 26	4 76	5 66	7 88
24	2 21	2 31	2 40	2 49	2 58	2 66	2 74	2 89	3 03	3 17	3 26	3 36	3 50	3 67	3 90	4 22	4 72	5 61	7 82
25	2 17	2 27	2 36	2 45	2 54	2 62	2 70	2 85	2 99	3 13	3 22	3 32	3 46	3 63	3 85	4 18	4 68	5 57	7 77
26	2 13	2 23	2 33	2 42	2 50	2 58	2 66	2 81	2 96	3 09	3 18	3 29	3 42	3 59	3 82	4 14	4 64	5 53	7 72
27	2 10	2 20	2 29	2 38	2 47	2 55	2 63	2 78	2 93	3 06	3 15	3 26	3 39	3 56	3 78	4 11	4 60	5 49	7 68
28	2 06	2 17	2 26	2 35	2 44	2 52	2 60	2 75	2 90	3 03	3 12	3 23	3 36	3 53	3 75	4 07	4 57	5 45	7 64
29	2 03	2 14	2 23	2 33	2 41	2 49	2 57	2 73	2 87	3 00	3 09	3 20	3 33	3 50	3 73	4 04	4 54	5 42	7 60
30	2 01	2 11	2 21	2 30	2 39	2 47	2 55	2 70	2 84	2 98	3 07	3 17	3 30	3 47	3 70	4 02	4 51	5 39	7 56
40	1 80	1 92	2 02	2 11	2 20	2 29	2 37	2 52	2 66	2 80	2 89	2 99	3 12	3 29	3 51	3 83	4 31	5 18	7 31
60	1 60	1 73	1 84	1 94	2 03	2 12	2 20	2 35	2 50	2 63	2 72	2 82	2 95	3 12	3 34	3 65	4 13	4 98	7 08
120	1 38	1 53	1 66	1 76	1 86	1 95	2 03	2 19	2 34	2 47	2 56	2 66	2 79	2 96	3 17	3 48	3 95	4 79	6 85
∞	1 00	1 32	1 47	1 59	1 70	1 79	1 88	2 04	2 18	2 32	2 41	2 51	2 64	2 80	3 02	3 32	3 78	4 61	6 63

Table 2 Significance of F at 0.01 Level

df_2 \ df_1	1	2	3	4	5	6	7	8	9	10	12	15	20	24	30	40	60	120	∞
1	4052	4999.5	5403	5625	5764	5859	5928	5982	6022	6056	6106	6157	6209	6235	6261	6287	6313	6339	6366
2	98.5	99.00	99.17	99.25	99.30	99.33	99.36	99.37	99.39	99.40	99.42	99.43	99.45	99.46	99.47	99.47	99.48	99.49	99.50
3	34.12	30.82	29.46	28.71	28.24	27.91	27.67	27.49	27.35	27.23	27.05	26.87	26.69	26.60	26.50	26.41	26.32	26.22	26.13
4	21.20	18.00	16.69	15.98	15.52	15.21	14.98	14.80	14.66	14.55	14.37	14.20	14.02	13.93	13.84	13.75	13.65	13.56	13.46
5	16.26	13.27	12.06	11.39	10.97	10.67	10.46	10.29	10.16	10.05	9.89	9.72	9.55	9.47	9.38	9.29	9.20	9.11	9.02
6	13.75	10.92	9.78	9.15	8.75	8.47	8.26	8.10	7.98	7.87	7.72	7.56	7.40	7.31	7.23	7.14	7.06	6.97	6.88
7	12.25	9.55	8.45	7.85	7.46	7.19	6.99	6.81	6.72	6.62	6.47	6.31	6.16	6.07	5.99	5.91	5.82	5.74	5.65
8	11.26	8.65	7.59	7.01	6.63	6.37	6.18	6.03	5.91	5.81	5.67	5.52	5.36	5.28	5.20	5.12	5.03	4.95	4.86
9	10.56	8.02	6.99	6.42	6.06	5.80	5.61	5.47	5.35	5.26	5.11	4.96	4.81	4.73	4.65	4.57	4.48	4.40	4.31
10	10.04	7.56	6.55	5.99	5.64	5.39	5.20	5.06	4.94	4.85	4.71	4.56	4.41	4.33	4.25	4.17	4.08	4.00	3.91
11	9.65	7.21	6.22	5.67	5.32	5.07	4.89	4.74	4.63	4.54	4.40	4.25	4.10	4.02	3.94	3.86	3.78	3.69	3.60
12	9.33	6.93	5.95	5.41	5.06	4.82	4.64	4.50	4.39	4.30	4.16	4.01	3.86	3.78	3.70	3.62	3.54	3.45	3.36
13	9.07	6.70	5.74	5.21	4.86	4.62	4.44	4.30	4.19	4.10	3.96	3.82	3.66	3.59	3.51	3.43	3.34	3.25	3.17
14	8.86	6.51	5.56	5.04	4.69	4.46	4.28	4.14	4.03	3.94	3.80	3.66	3.51	3.43	3.35	3.27	3.18	3.09	3.00
15	8.68	6.36	5.42	4.89	4.56	4.32	4.14	4.00	3.89	3.80	3.67	3.52	3.37	3.29	3.21	3.13	3.05	2.96	2.87
16	8.53	6.23	5.29	4.77	4.44	4.20	4.03	3.89	3.78	3.69	3.55	3.41	3.26	3.18	3.10	3.02	2.93	2.84	2.75
17	8.40	6.11	5.18	4.67	4.34	4.10	3.93	3.79	3.68	3.59	3.46	3.31	3.16	3.08	3.00	2.92	2.83	2.75	2.65
18	8.29	6.01	5.09	4.58	4.25	4.01	3.84	3.71	3.60	3.51	3.37	3.23	3.08	3.00	2.92	2.84	2.75	2.66	2.57
19	8.18	5.93	5.01	4.50	4.17	3.94	3.77	3.63	3.52	3.43	3.30	3.15	3.00	2.92	2.84	2.76	2.67	2.58	2.49

20	2.42	2.52	2.61	2.69	2.78	2.86	2.94	3.09	3.23	3.37	3.46	3.56	3.70	3.87	4.10	4.43	4.94	5.85	8.10
21	2.36	2.46	2.55	2.64	2.72	2.80	2.88	3.03	3.17	3.31	3.40	3.51	3.64	3.81	4.04	4.37	4.87	5.78	8.02
22	2.31	2.40	2.50	2.58	2.67	2.75	2.83	2.98	3.12	3.26	3.35	3.45	3.59	3.76	3.99	4.31	4.82	5.72	7.95
23	2.26	2.35	2.45	2.54	2.62	2.70	2.78	2.93	3.07	3.21	3.30	3.41	3.54	3.71	3.94	4.26	4.76	5.66	7.88
24	2.21	2.31	2.40	2.49	2.58	2.66	2.74	2.89	3.03	3.17	3.26	3.36	3.50	3.67	3.90	4.22	4.72	5.61	7.82
25	2.17	2.27	2.36	2.45	2.54	2.62	2.70	2.85	2.99	3.13	3.22	3.32	3.46	3.63	3.85	4.18	4.68	5.57	7.77
26	2.13	2.23	2.33	2.42	2.50	2.58	2.66	2.81	2.96	3.09	3.18	3.29	3.42	3.59	3.82	4.14	4.64	5.53	7.72
27	2.10	2.20	2.29	2.38	2.47	2.55	2.63	2.78	2.93	3.06	3.15	3.26	3.39	3.56	3.78	4.11	4.60	5.49	7.68
28	2.06	2.17	2.26	2.35	2.44	2.52	2.60	2.75	2.90	3.03	3.12	3.23	3.36	3.53	3.75	4.07	4.57	5.45	7.64
29	2.03	2.14	2.23	2.33	2.41	2.49	2.57	2.73	2.87	3.00	3.09	3.20	3.33	3.50	3.73	4.04	4.54	5.42	7.60
30	2.01	2.11	2.21	2.30	2.39	2.47	2.55	2.70	2.84	2.98	3.07	3.17	3.30	3.47	3.70	4.02	4.51	5.39	7.56
40	1.80	1.92	2.02	2.11	2.20	2.29	2.37	2.52	2.66	2.80	2.89	2.99	3.12	3.29	3.51	3.83	4.31	5.18	7.31
60	1.60	1.73	1.84	1.94	2.03	2.12	2.20	2.35	2.50	2.63	2.72	2.82	2.95	3.12	3.34	3.65	4.13	4.98	7.08
120	1.38	1.53	1.66	1.76	1.86	1.95	2.03	2.19	2.34	2.47	2.56	2.66	2.79	2.96	3.17	3.48	3.95	4.79	6.85
∞	1.00	1.32	1.47	1.59	1.70	1.79	1.88	2.04	2.18	2.32	2.41	2.51	2.64	2.80	3.02	3.32	3.78	4.61	6.63

Appendix E
Chi-Square Values

This table is taken from Table IV of Fisher and Yates, *Statistical Tables for Biological, Agricultural, and Medical Research*. Reprinted by permission of Addison Wesley Longman, Ltd.

Distribution of Chi-Square

df	Probability					
	20	.10	.05	.02	.01	.001
1	1.642	2.706	3.841	5.412	6.635	10.827
2	3.219	4.605	5.991	7.824	9.210	13.815
3	4.642	6.251	7.815	9.837	11.345	16.266
4	5.989	7.779	9.488	11.668	13.277	18.467
5	7.289	9.236	11.070	13.388	15.086	20.515
6	8.558	10.645	12.592	15.033	16.812	22.457
7	9.803	12.017	14.067	16.622	18.475	24.322
8	11.030	13.362	15.507	18.168	20.090	26.125
9	12.242	14.684	16.919	19.679	21.666	27.877
10	13.442	15.987	18.307	21.161	23.209	29.588
11	14.631	17.275	19.675	22.618	24.725	31.264
12	15.812	18.549	21.026	24.054	26.217	32.909
13	16.985	19.812	22.362	25.472	27.688	34.528
14	18.151	21.064	23.685	26.873	29.141	36.123
15	19.311	22.307	24.996	28.259	30.578	37.697
16	20.465	23.542	26.296	29.633	32.000	39.252
17	21.615	24.769	27.587	30.995	33.409	40.790
18	22.760	25.989	28.869	32.346	34.805	42.312
19	23.900	27.204	30.144	33.687	36.191	43.820
20	25.038	28.412	31.410	35.020	37.566	45.315
21	26.171	29.615	32.671	36.343	38.932	46.797
22	27.301	30.813	33.924	37.659	40.289	48.268
23	28.429	32.007	35.172	38.968	41.638	49.728
24	29.553	33.196	36.415	40.270	42.980	51.179
25	30.675	34.382	37.652	41.566	44.314	52.620

Distribution of Chi-Square (*continued*)

df			Probability			
	.20	.10	.05	.02	.01	.001
26	31.795	35.563	38.885	42.856	45.642	54.052
27	32.912	36.741	40.113	44.140	46.963	55.476
28	34.027	37.916	41.337	45.419	48.278	56.893
29	35.139	39.087	42.557	46.693	49.588	58.302
30	36.250	40.256	43.773	47.962	50.892	59.703
32	38.466	42.585	46.194	50.487	53.486	62.487
34	40.676	44.903	48.602	52.995	56.061	65.247
36	42.879	47.212	50.999	55.489	58.619	67.985
38	45.076	49.513	53.384	57.969	61.162	70.703
40	47.269	51.805	55.759	60.436	63.691	73.402
42	49.456	54.090	58.124	62.892	66.206	76.084
44	51.639	56.369	60.481	65.337	68.710	78.750
46	53.818	58.641	62.830	67.771	71.201	81.400
48	55.993	60.907	65.171	70.197	73.683	84.037
50	58.164	63.167	67.505	72.613	76.154	86.661
52	60.332	65.422	69.832	75.021	78.616	89.272
54	62.496	67.673	72.153	77.422	81.069	91.872
56	64.658	69.919	74.468	79.815	83.513	94.461
58	66.816	72.160	76.778	82.201	85.950	97.039
60	68.972	74.397	79.082	84.580	88.379	99.607
62	71.125	76.630	81.381	86.953	90.802	102.166
64	73.276	78.860	83.675	89.320	93.217	104.716
66	75.424	81.085	85.965	91.681	95.626	107.258
68	77.571	83.308	88.250	94.037	98.028	109.791
70	79.715	85.527	90.531	96.388	100.425	112.317

Glossary

academic theory—An academic theory is one that exists primarily for the sake of knowledge alone.

action theories—Theories that contend that our interpretation of other's behavior is more important and meaningful than the behavior itself. The individual's intentions (plans) leading to social behavior are also considered to be much more interesting than the specific behavior.

affective orientation—How people differ from one another in the ways they are aware of their emotions in communication activities. In other words, some people know when they are upset, and others aren't as aware of it.

analysis of variance—A method to assess the *variance among the group means* and compare it to the rest of the variance among this group of scores.

applied theory—An applied theory is one that we can use in solving a significant social or organizational problem.

attitude similarity—The degree to which two people hold attitudes that are the same.

average deviation—Tells us how far, on the average, each score varies from the mean.

behavior—Visible events or activities on any organism.

behaviorism—The point of view that mental events are unknowable and only overt behavior should be studied.

bureaucracy—The structure inherent in a large organization. Sometimes used to describe those who are responsible for maintaining the organization, and not actually functioning in a "line" position. Most of our large institutions have developed many layers of this activity.

cardinal numbers—What most of us think of when we use the word "number," in that some quantity is implied. A cardinal number can be thought of as the answer to the question "how many?" Cardinal numbers do not include fractions.

case study—Emphasizes one individual or group of individuals; the surrounding circumstances and previous events are explored and recorded, not simply one or two communicative behaviors in isolation.

chi-square—A statistical distribution derived from z scores, but is based on frequencies. It is an assumption-free test, that is, it doesn't depend on sampling from a normal population. It has its own set of probabilities and its own logic. χ^2 is related to z scores, in that $\chi^2 = z^2$ when z is normally distributed with a mean of zero and a standard deviation of 1. In short, χ^2 is a probability distribution similar to the other distributions we have seen, and can be used to analyze frequency data.

Chronbach's *alpha*—A coefficient of reliability different from odd-even and split half correlations. *Alpha* approaches reliability from the point of view of comparing variances between items to the overall variance.

coding—The research activity involved when given texts or activities are classified into categories and recorded.

coefficient of determination—The ratio of overall variance compared to the variance "around" the regression line. Usually expressed as R^2 (R-squared).

cohesiveness—This characteristic refers to the quality some aggregations have of "clinging" together. Cohesiveness can be created by a number of factors. Some typical ones are common goals, common background, liking for one another, and external forces or pressure. A group that is cohesive is one that has some force tending to hold it together. Casual aggregations lack cohesiveness.

communal—Common, or shared. One of the basic characteristics of science.

communication theory—A related collection of statements describing specific relationships among communication activities.

compliance gaining—One of the most common occurrences in interpersonal communication in which one participant wishes the other to do something, go somewhere, or think about something.

confidence interval—Describes the characteristics of a proportion derived from survey research. Since the survey is a sample, researchers do not have an exact estimate of the proportion in the overall population. The confidence interval is the range within which researchers are confident that the "true" proportion lies. Its calculation is done with z scores.

content analysis—The analysis of text for revealing characteristics, such as bias, preferences, and the like. Early techniques used in content analysis were simple: examining editorials, "slanted" news, and general quantities of coverage as an index to editorial position or bias in the news.

contingencies—When one number, or score is different depending on another number or score, it is said to be contingent on it. For example, if "affect orientation" differs with chronological age, we would say it is contingent on it.

convenience sample—A sample in which the requirements of randomness are sacrificed to save time, money, and/or effort. This is a sample in which the procedure is based on the physical and organizational proximity of the respondents.

conversational analysis—The study of interpersonal interactions in natural contexts, such as conversations. Emphasis is often on "episodes," rather than specific words or sentences. One basic premise of conversational analysis is that often the communicative purpose of individuals in actual conversations shows unintended motives or feelings.

correction term—In the analysis of variance, an intermediate calculation. It is calculated by squaring the total of the scores in the table divided by the overall total of people (or cases) in the table.

correlation coefficient—The square root of the coefficient of determination. This coefficient ranges from +1.00 to –1.00 and can be calculated independently of the regression analysis if this is all that is needed.

covariance—The degree to which two numbers *vary together.*

critical difference—The method of establishing a range for *statistical significance* to differences between means following the calculation of *F* in the analysis of variance. The critical difference is how large the differences between the means will have to be before it is considered significant.

culture—Individuals who share a common language, ethical standards, and geographical affinities are said to be members of the same culture.

degrees of freedom—Technically the degrees of freedom are an expression telling us how many numbers in the procedure are *free to vary.* Practically, the degrees of freedom are specified for each statistical test, usually based on the number of individuals or responses that went into calculating the statistic.

disinterestedness—A synonym for objectivity. Scientists should not distort what they do—or specifically what they observe in their study.

dyad—Two persons regarded as a pair.

empiricism—The point of view that asserts that only observable phenomena determine what is real and what isn't real, and leaves little room for differences of opinion.

error—Used variously in statistics to denote randomness or unpredictability.

error (Type I)—The mistake we make in the unusual circumstance of rejecting the null hypothesis when it is true.

error (Type II)—The mistake we make when we accept the null hypothesis when it is false.

expected frequency—In the chi-square test, the frequency that would occur by chance, or if your hypothesis isn't true.

exploratory research—Investigating, without preconceptions, what the state of affairs may be in a given problem area.

F test—A statistic invented by Sir Ronald Fisher, which compares whether one variance is significantly different from another. It is characterized by not one, but two different numbers for degrees of freedom.

field study—Usually taken to mean research that takes place in the actual place and situation where a particular phenomenon occurs, as opposed to a recording, a written account, or an artificial situation contrived in a research institution.

focus groups—A technique usually used in qualitative research. In a focus group, the researchers ask general questions and then let respondents say whatever comes into their heads.

frequency data—Derived from observations that are classed in one category or another. Frequency data are typically analyzed with the chi-square test.

frequency indexing—Refers to the practice of counting specific characteristics in texts. One of the basic techniques used in content analysis. If a newspaper mentions a particular issue more than another, the findings would be presented in a frequency index.

Guttman scale—A testing technique where each item represents a different level of strength, or commitment.

hermeneutic explanation—Occurs when researchers relate phenomena to larger categories of cultural and social significance.

hypothesis—Conjectural statement describing relationships between concepts. It is constructed in order to give shape and form to research. Often some causal relationship is implied in your hypothesis, but not necessarily. Typically a hypothesis takes the form: "If this theory is true, and I do X then Y will result." One of the principal functions of an hypothesis is to guide the research design and exemplify the theory in a way that gives the effort meaning.

induction—The mode of reasoning where we observe many specific instances and conclude from them a general principle.

inferential surveys—This type of survey is one in which we wish to make some judgments about the population as a whole. The sample that is drawn represents the population, and this substitution of sample for the whole is an *inferential* process.

information—Usually defined as the absence of entropy, or predictability. Information value is based on choices between two equally likely events, and is therefore measured in numbers based on the logarithm of the number two. Mathematically, it is a *logarithmic* function, that is, its alterations are usually expressed in terms of the logarithm (to the base 2) of the information content.

interpersonal communication—Direct, or face-to-face interaction, usually with a personal dimension. Almost always involves relational elements.

intersubjectivity—Refers to the process that scientists generally use to insure that they are talking about the same thing. It is the process of agreeing on the specific operations that will be representative of a given theoretical term.

item-total reliability—Calculated by deriving the correlation of each item score with the total score and averaging them.

laws—Highly specific statements involving the relationships between variables.

Likert scales—A procedure used in measuring attitude, which offers respondents an opportunity to agree or disagree with each item and a "mini-scale" to evaluate each item.

logical empiricism—A more modern view of logical positivism, which does not insist on restricting truth values as rigidly as positivists did. It also accepts that universal statements can never be verified and relies on confirmation from the accumulation of empirical tests. This accumulation does not constitute *exact proof*, but instead focuses on proof *with an acceptable level of probability*.

logical positivists—An early group of empiricists, who asserted that any definition not based on observation was meaningless. Positivists did not believe in "myths" such as democracy or communism.

mean—A standard descriptor of an aggregate (or group) of numbers. The mean or average is calculated by adding up all the scores and dividing the resulting sum by the number of scores in the collection.

mesokurtic—When a normal distribution has a small standard error we say it is mesokurtic.

metalogic—Logic about logic. When we discuss whether a statement is logical or not, we are using metalogic.

method of least squares—The technique used to calculate the smallest squared deviations from a predictive equation. The equation is solved using simultaneous linear equations.

mode—The number that appears most often in a distribution.

multiple correlation coefficient—An index of a relationship involving two predictors. Within each multiple correlation coefficient there are two regression coefficients, b_1 and b_2.

multiple regression—A form of regression analysis involving two regression coefficients, usually performed when researchers believe that a given effect has more than one cause.

narrative—As the name implies, is the telling of a story. When a story illustrates a particular characteristic of an individual, a group, or a corporation, it can be used as part of a qualitative investigation.

network—The general pattern in which an organization is put together.

nominal number—As the name implies, a number that serves primarily as a name, or an identifier. Social security numbers, or numbers on football jerseys are nominal numbers.

normal curve—The best estimate of the expansion of the binomial distribution where q=.5, p=.5 and n=infinity. A picture of a totally random series of events.

null hypothesis—Statisticians try to disprove hypotheses, rather than prove them. Therefore they formulate hypotheses about real events or real people in terms of the opposite. If we felt that people that applied to a given graduate program were better than the average student in grade point averages, we would test the idea by formulating a null hypothesis stating "Applicants are no better than average in GPA scores" and attempting to disprove it.

observed frequency—In the chi-square test, the frequency that actually occurred in your observations.

odd-even reliability—A reliability procedure that compares the odd numbers of the test to the even ones.

one-tail test—A test of the null hypothesis using only one end (or "tail") of the normal curve. If the research has an idea about the hypothesis to begin with, the statistical test would be *directional*, that is one-way.

operationalizing—When the researcher describes the specific steps taken to assess the concept or idea. For example, a "recipe" is the operational definition of a cake.

operationalism—A view that holds that scientific statements need to be grounded in specific actions in order to be meaningful.

ordinal numbers—A number that implies some kind of order, or a system of some kind.

organization—A fairly large group of persons, usually brought together for the purpose of performing some activity or enterprise.

parameter—A characteristic of a population, as opposed to a sample. The population mean is a *parameter* and a sample mean is a *statistic*.

platykurtic—A distribution with a large standard error is platykurtic.

polynomial regression—A useful kind of regression analysis that produces curved, rather than straight line relationships. It allows for different kinds of relationships between causes and effects.

population—The definition of what group is to be sampled. It is necessary to decide on what characteristics of the group become of interest to the researcher. Examples of populations are "middle aged adults who go to the grocery store at least once a week" or "women between the ages of 18 and 25 who watch television at least four hours per week" and so on.

positivists—*See* "logical positivists." The early positivists felt that for inductions to be valid, they should be couched in the same truth-statements as data statements. In other words, any inductive statement should be *operational* in the same sense that the data statements were, in other words, verified by controlled observation. This principle was introduced as a corrective to truth-statements which were justified on logical grounds alone, such as statements about an ideal metaphysical world.

power—The probability of making a Type II error (γ). Power is defined as $1 - \gamma$, or gamma. Usually power is a function of the number of cases in the sample and the hypothesized distance between the theoretical means.

quadratic equation—Equations involving expressions with exponents. They usually produce a curved line.

qualitative research—A form of exploratory research, usually involving in-depth analysis of a problem, individuals, or system.

quantitative research—Usually involves characteristics in which numbers can be assigned to assist in aggregating data. Usually involves ideas such as more or less; larger or smaller in specific characteristics.

questionnaire—A formal set of questions, in which respondents see the same questions.

random—The property of appearing by chance, that is, no number in a random array has any better probability of appearing than any other number.

random samples— A sample that is not biased in selection. Sometimes called a "scientific sample."

range—The distance between the largest and the smallest scores.

reductionism—The search for the simplest account of reality.

regression—The relationship of one variable to another, highly quantifiable by using the procedure of least squares.

replicable—Repeatable under different times and different circumstances.

research questions—Alternative form of an hypothesis, stated as a question rather than as a specific difference.

sample—A small group to represent the large group.

significance—The degree to which a specific statistical test deviates from chance.

simultaneous linear equations—More than one equation in a set which have unknown quantities.

split-half reliability—is calculated by taking the results of the first half of the test (questionnaire) and comparing it to the second half. The "halves" compared can be defined by any systematic procedure.

standard deviation—The square root of the variance.

standard error—Used interchangeably with *standard deviation.*

statistical notation—The specific systems that are involved in the use of numbers, primarily in aggregations.

statistic—The terms describing characteristics of the sample, as opposed to the population.

stratified sample—A sample in which a given characteristic of the general population is repeated in the sample.

stylistic analysis—A form of textual analysis. A standard system for defining styles, such as "listenability," "vocabulary diversity," "human interest," "realism," and "verifiability."

symbolic interactionism— A paradigmatic approach to knowledge which begins with the assumption that all life is a search for meaning, which is found in the way that each of us interacts with other persons, our institutions, and our culture. These interactions are *symbolic*, in that they take place primarily through language and symbols.

systematic sampling— This form of sampling uses a "system" to select cases, such an interval or some other device. For example a researcher might use a random number to start and then choose cases at a given interval, such as every tenth one.

t **test**—A comparison of means, based on the *t* distribution, which is a chance distribution (similar to the normal curve) formed by comparing the means of two different groups, and adjusting them according to their standard deviations.

test-retest reliability—The method of comparing the same test given at different times to the same population.

textual research—Examines the language used by an individual, a couple, a group, or a large organization. Usually done by obtaining transcripts or recordings of the text itself. This may come from direct recording, or from discovering texts in another source.

theory—A collection of statements, systematically arranged, that are used in explaining, evaluating and predicting any given phenomenon.

Thurstone scale—A test consisting of scaled items, which reflect independent judges' assessments of statement strength.

two-tail test— A non-directional test of significance.

variance—The most important measure of variability. It is the *average of the squared deviations from the mean.*

z score—This score is an arithmetic transformation of the "raw" score into standard deviation units.

Bibliography

Alexander, E. R., Penley, L. E., & Jernigan, I. E. (1992). The relationship of basic decoding skills to managerial effectiveness. *Management Communication Quarterly 6*, 58–73.

Allen, M., & Bourhis, J. (1996). The relationship of communication apprehension to communication behavior: A metanalysis. *Communication Quarterly, 44*, 214–226.

Allen, M., Hale, J., Mongeau, P., Berkowitz-Stafford, L., Stafford, S., Shanahan, W., Agee, P., Dillon, K., Jackson, R., & Ray, C. (1990). Testing a model of message sidedness: Three replications. *Communication Monographs, 57*, 275–291.

Altheide, D., & Johnson, J. (1980). *Bureaucratic propaganda*. Boston: Allyn and Bacon.

Anderson, J. A. (1987). *Communication research: Issues and methods*. New York: McGraw-Hill.

Anderson, J. A. (1996). *Communication theory: Epistemological foundations*. New York: Guilford.

Anderson, P. A. (1989). Philosophy of science. In P. Emmert, & L. Barker (Eds.), *Measurement of communication behavior* (3rd ed., pp. 3–17). New York: Longman.

Arntson, P. H., Mortenson, C. D., & Lustig, M. W. (1980). Predispositions toward verbal behavior in task-oriented interaction. *Human Communication Research, 60*, 239–252.

Asch, S. (1956). Studies of independence and conformity: A minority of one against a unanimous majority. *Psychological Monographs, 70* (416).

Asher, H. B. (1983). *Causal modeling* (2d ed.). Beverly Hills: Sage.

Ayer, A. J. (1956). *The problem of knowledge*. Baltimore, MD: Penguin Books.

Bem, S. (1974). The measure of psychological androgyny. *Journal of Consulting and Clinical Psychology, 42*, 155-162.

Berelson, B. (1952). *Content analysis in communication research*. New York: The Free Press.

Berger, C. R. (1988). Planning, affect, and social action generation. In L. Donohew, H. Sypher, & E. T. Higgins (Eds.), *Communication, social cognition, and affect*, (pp. 93–116). Hillsdale, NJ: Erlbaum.

Berger, C. R. (1995). *Communication failure, message plan adaptation, and cognitive load: Further assessment of the hierarchy principle*. Paper presented at the annual meeting of the International Communication Association, Sydney, Australia (May).

Berger, C. R., & Bell, R. A. (1988). Plans and the initiation of social relationships. *Human Communication Research, 15,* 217–235.

Berger, C. R., & Calabrese, R. J. (1975). Some explorations in initial actions and beyond: Toward a developmental theory of interpersonal communication. *Human Communication Research, 1,* 99–132.

Berger, C. R., Gardner, R. R., Parks, M. R., Schulman, L., & Miller, G. R. (1976). Interpersonal epistemology and interpersonal communication. In G. R. Miller (Ed.), *Explorations in interpersonal communication,* (pp. 149–157). Beverly Hills: Sage.

Berger, C. R., & Jordan, J. J. (1992). Planning sources, planning difficulty, and verbal fluency. *Communication Monographs, 59,* 130–149.

Berger, C. R., Karol, S. H., & Jordan, J. J. (1989). When a lot of knowledge is a dangerous thing: The debilitating effects of plan complexity on verbal fluency. *Human Communication Research, 16,* 91–119.

Berkoweitz, L. (1993). Toward a general theory of anger and emotional aggression: Implications of the cognitive-neoassociationistic perspective for the analysis of anger and other emotions. In Wyer, R. S., & Srull, T. K. (Eds.), *Perspectives on anger and emotion.* Hillsdale, NJ: Erlbaum.

Beyer, W. H. (1966). *Handbook of probability and statistics.* Cleveland, OH: The Chemical Rubber Co.

Booth-Butterfield, M., & Booth-Butterfield, S. (1990). Conceptualizing affect as information in communication production. *Human Communication Research, 16,* 451–476.

Bostrom, R. N. (1983). *Persuasion.* Engleewood Cliffs, NJ: Prentice-Hall.

Bostrom, R. N. (1990). *Listening behavior: Measurement and applications.* New York: Guilford.

Bostrom, R. N., Davis, W., Grant, N., & Einerson, M. (1990). *Don't stop me even if you have heard this one: A study of compulsive talkers.* Paper presented at the annual meeting of the International Communication Association, Dublin.

Bostrom, R., & Donohew, L. (1992). The case for empiricism: Clarifying fundamental issues in communication theory. *Communication Monographs, 59,* 109–128.

Bostrom, R., Humphrey, R., & Roloff, M. (1981). Communication and helping behavior: The effects of information, reinforcement, and sex on helping responses. *Communication Quarterly, 29,* 147–155.

Bostrom, R., & Waldhart, E. S. (1980). Components in listening behavior: The role of short-term memory. *Human Communication Research, 6,* 211–227.

Bostrom, R., & Waldhart, E. S. (1988). Memory models and the measurement of listening. *Communication Education, 37,* 1–18.

Bracewell, R. J., Fredericksen, C. H., & Fredericksen, J. D. (1982). Cognitive processes in composing and comprehending discourse. *Education Psychologies, 17,* 146–164.

Bradac, J. J. (1983). On generalizing cabbages, kings, and several other things: The virtues of multiplicity. *Human Communication Research, 9,* 181–187.

Bradburn, N. M., Rips, L. J., & Shevell, Steven K. (1987). Answering autobiographical questions: The impact of memory and inference on surveys. *Science, 236*, (April 10) 157–161.

Brandstatter, H., Davis, J., & Schuler, H. (Eds.) (1978). *Dynamics of group decisions*. Beverly Hills: Sage.

Bridgman, P. W. (1938). Operational analysis. *Philosophy of Science, 5*, 123–145.

Brown, J. (1960). *The motivation of behavior*. New York: McGraw-Hill.

Bruning, J. L., & Kintz, B. L. (1977). *Computational handbook of statistics*. Glenview, IL: Scott, Foresman.

Buerkel-Rothfuss, N. L., & Gray, P. L. (1990). Graduate teaching assistant training in speech communication and noncommunication departments. *Communication Education, 39*, 292–308.

Burger, J. M. (1990). *Personality*. Belmont, CA: Wadsworth.

Burggraf, C. S., & Sillars, A. L. (1987). A critical examination of sex differences in marital communication. *Communication Monographs, 54*, 277–294.

Burgoon, J. (1994). Nonverbal signals. In Knapp, M., & Miller, G. (Eds.), *Handbook of interpersonal communication*. (2d ed., pp. 229–338). Beverly Hills: Sage.

Burgoon, M., Hall, J., & Pfau, M. (1991). A test of the "messages as fixed effect fallacy" argument: Empirical and theoretical implications of design choices. *Communication Quarterly, 39*, 18–34.

Burns, K., & Beier, E. (1973). Significance of vocal and visual channels in the decoding of emotional meaning. *Journal of Communication, 23*, 118–130.

Burrell, C. (1994, November 26). MIT researcher faked study of antibodies. *Savannah News-Press*, p. 11a.

Bussey, J. (1991). *Characteristics of listeners in interview situations*. Paper presented at the annual meeting of the Southern Communication Association, Tampa, Florida (April).

Capella, J. N. (1990). The method of proof by example in interaction analysis. *Communication Monographs, 57*, 236–240.

Capella, J. N., & Palmer, M. T. (1992). The effect of partner's conversation on the association between attitude similarity and attraction. *Communication Monographs, 59*, 180–189.

Carbone, T. (1975). Stylistic variables as related to source credibility. *Speech Monographs, 42*, 99–106.

Carnap, R. (1953). Testability and meaning. In H. Feigl & M. Brodbeck (Eds.), *Readings in the philosophy of science* (pp. 47–52). New York: Appleton-Century-Crofts.

Cavalli-Sforza, L. L. (1991). Genes, people, and languages. *Scientific American, 265*(5), 104–111.

Chatham-Carpenter, A., & DeFrancisco, V. (1997). Pulling yourself up again: Women's choices and strategies for recovering and maintaining self-esteem. *Western Journal of Communication, 61*, 164–187.

Chesebro, J. (1984). The media reality: Epistemological functions of media in cultural systems. *Critical Studies in Mass Communication, 1*, 111–130.

Christophel, D. (1990). The relationship among teacher immediacy behaviors, student motivation, and learning. *Communication Education, 39*, 323–340.

Clair, R. B., Chapman, P. A., & Kunkel, A. W. (1996). Narrative approaches to raising consciousness about sexual harassment: From research to pedagogy and back again. *Journal of Applied Communication Research, 24*, 241–259.

Cochran, W. G., & Cox, G. M. (1957) *Experimental designs.* New York: John Wiley and Sons.

Craig, R. T. (1989). Communication as a practical discipline. In Dervin, B., Grossberg, B. J., & Wartella, E., (Eds.), *Rethinking communication*, (pp. 97–122). Newbury Park, CA: Sage.

Crick, F., & Koch, C. (1995, December). Why neuroscience may be able to explain consciousness. *Scientific American, 273*(6), 84–85.

Cronbach, L. (1951). Coefficient *alpha* and the internal structure of tests. *Psychometrika, 16*, 297–334.

Cunningham, F. (1973). *Objectivity in social science.* Toronto: University of Toronto Press.

Cushman, D. P., & Pearce, W. B. (1977). Generality and necessity in three types of communication theory. *Human Communication Research, 3*, 344–353.

Cushman, D., Valentinsen, & Dietrich, D. (1982). A rules theory of interpersonal relationships. In F. Dance (Ed.), *Human communication theory.* New York: Harper and Row.

Damasio, A. R., & Damasio, H. (1992). Brain and language. *Scientific American, 267*(3), 88–109.

Dance, F. (1982). *Human communication theory.* New York: Harper and Row.

Daniels, T., & Frandsen, K. (1984). Conventional social science inquiry in human communication: Theory and practice. *Quarterly Journal of Speech, 70*, 223–240.

Day, R. (1972). The interpretation of visual stimuli. *Science, 175*, 1335–1340.

Deal, T. E., & Kennedy, A. A. (1982). *Corporate cultures: The rites and rituals of corporate life.* Reading, MA: Addison-Wesley.

Deutsch, M., & Gerard, H. (1955). A study of normative and informative influences upon individual judgments. *Journal of Abnormal and Social Psychology, 55*, 629–636.

Dewey, J. (1933). *How we think.* Boston: D. C. Heath.

Donohew, L., Palmgreen, P., & Duncan, J. (1980). An activation model of information exposure. *Communication Monographs, 47*, 295–303.

Drug and Tobacco Use among U.S. Teens Continues to Rise. (1996, December 20). *Christian Science Monitor, 89*(19), 3.

Educational Testing Service. (1984). *Test analysis: Core battery.* Unpublished statistical report. Princeton, NJ: Educational Testing Service.

Edwards, A. (1976). *Linear regression and correlation.* San Francisco: W. H. Freeman.

Ellis, D. G. (1992). Syntactic and pragmatic codes in communication. *Communication theory, 2*, 1–24.

Ellis, D. G., & Armstrong, G. B. (1989). Syntactic and pragmatic codes in interpersonal communication. *Communication Monographs, 52*, 157–169.

Ellis, D., & Hamilton, M. (1985). Syntactic and pragmatic code usage in interpersonal communication. *Communication Monographs, 52,* 264–279.

Ewen, S. (1983). The implications of empiricism. *Journal of Communication, 33*(3), 219–225.

Fairhurst, G. T. (1992). The leader-member exchange patterns of women leaders in industry: A discourse analysis. *Communication Monographs, 60,* 321–451.

Feinberg, S. E., & Tanur, J. M. (1990, February 24). Combining cognitive and statistical approaches to survey design. *Science, 243,* 1017–1022.

Feldt, L. W., & Mahmoud, M. S. (1958). Power function charts for specification of sample size in the analysis of variance. *Psychometrika, 23,* 209–215.

Festinger, L., Riecken, H. W., & Schacter, S. (1956). *When prophecy fails: A social and psychological study of a modern group that predicted the destruction of the world.* New York: Harper and Row.

Fetzer, J. (1974). Statistical explanation. In K. Shaffner, & R. Cohen (Eds.), *Boston studies in the philosophy of science* (pp. 71–93). Boston: Philosophy of Science Association.

Fisher, B. A. (1978). *Perspectives on human communication.* New York: Macmillan.

Fiske, S., and S. Taylor (1984). *Social cognition.* Reading, MA: Addison-Wesley.

Fitch-Hauser, M. (1990). Making sense of data: Constructs, schemas, and concepts. In R. Bostrom (Ed.), *Listening behavior: Measurement and applications* (pp. 76–90). New York: Guilford.

Fitzpatrick, M. A. (1983). Predicting couples' communication from couples' self-reports. In R. N. Bostrom (Ed.), *Communication Yearbook* (Vol. 7, pp. 49–82). Beverly Hills: Sage.

Fitzpatrick, M. (1984). Marital interaction: Recent theory and research. In L. Berkowitz (Ed.), *Advances in Experimental Social Psychology,* (Vol. 18, pp. 1–47). New York: Academic Press.

Fitzpatrick, M. A. (1991). Understanding personal relationships through media portrayals. *Communication Education, 40,* 213–218.

Fitzpatrick, M. A., & Indvik, J. (1982). The instrumental and expressive domains of marital communication. *Human Communication Research, 8,* 195–213.

Fowler, E. R. (1993). *Survey research methods.* Beverly Hills: Sage.

Frentz, T. S., & Rushing, J. H. (1993). Integrating ideology and archetype in rhetorical criticism, Part II: A case study of Jaws. *Quarterly Journal of Speech, 79,* 767–781.

Frey, L. R. (1994). Revitalizing the study of small group communication. *Communication Studies, 45,* 1–6.

Ghiselli, E. E., Campbell, J. P., & Zedek, S. (1981). *Measurement theory for the behavioral sciences.* San Francisco: W. H. Freeman.

Gibson, J., Hanna, M., & Huddleston, B. (1985). The basic speech course at U. S. college and universities: IV. *Communication Education, 34,* 281–291.

Giesbrecht, M. G. (1972). *The evolution of economic society.* San Francisco: W. H. Freeman and Company.

Gilbert, S. J., & Whiteneck, G. G. (1976). Toward a multi-dimensional approach to the study of self-disclosure. *Human Communication Research, 2,* 347–355.

Girvetz, H. (1973). *Beyond right and wrong.* New York: The Free Press.

Goffman, E. (1955). On face-work: An analysis of ritual elements in social interactions. *Psychiatry, 18,* 213–231.

Goss, B. (1986). Personal communication.

Gouran, D. S. (1994). The future of small group communication research: Revitalization or continued good health. *Communication Studies, 45,* 29–39.

Graber, D. A. (1988). *Processing the news.* New York: Longman.

Guttman, L. (1944). A base for scaling quantitative data. *American Sociological Review, 9,* 139–150.

Guttman, N. (1997). Beyond strategic research: A value-centered approach to health communication interventions. *Communication Theory, 7,* 95–124.

Haidt, J., Koller, S. H., & Dias, M. G. (1993). Affect, culture, and morality, or is it wrong to eat your dog? *Journal of Personality and Social Psychology, 65* (4), 613–628.

Hanna, J. F. (1991). Critical theory and the politicization of science. *Communication Monographs, 58,* 202–212.

Hart, R. P. (1976). Absolutism and situation: Prolegomena to a rhetorical biography of Richard M. Nixon. *Communication Monographs, 43,* 204–228.

Hart, W. L. (1947). *College algebra.* Boston: D. C. Heath & Company.

Hays, W. M. (1973). *Statistics for the social sciences.* New York: Holt, Rhinehart, & Winston.

Hempel, C. (1965). *Aspects of scientific explanation.* New York: The Free Press.

Herr, P. M, Sherman, S. J., & Fazio, R. H. (1983). On the consequences of priming: Assimilation and contrast effects. *Journal of Experimental Social Psychology, 51,* 67–75.

Herman, E. S., & Chomsky, N. (1988). *Manufacturing consent: The political economy of the mass media.* New York: Pantheon Books.

Hernstein, R. J., & Murray, C. (1994). *The bell curve: Intelligence and class structure in American life.* New York: The Free Press.

Higgins, E. T., & Lurie, L. (1983). Context, categorization, and recall: The "Change of Standard" effect. *Cognitive Psychology, 15,* 525–547.

Hubner, K. (1985). *Critique of scientific reason.* (P. Dixon, & H. Dixon, Trans.). Chicago: University of Chicago Press (Original work published 1982).

Hull, C. S. (1943). *Principles of behavior.* New York: Appleton-Century-Crofts.

Hunt, P. J., & Hillery, J. M. (1973). Social facilitation in a coaction setting: An examination of the effects of learning over trials. *Journal of Experimental Social Psychology, 9,* 566–571.

Hunter, J. E., Hamilton, M. A., & Allen, M. (1989). The design and analysis of language experiments. *Communication Monographs, 56,* 341–363.

Huspek, M. (1991). Taking aim at Habermas' critical theory: On the road toward a critical hermeneutics. *Communication Monographs, 58,* 225–233.

Infante, D., & Rancer, A. (1982). A conceptualization and measure of argumentativeness. *Journal of Personality Assessment, 46,* 712–780.

Infante, D., & Wigley, C. (1986). Verbal aggressiveness: An interpersonal model and measure. *Communication Monographs, 53*, 61–69.

Jackson, S., & Jacobs, S. (1983). Generalizing about messages: Suggestions for design and analysis of experiments. *Human Communication Research, 9,* 169–191.

Jackson, S., O'Keefe, D. J., Jacobs, S., & Brasher, D. E. (1989). Messages as replications: Toward a message-centered design strategy. *Communication Monographs, 56*, 364–384.

Jacobs, S. (1994). Language and interpersonal communication. In Knapp, M., & Miller, G. (Eds.), *Handbook of interpersonal communication*. (2d ed., pp. 199–212). Thousand Oaks, CA: Sage.

Johannesen, R. (1980a). Perspective on ethnics in persuasion. In C. Larson (Ed.), *Persuasion: Reception and responsibility* (3rd ed.). Belmont, CA: Wadsworth.

Johannesen, R. (1980b). Teaching ethical standards for discourse. *Journal of Education, 162*, 5–20.

Johannesen, R. (1996). *Ethics in human communication* (4th ed.). Prospect Heights, IL: Waveland Press.

Jorgenson, J. (1994). Situated address and the social construction of "In Law" relationships. *The Southern Communication Journal, 59,* 196–294.

Kahneman, D. (1973). *Attention and effort*. Englewood Cliffs, NJ: Prentice-Hall.

Kardas, E. P., & Milford, T. M. *Using the Internet for Social Science Research and Practice*. Belmont, CA: Wadsworth.

Kearney, P., Plax, T., Richmond, V., & McCroskey, J. (1984). Power in the classroom IV: Alternatives to discipline. In R. Bostrom, (Ed.), *Communication Yearbook Eight*, (pp. 724–734). Beverly Hills: Sage.

Kelly, G. (1955). *A theory of personality: The psychology of personal constructs*. New York: W. W. Norton.

Kelly, L., & Keaten, J. (1992). A test of the effectiveness of the reticence program at the Pennsylvania State University. *Communication Education, 41*, 361–370.

Kelman, H. (1961). Processes of opinion change. *Public opinion Quarterly, 25,* 57–68.

Kerlinger, F. N. (1986). *Foundations of behavioral research* (3rd ed.). New York: Holt, Rinehart, & Winston.

King, P. E., & Behnke, R. R. (1989). The effect of compressed speech on comprehensive, interpretive, and short-term listening. *Human Communication Research, 15*, 428–443.

Kohn, A. (1992). *No contest: The case against competition*. New York: Houghton Mifflin.

Kolbert, E. (1995). The vocabulary of votes: Frank Luntz. *New York Times Magazine*, March 26, pp. 46–49.

Kreps, G. L., Frey, L. R., & O'Hair, D. (1991). Applied communication research: scholarship that can make a difference. *Journal of Applied Communication Research, 19*, 71–88.

Krippendorf, K. (1980). *Content analysis*. Beverly Hills: Sage.

Lange, J. J. (1993). The logic of competing information campaigns: Conflict in old growth and the spotted owl. *Communication Monographs, 60*, 165–182.

Lannaman, J. W. (1991). Interpersonal communication research as ideological practice. *Communication Theory, 1,* 179–203.

Lappako, D. (1997). Three cheers for language: A closer examination of a widely cited study of nonverbal communication. *Communication Education, 46,* 63–67.

Leathers, D. (1979). The impact of multichannel message inconsistency on verbal and nonverbal decoding behaviors. *Communication Monographs, 46,* 88–100.

"Leonardo's Lengths," (1994). *New York Times,* June 28, 1994, p. B11.

Lieberman, P. (1991). *Uniquely human: The evolution of speech, thought, and selfless behavior.* Cambridge: Harvard University Press.

Likert, R. (1932). A technique for the measurement of attitudes. *Archives of Psychology, 140,* 1–55.

Lindlof, T. (1991). The qualitative study of media audiences. *Journal of Broadcasting and Electronic Media, 35,* 23–42.

Lindlof, T. R. (1995). *Qualitative research methods.* Thousand Oaks, CA: Sage.

Lindquist, E. F. (1956). *Design and analysis of experiments in psychology and education.* New York: Houghton Mifflin.

Littlejohn, S. (1992). *Theories of human communication* (3rd ed.). Belmont, CA: Wadsworth.

Littlepage, G. E., & Pineault, M. A. (1981). Detection of truthful and deceptive interpersonal communications across information transmission modes. *The Journal of Social Psychology, 114,* 57–68.

Loftus, G., & Loftus, E. (1976). *Human memory: The processing of information.* New York: Wiley.

Lord, W. (1986). *The night lives on.* New York: Avon Books.

Marks, A. (1997, August 27). News media seek credibility. *The Christian Science Monitor, 89*(191), 3.

Marwell, G., & Schmitt, D. R. (1967). Dimensions of compliance-gaining behavior: An empirical analysis. *Sociometry, 30,* 350–364.

Matalin, M. A., & Carville, J. R. (1992). *All's fair: Presidential politics and elections.* New York: Random House.

Mayer, R. (1983). *Thinking, problem solving, and cognition.* San Francisco: Freeman.

McCroskey, J. C. (1970). Measures of communication-bound anxiety. *Speech Monographs, 37,* 269–277.

McCroskey, J. C. (1974). Measures of communication-bound anxiety. *Speech Monographs, 45,* 192–203.

McCroskey, J. C. (1977). Oral communication apprehension: A summary of recent theory and research. *Human Communication Research, 4,* 88–112.

McCroskey, J. C. (1978). Validity of the PRCA as an index of oral communication apprehension. *Communication Monographs, 45,* 192–203.

McGee, G. (1996). Young scientists need to feel a personal stake in ethics. *Chronicle of Higher Education,* August 2, p. B3.

Medhurst, M. J. (1994). Reconceptualizing rhetorical history: Eisenhower's farewell address. *Quarterly Journal of Speech, 80,* 195–218.

Mehrabian, A. (1972). *Silent Messages.* Belmont, CA: Wadsworth.

Mehrabian, A., & Ferris, S. R. (1967). Inference of attitudes from nonverbal communication in two channels. *Journal of Counseling Psychology, 31* (3), 248–252.

Mehrabian, A., & Wiener, M. (1967). Decoding of inconsistent communications. *Journal of Personality and Social Psychology, 6*(1), 109–114.

Melody, W. H., & Mansell, R. E. (1983). On critical and administrative research: A new critical analysis. *Journal of Communication, 33*(3), 103–116.

Merrill, J. C. (1965). How *Time* stereotyped three U.S. Presidents. *Journalism Quarterly, 42,* 565-571.

Merton, R. (1973). *The sociology of science: Theoretical and empirical investigations.* Chicago: University of Chicago Press.

Milgram, S. (1963). A behavioral study of obedience. *Journal of Abnormal and Social Psychology, 63,* 371–378.

Miller, G. R. (1980). On being persuaded: Some basic distinctions. In Miller, G. R., & Roloff, M. E. *Persuasion.* Beverly Hills: Sage.

Miller, G. R., Boster, F., Roloff, M., & Siebold, D. (1977). Compliance-gaining message strategies: A typology and some findings concerning effects of situational differences. *Communication Monographs, 44,* 37–51.

Miller, G., & Johnson-Laird, P. (1976). *Language and perception.* Cambridge: Harvard University.

Miller, G. R., & Sunnafrank, M. J. (1982). All is for one but one is not for all: A conceptual perspective of interpersonal communication. In F. E. X. Dance (Ed.), *Human communication theory* (pp. 220–242). New York: Harper & Row.

Miller, R. W. (1987). *Fact and method.* Princeton: Princeton University Press.

Mode, E. (1951). *Elements of statistics.* New York: Prentice-Hall.

Mortensen, C., Arntson, P., & Lustig, M. (1977). The measurement of verbal predispositions: Scale development and application. *Human Communication Research, 3,* 146–158.

Morris, C. (1946). *Signs, language, and behavior.* New York: George Braziller.

Motley, M. T. (1993). Facial and verbal context in conversation: Facial expression as interjection. *Human Communication Research, 20,* 3–40.

Mussachia, M. (1995). Objectivity and repeatability in science. *The Skeptical Inquirer, 19*(6), 33–38.

Myrdahl, G. (1967). *Objectivity in social research.* New York: Random House.

Newhagen, J. E., & Reeves, B. (1992). The evenings's bad news: The effects of compelling negative television news images on memory. *Journal of Communication, 42*(2), 25–41.

Nichols, R. (1947). Listening: Questions and problems. *Quarterly Journal of Speech, 33,* 83–86.

Nicotera, A. (1997). Personal communication to author via e-mail on November 6, 1997.

Osgood, C., Suci, P., & Tannenbaum, P. (1956). *The measurement of meaning.* Urbana, IL: University of Illinois.

Palmer, M. T., & Simmons, K. B. (1995). Conscious and nonconscious encoding of liking. *Human Communication Research, 22,* 128–159.

Pearce, D. (1972). God is a variable interval. *Playboy, 19,* 171–176.

Pedhazur, E. J. (1982). *Multiple regression in behavioral research: Explanation and prediction* (2d ed.). Fort Worth, TX: Holt, Rhinehart, & Winston.

Petty, R. E., & Cacioppo, J. T. (1981). *Attitudes and persuasion: Classic and contemporary approaches.* Dubuque, IA: William C. Brown.

Pfau, M., Parrott, R., & Lindquist, B. (1992). An expectancy theory explanation of the effectiveness of political attack television spots: A case study. *Journal of Applied Communication Research, 20,* 235–254.

Pinker, S. (1994). *The language instinct: How the mind creates language.* New York: William Morrow.

Poll on doubt of Holocaust is Corrected. (1994). *New York Times,* July 8, p. A7.

Pollock, D., & Cox, J. R. (1991). Historicizing "reason": Critical theory, practice and postmodernity. *Communication Monographs, 58,* 170–178.

Pomerantz, A. (1990). Conversation analytic claims. *Communication Monographs, 57,* 231–236.

Poole, M. S., & McPhee, R. D. (1994). Methodology in interpersonal communication research. In M. Knapp & G. Miller (Eds.) *Handbook of Interpersonal Communication* (pp. 42–100). Thousand Oaks, CA: Sage.

Poole, M., & Roth, J. (1989). Decision development in small groups: a test of a contingency model. *Human Communication Research, 15,* 549–590.

Postman, N. (1979). The technical thesis. *Vital speeches of the day,* January, 180–185.

Pratkanis, A. R. (1992). The Cargo-Cult science of subliminal persuasion. *Skeptical Inquirer, 16,* 27–38.

Ray, E. B., & Bostrom R. N. (1990). Listening to medical messages: The relationship of physician gender and patient gender to long- and short-term recall. In R. Bostrom (Ed.), *Listening behavior: Measurement and applications* (pp. 144–151). New York: Guilford.

Reardon, K. K., & Rogers, E. M. (1988). Interpersonal versus mass media communication: A false dichotomy. *Human Communication Research, 15,* 284–303.

Reich, R. B. (1992). *The work of nations.* New York: Vintage Books.

Reichenbach, H. (1936). *Experience and prediction.* Chicago: University of Chicago Press.

Reichenbach, H. (1959). *The rise of scientific philosophy.* Berkeley: University of California Press.

Renfrew, C. (1994). World linguistic diversity. *Scientific American, 270*(1), 116–123.

Reuben, B. D. (1993). What patients remember: A content analysis of the critical incidents in health care. *Health Communication, 5*(2), 1–16.

Rice, R. E. (1996, January). *Making a place for the new American scholar.* Paper presented at the American Association for Higher Education Conference on Faculty Roles and Rewards, Atlanta, GA.

Rokeach, M. (1960). *The open and closed mind.* New York: Basic Books.

Rorty, R. (1987). Science as solidarity. In Nelson, J. and others (Eds.), *The rhetoric of the human sciences* (pp. 38–52). Madison: University of Wisconsin Press.

Rorty, R. (1994). Does academic freedom have philosophical presuppositions? *Academe, 80,* 52–63.

Rorty, R. (1996, Winter). Remembering John Dewey and Sidney Hook. *Free Inquiry, 16*(1), 40–43.

Ross, P. (1991). Hard words. *Scientific American, 264*(4), 138–157.

Rubin, R., & Graham, E. (1988). Communication correlates of college success: A preliminary examination. *Communication Education, 37*, 220–239.

Ruud, G. (1995). The symbolic construction of organizational identities and community in a regional symphony. *Communication Studies, 46*, 201–222.

Schank, R. (1982). *Dynamic memory.* Cambridge: Cambridge University Press.

Schildhauer, J. (1985). *The Hansa: History and culture.* (Trans. K. Vanovitch). Liepzig, GDR: Druckerei Fortschrift Erfurt.

Schneider, D. E., & Beaubien, R. A. (1996). A naturalistic investigation of compliance-gaining strategies employed by doctors in medical interviews. *Southern Communication Journal, 61*, 322–331.

Schmandt-Besserat, D. (1990). Symbols in the prehistoric middle-east: Developmental features preceding written communication. In R. L. Enos (Ed.), *Oral and written communication: Historical aspects* (pp. 16–31). Newberry Park, CA: Sage.

Schutz, A. (1967). *Collected papers I: The problem of social reality.* (Ed. M. Natanson). The Hague: Martinus Nijhoff.

Schutz, A., & Luckmann, T. (1973). *The structures of the life-world.* Evanston: Northwestern University Press.

Scwarz, N., & Bless, H. (1992). Constructing reality and its alternatives: An inclusion/exclusion model of assimilation and contrast effects in social judgment. In Martin, L., & Tesster, A., (Eds.), *The construction of social judgment.* Hillsdale, NJ: Erlbaum Associates.

Searle, J. (1990). A classification of elocutionary acts. In D. Carbaugh, (Ed.), *Cultural communication and intercultural contact* (pp. 349–372). New York: Erlbaum.

Service survey. Royal Oak, MI, 1997.

Smith, M. J. (1982). Cognitive schema theory and the perseverance and attenuation of unwarranted empirical beliefs. *Communication Monographs, 42*, 116–126.

Smythe, M. J. (1995). Talking bodies: Body talk at bodyworks. *Communication Studies, 46*, 201–222.

Snizek, W. E., & Fuhrman, E. R. (1980). The role of theory in applied behavioral science research. *Journal of Applied Behavioral Science, 16*, 93–103.

Spitzberg, B., & Cupach, W. (1984). *Interpersonal communication competence.* Beverly Hills: Sage.

Stephan, F. F., & McCarthy, P. J. (1958). *Sampling opinions: An analysis of survey procedure.* New York: John Wiley & Sons.

Stiff, J. B. (1986). Cognitive processing of persuasive message cues: A meta-analytic review of the effects of supporting information on attitudes. *Communication Monographs, 53*, 75–89.

Sypher, B. D., Bostrom, R. N., & Seibert, J. H. (1989). Listening, communication abilities, and success at work. *Journal of Business Communication, 26*, 293–303.

Sypher, H., Palmgreen, P., & Rubin, R. (1994). *Measures in communication research*. New York: Guilford.

Taylor, C. A. (1991). Defining the scientific community: A rhetorical perspective on demarcation. *Communication Monographs, 58*, 402–420.

Thain, J. W. (1994, October). *Improving the Measurement of Language Aptitude: The Potential of the L1 Measures*. Paper presented at the Language Aptitude Improvement Symposium, Washington, D. C.

Thurstone, L. (1959). *The measurement of values*. Chicago: University of Chicago Press.

Thomas, L. T., & Levine, T. R. (1994). Disentangling listening and verbal recall: Related but separate constructs? *Human Communication Research, 21*, 103–127.

Toulmin, S. (1950). *The place of reason in ethics*. Cambridge: The University Press.

Tubbs, S. (1978). *A systems approach to small group communication* (2d ed.). New York: McGraw-Hill.

Tubbs, S. L. & Moss, S. (1987). *Human Communication* (5th ed.). New York: Random House.

van Fraassen, Bas C. (1983). Glymour on evidence and explanation. In Earman, J. (Ed.), *Testing scientific theories* (Minnesota Studies in the Philosophy of Science, Vol. X). Minneapolis: University of Minnesota Press.

Vangelisti, A. L., Knapp, M. L. & Daly, J. A. (1990). Conversational narcissism. *Communication Monographs, 57*, 251–274.

Verderber, K. S. & Verderber, R. F. (1980). *Interact: Using interpersonal communication skills* (4th ed.). Belmont, CA: Wadsworth.

Watson, K. W., & Barker, L. L. (1983). *Watson-Barker listening test*. Auburn, Alabama: Spectra Associates.

Watson, K. W., & Barker, L. L. (1984). Listening behavior: Definition and measurement. In R. N. Bostrom (Ed.), *Communication Yearbook Eight*, (pp. 178–197). Beverly Hills: Sage.

Wedell, D. H., Parducci, A. & Geiselman, R. E. (1987). A formal analysis of ratings of physical attractiveness: Successive contrast and simultaneous assimilation. *Journal of Experimental Social Psychology, 23*, 230–249.

Williams, L. P. (1964). *Michael Faraday*. New York: Basic Books.

Wilson, Edward O. (1994). *Naturalist*. Washington, DC: Island Books.

Yerby, J. (1995). Family systems theory reconsidered: Integrating social construction theory and dialectical processes. *Communication Theory, 5*, 339–365.

Zajonc, R. B. (1965). Social facilitation. *Science, 149*, 269–274.

Zobel, H. B. (1997, July 1). The crazy quilt in the courts. *Christian Science Monitor 89*(131), 19.

Index